WHEN LIFE TURNS TURTLE

JOURNEY OF A BOLLYWOOD TRAMP

RAJ SUPE

PLATINUM PRESS
PREMIUM FICTION

ISBN 978-93-52016-15-0
© Raj Supe 2016

Cover: Abhilasha Khandelwal
Layouts: Chandravadan Shiroorkar, Leadstart Design
Printing: Thompson Press

First Published in English in India 2016 by
PLATINUM PRESS
An imprint of LEADSTART PUBLISHING PVT LTD
Unit 25/26, Building A/1
Near Wadala RTO, Wadala (East)Mumbai 400037, INDIA
T + 91 22 24046887 + 91 96 99933000 F +91 22 40700800
E info@leadstartcorp.com W www.leadstartcorp.com

Ruskin Bond

Ivy Cottage
Landour Cantt.
Mussoorie
248179

"Does a spiritual life mean giving up everything in a material world? And is there more than one path towards spiritual enlightenment? These are some of the questions that assail Indraneel, the hero of Raj Supe's novel, in his quest for a more meaningful life. And, like other seekers before him, he hopes to find it on the banks of the Ganga at that spiritual haven, Rishikesh. All roads lead to Rishikesh! Will Indraneel find what he is looking for? He reflects the sincerity of the author, who has learnt to battle with the conflicting demands of the material and spiritual world. There is no better place than the banks of a great and sacred river to meditate and contemplate and come to terms with the contradictions in our natures. The author's fluent narrative and genuine search for truth should bring him many readers."

Ruskin Bond
September 20, 2015

ABOUT THE AUTHOR

RAJ SUPE (*aka* Kinkar Vishwashreyananda), is a poet, storyteller and novelist. An MBA, he has had a career in advertising, research and creative consulting, before turning to literary and spiritual pursuits. Some of his literary works include the spiritual memoir, *Pilgrim of the Sky*; the anthology *Hundreds of Shells*; and translations such as *Cloudburst of A Thousand Suns,* and the Sahitya Akademi awarded *Rainbow at Noon*. He has also worked on film scripts and plays.

His writings convey the passionate intensity of a seeker and the sincerity of one who hopes for an ideal mix of traditional mythic imagery and the urgencies of modern life. In the words of a leading poet, 'he has the anonymity of the saint-poet on the one hand and the self-expression of the modern writer on the other'. Raj is Editor of the spirituality e-magazine, *The Mother* [www.themotherdivine.com], as well as the co-founder of *Foundation for Contemplation of Nature* [www.foundnature.com].

Raj was initiated into the Order founded by Sri Sitaramdas Omkarnath and met his Guru in the person of Kinkar Vitthal Ramanuja. He now leads a simple life on the banks of the Ganges.

FOREWORD

I read Raj Supe's *When Life Turns Turtle* with a mixture of familiarity and strangeness. Familiarity because the protagonist, Indraneel, belongs as I do, to the world of films, and because his sojourn takes him to the mountains. I too, lived my youth in the mountains of Himachal. Strangeness because Raj introduced me to the world of rituals and beliefs – a world which, having read the novel, I now have a better understanding of.

The world that Raj creates is vividly described with a true artiste's eye for detail; his descriptions of the sights and sounds of Rishikesh and its environs are always noteworthy. I missed the flowers and the birds but that does not really subtract anything from the world Raj has created!

The torturous journey Indraneel undergoes to cleanse himself and shed all the clutter he has accumulated in his life in films, in Mumbai, is described with a firm grip on the mental, physical and (particularly) emotional aspects that constitute his past. The journey itself becomes a metaphor for the transformation Indraneel undergoes before he is healed and reborn in his new avatar.

Of particular note is Raj's concentration on the mighty river Ganga, as both a physical river and the spiritual mother of those who come into contact with her. The river itself is a metaphor for the forces that shape human life – those who dwell by her banks and those who come from thousands of miles away to experience life on a higher, purer plain – a life for those who are willingly 'initiated', and choose an existence free from the bondage of this earth, where money and other human beings suck one dry. An existence whereby, after years of rigorous physical practise of yoga and meditation, one can begin to see the path that god has designed for the enlightened to follow.

Helped by his 'closet guru' friend, Shaman, who lives in Rishikesh, Indraneel embarks on a journey unlike any he has ever undertaken or experienced.

Set in the 'belief land of Rishikesh', Raj's story leads the reader through light and shadow to the goal Indraneel has set for himself – a life of spiritual bliss. A gallery of interesting characters people the landscape Raj crosses in his quest. From each one he takes a piece of the jigsaw puzzle that will become a picture only when it is complete. Supporting the story is the Ganga, perennial river of India's mystical past and angst-ridden present. The Ganga is history's witness, a living goddess, now turbulent and destructive, now gentle as a mother's enfolding arms. The only currency she accepts is belief and self-surrender.

With insights into human character, observations of natural phenomena, and generous doses of spirituality, Raj serves up a rich repast from which no reader can depart unfulfilled.

~ BENJAMIN GILANI

1

Indraneel woke abruptly to the thigh-tingling vibration of his cell phone. Jerkily, he got to his feet and pulled it from the front pocket of his faded grey jeans. His head felt befogged as he peered at the screen. Arunodaya had forwarded a joke: *So my English is weak. So what if I don't know what apocalypse means? It's not the end of the world!*

In spite of himself, Indraneel smiled. 'Humour and beauty do not seek permission to work on the heart,' he thought wryly. He closed the WhatsApp window and the home screen immediately lit up with the wallpaper of Avani's face. It was a low-light image, capturing her as she bent down to blow out the candles on her birthday cake. With a soft and sorrowful look, Indraneel ran his thumb over the picture gently. 'She is beautiful!' he thought for the millionth time. 'And so unaware of her looks!'

Indraneel put the phone back in his pocket. His body felt painfully cramped from the long wait at the terminal for his flight to Dehradun. He had flown in from Bombay at an ungodly hour and his connection had been indefinitely delayed. He stretched his long, lean body, lifting his hands high above his head. At 6' 2" he didn't have an ounce of extra fat. He felt somewhat better though his back still hurt from the unnatural sleeping posture in the airport lounge chair. His eyes felt gritty and burned from lack of sleep.

Following his bitter break-up with Avani, Indraneel had barely slept. When he did, it was more of an alcohol-induced stupor. Painful memories tossed about in his mind endlessly; snatches of conversation played on and on; bittersweet images rose unbidden.

Indraneel walked to the end of the corridor to the restroom. The bright lights of the new-age bathroom felt overwhelming as he squinted at his reflection in the shiny mirrors. Pulling off the band which held back his unruly locks, he ran a hand over his head in an attempt to smoothen his long, curly hair before putting the band back on.

'I look terrible,' he thought with a strange sense of detachment. Red, swollen eyes and a three-day stubble on his chiselled but gaunt face, stared back at him. He looked every day of his 38 years. His once youthful features were weighed down by the deep sorrow in his dark eyes. His mouth tasted like cotton wool.

'I really should cut down on the smoking and drinking,' he told himself half-heartedly.

Heaving the heavy bag containing his precious camera onto the granite washbasin counter, Indraneel rummaged through it and found what he was looking for – a cigarette. His body craved a nicotine fix. He raised the slim roll towards his lips and then stopped mid-air. Avani had wanted him to quit. Indraneel sighed and put the cigarette back into the packet. He groped blindly in the bag, searching for something else. His hand closed over a blister-pack of fruit-flavoured Orbit chewing gum. The sharp minty taste helped clear his head.

He pushed back the cuff of his expensive but now crumpled Burberry shirt, and glanced at the face of his wafer-thin Rolex wristwatch. It was time he headed to the departure gate.

Indraneel had a sea of humanity for company as he walked to Gate 21 – women attempting to restrain their children from running up the escalators, young men, old men, working professionals... and then there were hordes of giggling teenagers at the newly opened Starbucks outlet. Indraneel glimpsed the logo of his alma mater, Massachusetts Institute of Technology, emblazoned on a young man's T-shirt. How many years had passed since he graduated? He tried to calculate but his mind refused to cooperate.

Life moved on irresistibly around him. Only his seemed to have stopped. His mind backpedalled to a more innocent time

2

Indraneel first saw Avani at Prabhu Da's rehearsal...

He put the bottle of Johnnie Walker Blue Label he had picked up at the Paris dutyfree, into a neat carry-bag. It was for Prabhu Da, whose birthday he had missed. He had seen online pictures of the bash; quite a few celebrities in attendance. But this particular gift would be welcome any day of the year, Indraneel thought with a knowing grin.

When he arrived at the acting studio, he saw 20 young actors standing in a circle around Prabhu Da – a fair, plump, curly-haired 70-year-old, barely 5' 3" tall. His dark eyes sparkled, full of mirth, and he sported a pair of trademark Gandhi moon-spectacles, balanced on his head. He wore a nondescript round-necked T-shirt and flower-printed cargo pants. Despite his odd attire, he had an unmistakable intellectual air.

Prabhu Da held the firm conviction that one could not act if one could not speak. In his workshops, actors were given four clear directives:

1. Know the words perfectly.

2. Pronounce the words perfectly.

3. Enact the words perfectly.

4. Play with the words perfectly.

According to him, this constituted 90 per cent of acting. The rest followed naturally. The Naseers of the world loudly vouched for his formula.

While the students stood ranged around the circumference of the imaginary circle he had made one of them draw, the Master sat in a half-lotus posture, like the nucleus of a cell.

Presently, he addressed them. "Meisner calls it 'living truthfully in imaginary circumstances', right? He asks the actor to be spontaneous. He is telling you to be honest. He is asking you to invest emotionally in the scene. But how do you do that?"

"By substituting? By thinking what I would do if I was Juliet?" A young girl spoke up enthusiastically.

"Bravo! Strasberg *ki aulaad* [offspring]. Darling, did I ask you?" Prabhu Da spewed irritably.

"Da... but Da.... you said: *But how do you do that?*"

Prabhu Da looked straight into her eyes. The girl cringed.

"Yes, I said that. It was a monologue. I was talking to myself. If you had not interrupted, I would have answered myself. Who is the teacher here?" his voice boomed. "Prabhu Da is the teacher...right?" he reiterated, stressing who was in charge.

"Right, Sir."

"Then keep quiet until I specifically ask you to speak. This is my own vocal training – getting actors to listen...and shut up."

"Sorry Da..." the girl squeaked, drawing imaginary circles on the studio floor with her toe.

"Welcome..."

The girl was relieved. She stopped drawing circles and looked up, happy he had accepted her apology.

"Darling, I'm not talking to you even now. I was welcoming that gentleman over there." Prabhu Da waved a hand in Indraneel's direction.

Indraneel quietly sank into a chair in one corner, gesturing to his mentor that he would wait.

But Prabhu Da had other ideas. "Listen, all of you. Do you know that guy?"

Most of them nodded and murmured, 'Yeah'. One girl blushed and said a little breathlessly, "Isn't he Indraneel Barua, the film-maker? I've seen him on TV."

"That's him. Meet Indraneel Barua."

Prabhu Da looked around impatiently and then bellowed, "Where is Avani?" He turned to the others. "Where did Avani go? Someone go and fetch her!"

There was a flurry of activity as several students hurried off to find the missing Avani.

Prabhu Da beckoned Indraneel closer. "I want you to meet Avani, Indraneel. You know, she is not a fake. She is my favourite, my muse, the most..."

A soft voice interrupted. "Da, your Irish coffee." Avani handed him a cup.

"Ahhh Avani!" Prabhu Da's face lit up.

Indraneel turned to look at Da's muse. He was struck by the beauty of the woman standing there. Slender and tall, she wore a green dress that left her shoulders bare. There was something more than beauty here. In his profession Indraneel had seen women with greater beauty, but Avani exuded something more... innate. Magnetism? He groped for the right word but it eluded him.

Prabhu Da gestured for her to sit and then introduced Indraneel. "This is *the* Indraneel Barua, *apanaa shaagird* [my student]!"

Indraneel offered his hand with a casual, "Hi!"

Avani shook his hand and responded in a well-modulated voice, "I'm Avani."

Indraneel smiled. "Da's muse..."

Avani blushed. Indraneel suddenly realized he was still holding onto Avani's hand and quickly let it go. He also noticed she had not taken her eyes off him. The attraction was mutual and instantaneous.

Oblivious to what was happening between his two favourite people, Prabhu Da went on happily. "Indraneel, I want you to give these people some *gyaan* [knowledge] on Method Acting," he said.

"Da, why me? That's your department, not mine." Indraneel spoke quietly, trying not to attract any more attention.

"*Arrey yaar*, you've learnt so much from me. Can't you quote a bit of that?" Prabhu Da prodded.

"Honestly, I don't remember much of it."

"Everything's in trying, my dear friend! Start.. tell them whatever you know. I'm sure there was something you learnt from this *Socrates*." The emphasis was deliberate, self-believing.

Indraneel tried once again to wiggle out of it but Prabhu Da would not take no for an answer. The students, still in their circle, gazed at Indraneel with undisguised eagerness.

"Okay...okay...I'll tell you what fascinated me most and what I learnt from Prabhu Da's workshops. Honesty will speak," Indraneel began, clearing his throat.

"Yes, honesty is what I ask," Prabhu Da encouraged.

"I don't understand many of the acting Gurus like Stanislavski, Strasberg, Meisner, Stella Adler and so on. All those things about method and mining emotions just escape me. Someone told me that method actors immerse themselves in their characters..."

"Is Amir Khan a method actor then?" a student asked.

Indraneel did not respond immediately. "Well, I was told method actors get into the character to the extent that they remain in character off-stage and off-camera too, for the duration of the project... And I thought, wow! That is why Amir Khan appears in his adverts looking like the character of his forthcoming movie. Remember the side-locks of *Dil Chahata Hai* and the curls falling on his shoulders for *Mangal Pandey*? That look was exactly what you got in the ads as well. Now, I don't know if Amir did method after QSQT but that's what I thought he did."

The students were engrossed. Indraneel continued. "Then there was talk about Strasberg every time I came to Prabhu Da's workshop. But the only reason I paid attention to Strasberg was because his students included Marlon Brando, Robert De Niro, Al Pacino, Dustin Hoffman, Marilyn Monroe and Jack Nicholson. When I began, I would walk around with Stanislavski's books tucked under my arm – *An Actor Prepares*, *Building a Character* and *Creating a Role*. In fact, I remember when I met Prabhu Da for the first time, I had a copy of..."

"*An Actor Prepares*," Avani interjected with a grin.

"Well, she's right. I *was* carrying that book... How did you know?" Indraneel asked, intrigued.

Avani did not reply, she just looked at Prabhu Da, not wishing to speak without his approval.

"Answer the question girl," Prabhu Da said forcefully.

Avani swallowed and then said somewhat shyly, "I'm a great fan of yours and have long wished to act in your films, or assist you, some day. I learnt this nugget from a magazine interview."

Indraneel was pleased to know Avani had that degree of interest in his work. He continued to gaze at her.

"Indraneel! Tell them what you learnt from my workshops. Let's not get caught up in Avani's admiration and ambition," Prabhu Da ordered brusquely.

"Yes, I'm coming to that," responded Indraneel hastily. "What I learnt was the concept of truth in acting. First and foremost, Prabhu Da believes the script is king. The words of the script are potential actors, who we bring into motion. If you don't believe in the truth of the script, there can be no truth in the play. As an actor, you have to submit to the script..."

"*Surrender* to the script," Prabhu Da corrected.

Indraneel had a heightened consciousness of Avani's presence; he could feel her eyes staring at him.

"Yes, the actor must surrender to the script like a believer surrenders to the words of the *Gita* or the

Bible. It's only then that the truth is revealed. And that is also where the problem lies. Often, actors don't believe in the script. The audience may think it is just a play, not reality, but for an actor to think that is shame and suicide."

"Let me underline that. If an actor thinks what he is portraying is fiction, it is shame and suicide... Are you getting what he is telling you?" Prabhu Da roared.

"Yes..." the group nodded.

"Go on..." Prabhu Da urged.

Indraneel was actually enjoying this. He had spent a great deal of time reflecting on these things after the workshops. Throughout his directorial career, he had built theories in his head. Some things had been learnt and internalised, others discovered.

"Get to the truth..." Prabhu Da urged.

Indraneel looked at his hushed audience. "So the actor has to believe the script is true; that the things which happen are true. And then he must start to feel and act them out until the truth in the script is really discovered. I myself did not believe this until Prabhu Da demonstrated it to us. He made us slog for three weeks; I still remember how painful it was. We all felt he was trying to extract juice from dry pulp. One afternoon, he distributed the pages of a play."

"Kalidas' classic, *Meghduta.*" Prabhu Da added.

"Yes, it was *Meghduta.* But he didn't reveal that to us at the outset. He just randomly distributed pages from the play and asked us to memorise the lines and keep thinking about them until we could recite them in our dreams. He wanted us to improvise on the script."

"Improvise on Kalidas's script?" Avani asked, surprised.

"Yes, *the* script."

"But he gave you the script," Avani persisted.

"That was precisely the point. He gave it to us but there was no title and all the names had been changed. Some parts were deleted. It was incomplete. We had no clue it was Kalidas or *Meghduta*. It was just a script. He asked us to feel the words and tell him if we found any images or words that would make it more complete. We didn't know what to do. I mean, here was a script...what did he mean by making it more complete? 'Work on Truth not imagination,' he told us. 'Imagine the truth'."

Indraneel paused to take a sip of water from the glass on the table nearby.

Avani sat in rapt attention, drinking in every word. "He is so good, *na*?" she whispered to Rekha, the girl beside her.

Rekha winked and whispered back, "Drooling over him?"

Avani asked her to shut up and listen.

"So we had to stick to the confines of the given script and think up 'possibilities of truth'," Indraneel told them. "When we were done, he distributed the original Kalidas script, including the parts that had been deleted. Unbelievably, at least half of us had stumbled upon the exact words of the original. How did we actually write some of Kalidas's words in the 21st century?"

"That's amazing!" Abhimanyu, one of the older students, exclaimed involuntarily.

Indraneel nodded in agreement. "I continue to be amazed though many years have passed since then. He taught us that fiction too, has a reality. It comes from a *real* writer, writing the truth as he knows it. Anyone can touch that truth. What it means is that a work of art is not a work of fiction. It has a reality which comes from the core truth of its creation. If we can touch that underlying creative process, we gain the key to the truth. Am I making sense?"

Indraneel paused to study the reaction on the faces around him. Some showed understanding and awe, others wore bemused looks that said, 'What am I missing here?'

"How simply and beautifully you explained it to them, Indraneel. I'm impressed!" Prabhu Da exclaimed, patting Indraneel on the shoulder. "I doubt if I could have communicated it so well myself." He turned to his students. "My darlings, wasn't he brilliant? A round of applause please!"

Indraneel felt embarrassed by the lavish praise. "You flatter me, Da. I merely repeated what you, the best of teachers, taught us."

"Yes, but you milked great learning from my theory, and that delights me. People like me are theorists, you see. We keep churning out theories. Yes, theories are nice but they are just theories. It's people like you who gather the honey, not the flowers. Come! Let's go and celebrate your return from France."

Prabhu Da had forgotten the ring of students. One of them cleared his throat and asked, "Da, what is the exercise for today?"

"Nothing! Class is over. Just keep thinking about what this man has just said."

The students picked up their bags and began to disperse, leaving indistinct 'Bye Da...' 'Bye Sir...' hovering in the air behind them.

As they walked to the car park, Indraneel showed Prabhu Da the top of the bottle he was carrying in his sling bag.

"Whiskey! For me?" Prabhu Da was as happy as a child on his birthday.

Indraneel cast him a who-else-but-you look and turned away, searching for Avani in the parking lot. She had been the last to leave the Studio, turning off the lights and air-conditioners.

Now she came up to Indraneel and said with genuine warmth, "It was such a pleasure to meet you."

Feeling absurdly tongue-tied, Indraneel murmured thanks, secretly wishing he could have spent more time with her. He almost asked her if she needed a lift, but then decided on silence.

A little flame kindled in his heart.

3

Indraneel helped Prabhu Da into the gleaming black SUV he drove.

Hoisting himself into the luxurious interior with some effort, Prabhu Da cursed Indraneel's big vehicle. "This isn't a car it's a bloody black beast! I prefer auto-rickshaws. They flit like butterflies from place to place." He continued muttering as he fumbled with the seatbelt.

Indraneel laughed. "Butterflies and auto-rickshaws, Da? What a comparison! They are more like infernal locusts than flitting butterflies."

As he reversed, Indraneel saw Avani walking out of the compound. His eyes were drawn to the gentle sway of her hips. Busy talking on her phone, she didn't notice them as they went past.

"Should we offer her a lift?" Indraneel asked hopefully.

Prabhu Da wasn't really listening. He was busy reading the label on the whiskey bottle. "Give a lift to whom?" he mumbled.

"Avani," Indraneel said, pointing.

"Avani? Oh, no need. Aman will pick her up."

His curiosity piqued, Indraneel prompted as casually as he could, "Aman?"

"Aman Vora, a boy from Gujarati theatre," Da explained off-handedly, and then added, "Enough of Avani. Drive straight to Arunodaya's place."

They drove on in silence. Prabhu Da napped, clutching the wine bottle like a child with a precious new toy.

Soon they were ringing the bell of the ground floor apartment. Arunodaya was recovering from the flu. He was tall like Indraneel, but while Indraneel was classically handsome, Arunodaya had the look of a famished wolf. A distinctly idealistic fire burned in his eyes. Following his bout of flu he looked more famished than ever.

Arunodaya's father had wanted him to join the family diamond business. But Arunodaya hated commerce of any kind. He had artistic leanings and was too proud to allow his father to sponsor him. So Arunodaya left home, much to the dismay of his parents, Kapil and Rohini Garg, and his young sister, Vaz. He moved into a one-room hole in Amboli, a lower middle class neighbourhood. It was quite a change for the affluent South Bombay boy. The going was rough but Indraneel stood by him all the way.

"Welcome! Welcome!" Arunodaya exclaimed, happily, hugging Indraneel. "How was Paris?"

Indraneel extricated himself from his friend's bear hug. "Good. I saw the pictures you posted of Prabhu Da's birthday party."

"When did you see them? You just flew in this morning."

"Online." Indraneel sat down in a white plastic chair.

"Aha! My second home!" Prabhu Da plonked himself down on the small sofa. "Now quick, Arunodaya, three glasses please!" He proceeded to open the bottle and smell the heady aroma appreciatively.

Arunodaya found two glasses and set them down. "Da, I'm still on medication, so nothing for me."

Indraneel was not much of a drinker. "Just a small one," he told his gangly friend, indicating a small measure with finger and thumb.

They sat around the small table, Prabhu Da drinking the expensive whiskey like it was country liquor; pouring it down his throat, glass after glass.

Indraneel barely touched his drink. Last year he had been approached with a proposal to produce and direct the largest play ever to be staged in India, but he had refused. The flak his decision had drawn had made Indraneel wonder if he had indeed grown inimical to theatre. Or so the theatre fraternity said. He watched plays for Arunodaya's sake. They were school friends. Their families went way back. They had acted together at the beginning of their careers. Indraneel considered it his moral duty to watch every play Arunodaya worked in. They had night-long sessions discussing what worked and what did not, scene by scene. Indraneel had been approached recently to produce another play, but had once again refused. He simply had no time.

In his characteristically straight forward way, Arunodaya asked, "Indraneel, why did you refuse? The producer approached me to convince you. I thought you'd sign."

"Hmm..."

"Did you die?" Arunodaya demanded, incensed.

"What do you mean?"

"The question is simple: Did you die?"

"Nonsense! You can see I'm alive and kicking."

"Then why did you refuse the play? Sold out to cinema, huh? No allegiance to theatre, is that it?"

"Arunodaya, come on..."

"No, no....you lost it. You became a worm. A reptile! When one ceases to see the point of theatre one's grey matter has been put into formaldehyde. Dead but preserved like pickle."

"Look Arunodaya, I want to focus on cinema. I've just given it four years, and made three films. Theatre takes a lot of time; it's not my scene. I can't just keep sitting at Prithvi Theatre café, being charmed by three-sentence reviews in *Mid-day* and expecting other people to pay my bills. In the last four years I've made a life for myself. Tell me, could you have produced your last play if I was still struggling in theatre?"

"Don't remind me of the debt you've placed me under. Actually Indraneel, your money be damned. I'd love it if both of us starved doing theatre, than my going solo and you paying for it by doing a reptile brand of successful cinema."

Indraneel was the last person to seek credit for his generosity. He was also the last person to make a contrary point. "Maybe you're right," he observed, and let it pass.

Nothing gave Indraneel more pleasure than seeing Arunodaya do well in theatre; he expected great things from him in the future. That he himself was uncomfortable in the genre was something else.

Arunodaya was quick tempered; something in his head frequently snapped. But he knew Indraneel well and felt rather protective of his friend. He often acted as his alter ego, fierce critic, and conscience.

Indraneel appreciated that. As artists and human beings, they respected each other.

Prabhu Da was now happily drunk, the whiskey bottle almost empty. Slurring his words a little, he asked Indraneel, "*Kya picture banaa rahaa hai aaj kal* [Which movie are you making nowadays]?"

It was the question he constantly asked and Indraneel answered numerous times. But Prabhu Da invariably forgot the answer, almost immediately. Nevertheless, the fact that the Master had asked warmed Indraneel's heart.

"Da, I'm finalising a new script for a film called *Struggler*." Changing the subject, he said to Arunodaya, "By the way, I met Avani at the Studio this evening. Dude, is she sexy!"

Arunodaya was annoyed by this crass remark. "Indraneel, don't even think about it," he warned.

"Think about what?"

"She is a simple, small town girl with a real passion for theatre. Don't mess with her," Arunodaya said succinctly.

"Whoa...whoa...you're overreacting." Indraneel held up both hands, laughing in mock horror.

Prabhu Da spoke up. "What he's saying is don't lure her with the slimy glitter of cinema."

"You'll have an affair and ditch her! Worse, break her heart!" Arunodaya added, solemnly nodding his head.

"Back off guys!" Indraneel cried in self-defence. "What if *she* breaks my heart?"

"Movie-makers don't have hearts," Arunodaya scoffed.

Prabhu Da's hands shook a little as he lifted his glass, spilling some of the whiskey on himself. Imitating Indraneel he intoned with an exaggerated, dramatic flourish, *"Mere paas gaadi hai, banglaa hai, paisa hai, izzat hai...tumhaare paas kya hai* [I have car, house, money, respect...what do you have]?"

"Mere paas draaMaa hai [I have draMa]!" was Arunodaya's swift and witty response.

The three men threw back their heads and laughed till they cried.

4

Fourteen months later....

Indraneel's 14th floor office space had the aura of lived-in luxury. It was located in another wing of the same Cuffe Parade complex as his residence. Originally a three-bedroom apartment, it had been converted to suit Indraneel's needs. The erstwhile living room, with its imposing view of the sea, was his personal office. It was a masculine room with light grey wall-to-wall carpeting – the kind one's feet sank into. The sofas were black leather, and red leather bean bags sat around erratically. The soft grey walls were stark, with just one large painting of an astonished Yashoda Ma, gazing at the whole universe in baby Krishna's open mouth. It was an unusual painting of a well-known subject. Indraneel had commissioned it some time ago. His desk was devoid of personal photos or mementos. It was neat and clear, with the exception of his iMac.

The reporter from *Style & Screen* arrived at 11am, as scheduled. Indraneel's assistant ushered her in saying, "Sir is expecting you."

Used to interviewing film personalities and movie moguls, Shalini Shinde was privy to their opulent lifestyles. She was nevertheless impressed by the expansive sea view from Indraneel's office. Inherited money or earnings from the blockbuster, *Lukkhey*? She guessed it was the former.

Indraneel rose to greet Shalini and they shook hands. She sat down on one of the black sofas.

Wearing a white Lucknawi *chikan*-work *churidar-kurta* [Indian dress], with a multi-coloured *dupatta* [stole], numerous silver bangles jangled on her wrists.

"What a fabulous view!" she said with complete sincerity. "You look good too!" she added, a smile tugging at her rather hard mouth.

"Thank you!" Indraneel had showered and was wearing a deep blue Ralph Lauren full-sleeved shirt and tan chinos. He preferred to dress more formally for work.

There was a knock on the door and a smartly dressed girl came in and asked Shalini, "Ma'am, what would you like to drink?"

The girl offered options from cappuccino to smoothies to white wine.

"A Diet Coke, please," Shalini replied.

"And to eat? We have chicken sandwiches, rolls, *kachoris* [fried snack] and *aloo tikkis* [potato cakes]."

Shalini looked at Indraneel and smiled, asking playfully, "*Iraadaa kya hai* [What's your intention]? You want to make me fat?"

"Journalists write good things when their stomachs are full," Indraneel joked.

Shalini opted for the *kachori* and Indraneel asked for a black coffee.

"Shall we begin?" Shalini suggested, taking the Dictaphone out of her cavernous bag.

"Sure!"

"You are perhaps the youngest director to have been so successful, with just two films. Your first film, *Lafangey*, made you a critically acclaimed director. You also made 100 *crores* [10 million]. How did it feel?" Shalini tapped her fingers on the armrest.

"While these things made me happy, everything was so unexpected. I was not entirely prepared for it. Success came like a storm. Half the happiness was lost in getting my bearings."

"May I put my feet up?" Shalini asked. This was getting interesting.

"Please do." Indraneel gave a casual wave.

Shalini slipped out of her glittery flip-flops and wriggled her toes into the luxurious carpet before tucking them beneath her on the large black sofa. The food arrived.

"But it's a sweet anxiety?" she asked, helping herself.

"Yes. But frankly, I spent the whole time asking myself: Am I worth all this?" Indraneel admitted, gazing out at the somewhat turbulent sea.

"Come on! You deserved it for great work," Shalini commented, playing with her hair.

Indraneel paused to blow on his coffee before taking a sip. "Shalini, I'm not a deluded soul. I know my place. I didn't work hard on *Lafangey*; I was just plain lucky. I can list 100 directors who were and are my superiors in craft and skill."

"Don't you think you are too hard on yourself? I love your work. Your films have gone to festivals and won awards. Isn't that enough?"

"No. It's not enough."

"Then what is enough?"

"Nothing is enough really. But some people do great stuff and that seems like enough at that moment. It's not about success, because success fails you. It's not about getting rich, because money beggars you. And it's not about fame, because fame shames you."

"You're a philosopher!" Shalini stirred the clinking ice cubes in her Coke with a straw.

"Don't abuse philosophers. I'm not an Aristotle, Russell or Kapila," Indraneel remarked softly.

"Kapila?"

"A Vedic sage credited with being one of the founders of the Samkhya School of philosophy."

"It's a pleasure talking to such an informed man, Mr. Barua."

"Hardly, just enough to distinguish myself from the beasts. Actually, reading on philosophy and spirituality is a hobby. It makes me feel self-important and unimportant at the same time," Indraneel mused.

"By the way, where did you go to college?" Shalini was openly curious now.

"In the U.S. – MIT."

"Wow! No wonder you are so unfilmy! That was a great place to start... but when it came to films, was it a struggle? How difficult was it for you to break into film direction after your stint with an event management company?"

"I was one of the fortunate few. I never had to sleep at railway stations, Mahakali caves or in youth hostel lobbies. I never lived on bananas or *baidaa* [egg] rice. I was well provided for. I worked with the California-based Pico Group; it's among the world's top 50 event management companies. I've had a cushy life, which is perhaps why I'm so impressed by struggle and fight. It fascinates me," Indraneel said candidly.

"That explains *Lafangey*, *Lukkhey*, and now *Struggler*. You only take losers as your themes?" Shalini probed curiously. The *kachori* was so crisp and fresh that she dropped a cascade of crumbs as she bit into it.

Indraneel promptly offered her a napkin. "Not losers, strugglers... My trilogy is about rising from nothing," he corrected.

Wiping her fingers Shalini shot off another question. "So your characters struggle to survive. That's intriguing. Now I can see the progression. Your three films portray three states – destitute; wastrel, somebody. Did I get that right?"

"Absolutely!"

"How do you know this struggle so well?"

"I don't but I am trying to. Things have been pretty easy for me. Success came quickly. I look for failure and transcendence in my subjects; something low and mean, close to death, or something high and elevating, close to immortality. Those are the subjects that interest me."

Shalini, who was sipping on her Diet Coke, was surprised. "You're very different!"

"Difficult?" Indraneel smiled.

"No, I said different."

"No, I'm not different. I'm not Martin Scorsese, Gurudutt or Alfred Hitchcock. I am run of the mill."

Indraneel offered Shalini another tissue to catch the crumbs from the *kachori* she had picked up.

"How is *Struggler* shaping?"

"Very well. It's almost done. Just about three-four days of patch work left," Indraneel answered confidently.

Other questions followed. Shalini was reasonably impressed by what she heard. Certainly he was different from her usual interviewees. Finally they shook hands and she left, thanking him for his hospitality. She thought him both well-mannered and respectful of women. He hadn't said one shady thing. In her line of work, where one met such dogs, he was a man of good breeding. She wondered what the hell he was doing in the film industry. Having met him, she had forgotten the essential merit of his films. Somehow the person loomed larger.

5

Indraneel felt dog tired. He had been flying for over 30 hours, returning from the Toronto Film Festival. The Indian film-makers at the festival had got under his skin with their shallow hypocrisy and narcissism. 'Grow up!' he wanted to say, but didn't. Although he flew business class, he longed for a shower and a bed. At over 6', he really needed to stretch out after a long flight.

Despite the debilitating fatigue, his mind was on Avani as he got into the prepaid cab. He was soon on his way to her Lokhandwala apartment. He closed his eyes and allowed his mind to drift. Would she be awake? She had answered his WhatsApp saying she was waiting for him. But that had been an hour ago. Getting his luggage had taken forever. What would she be wearing?

The week away from her had been difficult. He had missed her intensely. 'She is perfect for me,' he thought. He planned to take their relationship to the next level but the time they had with each other was so short. He wanted to propose but the insane, brutal schedules of their busy lives did not make for the perfect moment. Soon...he told himself. It had to be memorable and perfect.

The movement of the cab lulled him to sleep. The next thing he knew was the cabbie asking, "Which building, *saab*?"

Indraneel pointed to a squat building with peeling paint, coming up on their left. The cabbie demanded an extortionate sum, far higher than the meter reading, but Indraneel merely sighed and paid him off. He was too tired to argue. He got out, heaving his backpack after him.

It was a little after 1 am. The building was old and had no lift, but Indraneel, elated at the prospect of seeing Avani, did not mind carrying his bag up three flights of stairs. The stairway was ill-lit and dirty, with a stray dog asleep on one of the landings. Indraneel hardly noticed. He finally arrived at her door, his heart pounding from exertion and anticipation. He dug into the backpack and found the key. It turned silently. He hoped she had not put on the deadlock and bolted the door. She had not. The door swung open.

There she was! All the lights were off except for a small table lamp. She wore only a long and faded T-shirt which had once sported a large Garfield saying: *I don't know. I don't care.* She sat on a low stool, talking into her phone. Her long, wavy hair glowed in the lamplight. Indraneel's eyes drank it all in – the delicately chiselled features, the twinkling eyes and bow-shaped lips, the habit she had of chewing at her lip when nervous.

"Yes, I'll be there…" When she saw him her face lit up but she quickly put a finger on her lips, gesturing to him to remain silent.

Indraneel wheeled in his bag and closed the front door quietly. He heard her say in her melodious voice, "Yes, 5 pm suits me just fine."

As he opened his backpack to pull out the gift he had got her, he suddenly found himself being hugged from behind in a vice-like embrace, her face pressed to his back. He savoured the moment and then asked gently, "Missed me?"

Turning her around, Indraneel hugged her tight. When his lips touched her eyes, he found they were moist. Immediately he pulled back, asking with concern, "Why are you crying, baby?"

She hugged him and mumbled into the crook of his neck, "I missed you so much!"

He crushed her to him. She felt so soft and fragile. Finally he loosened his grip. Avani wiped her eyes and asked if he wanted a drink. His fatigue melted away as he nodded.

"Dinner?" she asked.

Indraneel's stomach rumbled. "A snack would be great."

She poured him his favourite whisky, handed him the glass and went to heat up some *poha* [savoury snack]. An appetising aroma soon filled the room.

The gift he had bought her was a white and pink gold charm bracelet. It had teddy bears playing different musical instruments. He went into the kitchen, put one hand gently over her eyes and slipped the bracelet onto her wrist with the other.

"What is it?" Avani asked excitedly, trying to see between his fingers.

Indraneel released her and Avani ran over to switch on another light in the miniscule kitchen to get a better look at her present.

"It's beautiful!" she breathed, and then stopped short. "I can't accept something so expensive," she said in a pained voice.

Indraneel remained unfazed, simply giving her another hug and a quick kiss. He was happy she liked the bracelet.

Avani served the *poha* and they both sat down at the dining table. Indraneel began to eat hungrily. He suddenly felt famished and the *poha* was delicious.

Avani smiled, watching him eat. Between spoonfuls, Indraneel offered her a sip of his drink. She took a large gulp and blinked.

"I didn't realise I had made it so strong!"

Indraneel merely smiled and continued to eat.

"I have something to tell you," said Avani.

Indraneel was mildly curious. Relaxed now, with food in his belly and a drink in his hand, he asked, "What is it?"

Avani began to clear the plates. "I'm pregnant."

Indraneel froze. "Are you sure?" he finally asked.

Avani pulled out a report from a nearby cabinet and handed it to him. He looked at it. Without missing a beat he said, "We'll keep the baby."

"Indraneel, we've known each other for barely a year. You are not even divorced yet. This is not a joke," Avani's voice almost broke.

"Yes I know all that but we can work something out." Indraneel came to her side. Putting an arm around her he walked her the short distance to the living room and made her sit down on the sofa. He wanted to tell her right then that he wished to marry her but he knew it was not the right time to propose. He didn't want her to think he was offering marriage because she was pregnant. He loved her. The more he thought about it the more sure he was, though the points she had made were valid too.

"I'm not ready to be a mother yet, Indraneel. You know I want to be a successful actress. I'm getting such good offers! In fact, I'm auditioning for Yash Raj Films the day after. I can't imagine supporting a child when I can barely support myself." Avani was beside herself.

"Calm down...I'll support you..." Indraneel responded, trying to placate her.

"It's not just the money. I barely know you! In the year we've known each other, it's always been about sex. You never had the time to sit and talk, to get to know me as a person, find out about my dreams and aspirations. It's always been about you...only you."

Indraneel remained outwardly calm though he could feel his anger rising like an uncoiling serpent. She had grossly misunderstood him. His voice was measured as he said, "Yes, initially in any relationship it's always physical. I agree we've not had the time to talk things out... I live in Cuffe Parade with my parents and you are here. The commute is a pain. But we can rectify the situation." He stopped, studying her reaction, and then continued. "I'll buy you a place in Worli or Bandra..."

Avani cut him off in mid-sentence. "I'm not your bloody mistress!" she fumed. "Don't try to buy me..." Her eyes flashed fire and then welled with angry tears. "First thing tomorrow I'm going to terminate this pregnancy."

Indraneel was shocked by her declaration. He had never thought of her as a mistress; she was looking at the whole situation perversely. "I love you Avani," he said gently, trying to be reasonable. "It's our baby you're talking about. We have a great thing. Let's not make a hasty decision."

Avani was crying in earnest now. He went to her, hugging her close. She sobbed into his shirt saying, "I love you too... it's just that I'm scared."

Indraneel carried her to the bedroom; she felt as light as a feather. Placing her on the bed, he switched off the light and pulled her close to him.

"Let's talk about it tomorrow. We can discuss whether you want to carry this child to term or not... after five days. Let's give ourselves some space to think."

"Three days..." said Avani.

"Five."

"Three…" she insisted.

"Okay, three!" Indraneel smiled. He was confident he would be able to convince her to keep the baby. After all, he wanted Avani to be his wife. Life was a gift from God; abortion was murder.

It was barely 6 am when Indraneel awoke. There was a cacophony of different noises – the traffic outside, a pressure cooker whistling, children yelling, a TV blaring, someone dragging something in the flat directly above. Avani was still asleep. She looked like a child. Indraneel placed a gentle hand on her flat stomach. 'My child lives...' He felt overwhelmed by the thought.

Avani woke and smiled up at him just as his phone rang. It was his cab, asking for directions. He had forgotten he had ordered the cab to take him back to Cuffe Parade. Indraneel rose from the bed reluctantly, kissed Avani on the forehead and told her to go back to sleep.

"Five days okay?" he reminded her, smiling.

"Three," she mumbled into her pillow.

6

Indraneel picked his shirt off the floor of Avani's tiny bedroom. Giving it a shake he glanced ruefully at the wrinkles before thrusting his arms into the sleeves. He contemplated changing but decided against it and finished tucking the shirt into his jeans. Letting himself out of flat, he carried his backpack down the three floors and made his way to the waiting cab.

There was a buzz of life on the streets, people going about their lives with purpose and determination though it was just 6.30 in the morning. He enjoyed observing people. A raucous fight had broken out between two *koli* fisherwomen at the municipal water tap. Hurling plastic pots at each other, they screamed abuse at the top of their voices. He remembered reading somewhere that the next world war would be about water.

Indraneel flipped open his phone and began answering emails and messages. It was still too early to return calls. The traffic was sparse and they got to Cuffe Parade in record time. He paid off the cabbie and alighted. As he walked towards the air-conditioned foyer, the uniformed watchman saluted. Indraneel nodded in acknowledgement.

There was no need to wait for the lift, it was right there. Pressing 27, Indraneel caught his own reflection in the mirrored interior of the elevator. He looked dishevelled. It was not that he was afraid of his parents; they would not judge him for being with a woman; he was almost 40, but he loved and respected them deeply, and did not wish to embarrass them. They had suffered enough from the insensitivity of his soon-to-be ex-wife, Chitra.

Indraneel chose not to tell his parents that he had flown in last night. While he didn't wish to lie to them, it was better for now that they didn't know he was seeing Avani, when things were still so new between them. He believed a nascent relationship needed privacy and space to thrive. He didn't want the scrutiny of others. Not right now.

The tinkle of the elevator bell told him he had arrived at his floor. It was just a few steps to the apartment, the only one on the floor. He was about to press the bell when the door opened and his father's long-time chauffeur appeared with the keys to the cars parked in the garage.

"Morning Govind," Indraneel called as he walked in.

He could hear his mother chuckling in response to something his father had said at the dining table. They were still unaware of his presence. He loved the easy camaraderie between his parents. They were in their 60s; childhood friends who had married.

Indraneel took in the breakfast scene. Revati, his mother, was a short woman, impeccably dressed in a blue crepe *salwar kameez*. Solitaire diamonds glittered on her earlobes and fingers. The diamond bangles on her wrists caught the early morning sun streaming in through the large French windows as she buttered her toast.

His father, Balarama Barua, was a tall and fit man with a full mane of silver hair. Both his parents came from wealthy backgrounds, were well-read and soft-spoken. Balarama ran a business importing medical equipment into India. He loved his work and travelled a lot.

Revati was a well-known painter who worked in the delicate medium of water colours. She owned and ran an art gallery called Kadambari, and often held shows for talented, underprivileged artists. She was currently showcasing works by the Hobo Gujjars of Uttarakhand.

When Revati looked up and saw Indraneel, she gave a small yelp of joy. "Indoo...!" She cast aside her napkin and came running to hug him.

Her head barely reached her son's shoulder but Indraneel felt like a child again. Bending down he kissed his mother on both cheeks.

"Hey Indoo....come on in!" his father called.

Big Gomati emerged from the kitchen. She was only a few years older than Indraneel, but already she was a grandmother. Though her children were well-settled, she chose to remain with the Baruas. *"Chote Saab aa gaye* [Young Sir, you have come]?" she now said, her still unlined face wreathed in smiles.

Indraneel smiled back at her and then turned to hug his father, who sat addressing a plate of cut fruit.

"What would you like to eat? You must be famished. These flights mess up the body clock no end," Balarama complained, shaking his silver head sadly.

The dining table was laden with food. Hash brown, baked beans, fresh toast, cut mango, watermelon and pineapple, a pitcher of freshly squeezed orange juice, curls of butter, peach preserve... Indraneel contemplated what to eat.

His father glanced at him. *"Beta*, you look tired."

Big Gomati returned with crockery and cutlery and set another place at the table. The porcelain plate, silver cutlery and crystal glassware, were all

WHEN LIFE TURNS TURTLE

arranged with military precision. Black coffee, just the way he liked it, materialised as if by magic.

His mother fussed over him. "What can I serve you?" she asked, running a hand over Indraneel's unruly hair.

"Nothing right now, I'm good. Just coffee."

His father was eating pancakes.

"There is no order to his eating," Revati commented, hiding a smile.

Big Gomati brought in fresh pancakes and placed them on Indraneel's plate without asking. He smiled at the love and warmth of his family, ate the pancakes and washed them down with black coffee. He longed to sleep. He rose from the table and told his parents he was going to take a nap.

A short flight of steps led to his room. Despite having left Avani just a short time ago, he felt a sudden pang of longing. He called her even before got to his room. She picked up on the second ring. She was in an auto-rickshaw, on her way to a light rehearsal of the play which was opening on Friday. There was a lot of road noise in the background.

"I'll be switching off my phone...I've got to get some sleep," Indraneel told her. If she needed to reach him urgently she could always call the landline.

Indraneel showered and switched on the AC. The shirt he wore was loose; he had lost weight. He prided himself on his trim figure and worked out at the gym regularly, but after he began seeing Avani and started filming *Struggler*, there had been no time. He usually began his day breakfasting with his parents. That was the only time he saw them. If he was shooting in the suburbs, he often left home by 8 am, winding up at Avani's place for dinner. Or they went out. Either way it was usually past 2am when he finally left her place to return home. Sometimes he stayed over.

'I should get a driver,' Indraneel thought for perhaps the hundredth time. He loved to drive but the lack of sleep was beginning to tell on him. He seemed to be living on adrenaline, coffee and love. He needed to slow down.

His eyes fell on the silver Balakrishna his grandmother had given him many years ago. Though the Lord was dust-free, he no longer enjoyed the daily bath, anointing with sandal paste and changing of clothes that Indraneel had once performed. Without thinking, Indraneel went back down to the hall, barefoot. An arrangement of fresh flowers in a large cutglass vase stood in colourful splendour. He pulled a blush pink rose from the arrangement, then remembered his grandmother telling him that yellow or *pitambari* was the Lord's favourite colour. Indraneel put the pink rose back and looked for a yellow one.

Balarama looked up from the newspaper he was reading. Noticing his son's odd behaviour, he asked what Indraneel was doing.

"If you are smuggling that rose to a girlfriend tucked away upstairs, take a few more. A single rose will not cut much ice," he laughed, winking at his son.

Indraneel found a yellow rose. He smiled at his father's words but did not stay to prolong the conversation. Back in his room, he offered the perfect flower to Balakrishna, contrite at having neglected him. Then he fell onto his bed and was asleep the moment his head touched the pillow.

7

There was a loud pounding on the bedroom door. Indraneel opened his eyes, startled and disoriented. He could not tell the time as the thick drapes remained drawn across the large picture windows. Gingerly he walked to the door and opened it, wondering what the freaking urgency was.

Big Gomati stood with the cordless phone in her hand, a worried expression on her face. "*Lily madam ka phone hai. Madam ne bola bahut urgent hai, saab ko jagaao* [Madam Lily said it was urgent and to wake you]."

Lily had been Indraneel's PA for three years. She was young, smart and efficient. He knew she would discriminate between what was urgent and what wasn't. He took the phone.

"I'm sorry to disturb you, Sir...but Shahabuddin has committed suicide," Lily told him without preamble.

Indraneel was shocked! Lily added that Shahabuddin had hung himself in the apartment he shared with two other actors. All three were part of the *Struggler* cast.

"I'm coming to office right away," he told her.

Indraneel glanced at the grandfather clock in the hall; it was past 6 pm. He had been asleep for ten hours. He raced up the stairs to his room and quickly changed into a plain white, collared T-shirt, and then hurried across to his office in the neighbouring wing. Most of the film cast and crew were already there. The movie had a cast of newcomers, many of them very young. But it was a close-knit group and the news had shattered them. Lily had organized tea for everyone.

As soon as they saw Indraneel, everyone converged on him, speaking at once. The babble of voices hit Indraneel but he did not ask them to stop. He understood their need to express their overwrought feelings.

When there was silence again he asked, "Which hospital was he taken to?"

"Cooper," several voices replied together.

"Who took him?"

"Ahmed and Gopi," Lily answered. "They're still there with the body."

Indraneel quickly made a decision. "Let's go to the hospital."

It was a frustrating drive through the stalled, rush hour traffic. Indraneel drove his SUV, some of the actors riding in the vehicle with him. The others followed on their bikes. Mohan, one of those in the car, told him Shahabuddin had recently been ditched by his girlfriend, Dolly. He had been so dejected that he had wanted to end his life.

Indraneel felt angered by the utter futility of such a death. He was pro-life. A deep sense of melancholy settled upon him. How could anyone end his precious life because of a woman? What a waste! Shahabuddin had been so talented...on the verge of a big break.

"Where was Shahabuddin from?" he asked.

Someone said Badayun, a small but historical town in Uttar Pradesh. Apparently he had two sisters.

Indraneel called a friend on the hands-free. "How does one reach Badayun in the shortest possible time?"

"Fly to Delhi and drive from there," his friend advised.

Indraneel briefly explained the situation, telling him that he needed to transport the body to Badayun.

"Could you check and let me know when the last flight for Delhi leaves?"

Then he called Avani to tell her he wouldn't be able to meet her for dinner as planned. He realised he had not spoken to her for many hours, having been asleep and now this. She was pregnant with his child...the thought filled him with warmth and happiness. But her phone was switched off. Before he could leave her a message, his travel agent friend called back with the information that there were flights to Delhi almost every hour.

Indraneel called Ahmed at Cooper hospital. "Find out what the formalities are to get the body released. Start the documentation process so we can fly to Delhi today."

"Okay Sir," Ahmed responded quietly.

"And don't worry about money; just get the work done." Indraneel's tone was almost a command.

Lily, in the back seat, leaned forward. "Sir, I just checked. There is a flight leaving at 2 am, which should suit us fine."

"Talk to whoever you need to and see that the body goes on that flight," Indraneel responded in a businesslike way. "Also, book tickets for all those who wish to go...we will travel and stay together."

Consulting the others, Lily noted down the names and ages of the people who would be travelling and then called the travel agent.

When they arrived at the hospital it was 8.30 pm. The media was out in full force. Five OB vans stood parked on the road and journalists were trying to talk to anyone willing to give them a sound bite.

"Sir, take the car in through the side entrance. I just spoke to the Chief of Security at the hospital. They will wave us through without stopping us," Lily told Indraneel quickly.

Indraneel drove the gleaming SUV through the narrow rear passage, eluding the hungry media. 'Sometimes the media is so ruthless,' he thought. 'Like a pack of hungry wolves when it comes to chasing a story.'

One of the others offered to park the car. The rest got down and made their way to the morgue. Indraneel heard someone running towards them. Much to his dismay, he saw Shalini Shinde, the journo from *First News* and *Style & Screen*, with her cameraman in tow. Before he could gather his wits, she had thrust her mike into his face and instructed her cameraman that she wanted a tight close-up.

Indraneel schooled his features into an expressionless mask but his eyes followed the actors anxiously waiting for him.

"We have with us the film director, Indraneel Barua, who was Shahabuddin's mentor...." Shalini began, speaking into the camera.

Indraneel put his hand out to cover the lens. "Shalini...I'm not up to this right now...another time?"

She sighed. "Indraneel, the time is now! Later just won't do. A short sound bite – all I want is your reaction."

"Shalini, it's a rough time for us. I really need to go in." Indraneel gestured towards the entrance. "There are a million things to do and I'm running against a deadline."

Shalini's face clearly showed her frustration. "Indraneel, it won't take five seconds! I just want a reaction."

He paused and then nodded. He didn't have the time to argue with her. He spoke one sentence with deep feeling: "I will miss you, Shahabuddin my friend."

Shalini thanked him and turned back to the camera, giving brief biographical details of Shahabuddin's short life. Indraneel hurried towards the morgue. The thick smell of formalin almost made him gag.

The doctor in charge came over and shook his hand. "I saw *Lukkhey*...I love your films," he commented enthusiastically, seemingly oblivious to the tragedy of a young life lost to suicide.

But in that moment Indraneel was only thankful for the fame that could help him cut through the red tape. He accompanied the others to view the body. Only Shahabuddin's face was visible – wiped clear of all the agony and trauma of his young life. Despite the violence of his deliberate end, he looked peaceful...at last. A few of his fellow cast members broke down.

Indraneel felt his head throbbing with anger. A young life eliminated! Life was a precious gift. Suddenly he remembered Avani. He walked away from the others and called her. Her mobile was still switched off. As he was messaging her, his mother called. Indraneel apprised her of the situation.

"Mom, pack me an overnight bag with some clothes and send it to me with Govind. He can bring back my car."

"Indoo, do what you can to help the family," his mother urged before asking gently, "Where is his family?"

"In Badayun, UP."

"May his soul rest in peace," she sighed sadly.

Lily, who had been on the phone continuously, told Indraneel she had booked 17 seats on the flight and made arrangements for the conveyance of the body as well.

"Is there anyone else who would like to go?" Indraneel asked.

Lily shook her head and went off to the hospital office to speed up the paperwork needed to make the flight on time. She bribed and cajoled, working against the clock.

Indraneel spoke to Shahabuddin's family in Badayun, telling them they would be in Badayun by morning. The young man's mother was too distraught to speak but his father listened stoically, not saying a word.

Crowds of young people, all known to the promising actor, thronged the hospital to get a glimpse of their friend. Shahabuddin had won a theatre award recently and there were rumours that his role in Indraneel Barua's film would probably get him into Yash Raj Films. As word of his death spread, the crowd of mourners swelled.

Many people came up to speak to Indraneel. With all that was going on, he had no opportunity to call Avani again. Nor did he have time to wonder why her phone was uncharacteristically switched off.

It was past 10 pm when Govind arrived. Shahabuddin's body was finally loaded into an ambulance and they left through the same side entrance they had come in by, leaving the media in the dark.

As they arrived at the airport, Indraneel thought of the irony of being back there in less than 24 hours. Picking up his bag he instructed Govind to drop Lily home.

"Sir, I can take a cab back," Lily assured him.

But Indraneel insisted. "Lily, Govind will drop you home." Then he made his way towards Departures.

Money takes care of many things in India, particularly bureaucratic red tape. Before they knew it, they had all boarded the flight. For some of the young cast, it was their first time on a plane and they briefly forgot their grief in the excitement of flying.

Indraneel sat in economy with the others. He was glad he had slept when he had the chance. Anger continued to simmer within him. He wondered how he could have failed to see the signs of self-destruction in the boy. How had it escaped him on the sets? 'I was shooting a guy who was contemplating death as he faced my camera! Am I that imperceptive?' he wondered dejectedly.

Actors were temperamental and unstable people. He was glad he had not heeded Prabhu Da's many pleas to be an actor. They were so self-involved they could not think beyond themselves. He knew thousands of young people came to Bombay every day to try their luck but only a miniscule number ever made it to even a non-speaking role in films. They faced rejection every day; their financial condition precarious; their angst and frustration a slow burn, threatening to engulf their very souls. Though he had never had to struggle for anything, Indraneel felt deep empathy and tried to cast newcomers when he could.

Putting his head back, Indraneel closed his eyes. He woke to the announcement that they were about to land in Delhi. The others were peering down at the glittering lights spread below them like a celestial carpet of twinkling diamonds. The plane banked, skimming the buildings as it descended towards the runway. The awe and wonder in the young boys around him made Indraneel smile as he marvelled at the beauty of the human spirit. If the circumstances had been different, he would have indulged these struggling actors with a tour of the capital.

Lily had organised an ambulance to transport the refrigerated box with the body. They got into the small, air-conditioned mini bus which was also waiting, and the ambulance followed.

When they reached Badayun, it was 8 am. The sun was already blazingly hot. The whole village had gathered and there was a sea of women in black *burkhas*. The sound of their wailing tugged at the core of Indraneel's being. What a waste!

Shahabuddin's mother came forward and fell at his feet, thanking him for bringing home their boy. A slight woman, bent like a gnarled root, she kept mumbling, "Why did he do it?"

Indraneel felt sad and helpless. He gave Ahmed some money and told him to take care of the funeral expenses.

They all attended the last rites at the Muslim burial ground. The handkerchief on Indraneel's head had once been pristine white but was now damp with sweat. The molten sun seemed to burn into the mourners standing around the freshly dug grave. There was not a single tree for shade, just hard, bare earth.

Though the rituals were different from those he was familiar with, and the language Arabic, the basic human grief around him struck a deep chord within Indraneel as the body was lowered into the earth, covered in a simple white burial cloth. The finality of the sound of falling earth filled him with a deep sense of pathos. Shahabuddin's life was over.

Suddenly, the high pitched, collective wailing of the women shattered the silence. Indraneel did not wish to intrude on the family's grief and loss. He told the actors they should go back to Delhi, and return to Bombay from there. Once back, they would finish the film. Just two days work remained on it. Even the dubbing was almost done. Although it had been a small part, Shahabuddin had delivered a stellar performance in *Struggler*. Now death had claimed him.

Getting into the front seat beside the driver, Indraneel tried Avani's number again. She picked up after three rings. She sounded sleepy but happy to hear from Indraneel. He briefly told her what had happened, surprised that she didn't already know about it from the media.

They stopped at a small but surprisingly clean wayside hotel called Padma Palace. In his room, Indraneel opened his backpack. His mother had packed his shaving kit as well as his chewing gum. He smiled at her thoughtfulness. Bone tired, his body still on Mountain time, he could barely keep his eyes open.

He called Lily and asked her to book him on a return flight to Bombay that evening; then to speak to the others and arrange for their return as well. Within minutes he received a mail from Jet Airways, confirming his booking. He looked at his watch –

he could catch a couple of hours sleep. Setting the alarm on his phone, he flopped onto the bed spread-eagled, on his stomach.

8

Once again Indraneel found himself in a cab, heading towards Avani's apartment. This time, it was late evening and the traffic heavy. Horns blared and tempers ran high. A steady drizzle didn't help. His mind was strangely blank as he gazed at the chaos and confusion he was trapped in.

It took him two hours to get to Lokhandwala. The hectic travel, the gloom and the stress of the last few days were finally getting to him; he felt on edge and irritable. Indraneel called Avani. She said that she too, was stuck in traffic, on her way back from Bandra.

Dragging himself up the stairs, Indraneel opened the door of Avani's flat. There was something infinitely sad about an empty house, he thought, feeling low. A stiff drink seemed like a good idea. He always kept a bottle of his favourite whisky at Avani's. He poured himself a drink in a tea cup since he could not locate a glass, and settled down in front of the TV to surf channels.

A newspaper lay on the centre table; he had had no time read one. Picking it up, Indraneel saw Avani's medical file from Cooper Hospital lying below. Setting aside the newspaper, he opened the file. The gynaecological report said her pregnancy had been terminated. Indraneel couldn't believe his eyes. He glanced at the date. Yesterday! How could she not have told him? How could she have made such an important decision by herself? He felt excluded and lonely. How could she have killed their child?

Just then he heard the lock turn in the door. Indraneel closed the report and put the file back under the newspaper. Avani walked in but did not come to him. Drenched from the rain, her jeans and yellow *kurti* were plastered to her skin.

"I need to get out of these wet clothes," she said, discarding her soggy high heels on the doormat.

Indraneel poured himself another drink – a stiff one. He felt ridiculous drinking scotch from a tea cup.

Avani emerged dressed in shorts and an orange spaghetti top. She hugged him and commented, "You look like hell! Come...we can talk in the bedroom."

Indraneel waited to see whether she would tell him about the abortion. Picking up the tea cup and whisky bottle, he walked into the tiny bedroom and sat down on the bed, watching her intently. Avani stood before the mirror, taking off her make-up with baby lotion. She too, looked tired. Dark purple shadows emerged below her eyes as she removed her make-up.

She spoke to Indraneel's reflection in the mirror. "Had you finished shooting Shahabuddin's part?"

"Yes, he'd packed up. The shooting was done." The longer she talked about other things, the angrier Indraneel felt. He gulped down his second drink and poured himself an even stiffer one.

Avani suddenly laughed. "Indraneel, why are you drinking from a tea cup?"

Her laughter was the last straw for Indraneel. He jumped up and gripped her by the shoulders. "Avani, when were you planning to tell me about the abortion?"

There was such anger burning in his eyes that Avani pulled back for a moment. She had only seen gentleness in him before. Pushing his hands away, she turned away. "So you saw the report? There's nothing to hide."

"Why didn't you wait?" Indraneel asked, his voice husky. "I thought we agreed to think about it?"

"I did think about it..." Avani was unruffled by his obvious anger. "I'm not ready for a child, Indraneel. I have everything going for me right now. I can't complicate things by being pregnant and getting fat. I didn't want that at all. There is nothing more to be said."

Indraneel felt overwhelmed by sadness. "You killed our baby, Avani...our son or daughter. How could you do it?"

"Cut the drama, Indraneel. Save it for your movies," Avani retorted coldly. "And stop calling it a baby. It was barely the size of a mustard seed."

"Avani, it was our child, conceived in love. You could have waited to talk to me."

"Conceived in lust, Indraneel," Avani retorted, angry that he was still arguing. "Get real. Love happens when you know a person. We barely do. You never have time to talk to me. As I told you the other day, it has always been about sex for you."

Indraneel attempted to reason with her. "Yes, I have not spent enough time talking, I agree. But you are a sexy woman and I am attracted to you."

But Avani was beyond reason. "Even whores are sexy."

Indraneel looked at her in disgust. "What are you talking about and what am I talking about? You are losing it, girl."

"*I* am losing it?" Avani was livid now. "You come here to smoke and drink because you can't do that at your parent's place, which is like a jail to you – no booze, no fags, no girlfriends. This arrangement suits you because you also get to have sex. You are scared of your parents! I have never heard of a 40-year-old living with his parents. You are a mama's boy!"

Indraneel's body quivered with indignation. He caught Avani by her hair and raised his hand to slap her. But something pulled him back and his hand fell to his side. He let her go and turned away.

But Avani had not finished. "When there was talk that you beat your wife, Chitra, I thought it a fabrication. But now I know what you are capable of....so hit me!" she challenged.

Indraneel punched the wall hard. The pain in his knuckles somehow soothed his anger. He swallowed the remains of his drink. Pouring himself some more whisky, he walked to the fridge to get ice cubes.

Avani followed him to the kitchen. "I want to be an actress. I know I have it in me. I can't just throw it all away because I got knocked up."

Indraneel drained the tea cup of neat whisky and stared down at the rapidly melting ice cubes in it.

"Knocked up?" he asked scornfully. "A child is a gift from God. Life is precious!"

Avani held up her hand, gesturing for him to stop.

"Enough *yaar*! Go tell that to the watchman who has six kids. Gifts from God!" she jeered. "You have lived in paradise. You have no idea about the real world. You are rich, educated; your parents are alive and still married to each other. They have provided you with every comfort; you don't know what it is to struggle."

Indraneel smiled sardonically. "Why the hell should I feel bad that I have a normal life? My parents love me, they provided for me. Why should I be apologetic for not being emotionally damaged or for being wealthy? Why must I belong to the club of glorified struggle and poverty to understand the 'real' world?"

Indraneel poured the last of the whisky into the tea cup. Avani was totally agitated

"Indraneel...I have struggled really hard to get here." Avani looked around her at the small apartment. "Earlier I shared a dump with three girls. You know how hard I work to send money to my mother every month. She has only me. I'm on the brink of making it...I can't throw it all away to have a child."

"It's time *you* got real, Avani. Thousands of young and beautiful girls come to Bombay to try their luck. Look at yourself in the mirror. You are beautiful, but you are not in competition with Katrina Kaif. And as far as my coming here to get laid is concerned, many women are ready to sleep with me. You know that."

"So I'm not good enough to be cast in your films but I'm good enough for you to go slumming with?" Avani's voice trembled with rage. "Sometimes I feel you think of me as a research subject for your work."

Indraneel was angry; he gripped the tea cup so tightly that it was in danger of shattering. But his voice was cold. "Credit me with some scruples and morals, Avani."

"Scruples?" she sneered, her pretty features distorted. "The first time you kissed me you knew I was seeing another man."

Indraneel was both drunk and angry, a dangerous combination. His retorted with uncharacteristic disdain. "How sensitive of you! If memory serves, you kissed me right back. You know as well as I do that you would have willingly slept with me that evening. You were more than willing." He laughed cynically.

"You are a cheap bastard!" Avani yelled, shaking with anger. "I've given this relationship *so much*. Because of you I barely slept. I look like an old hag with bags under my eyes. You always want food from outside, and I gain weight. I have no time to go to the gym or spend time with my friends. You have isolated me as your exclusive plaything." She went over to the sink and began washing the dirty dishes with exaggerated aggression.

Indraneel surprised her with his next words. "I want to marry you Avani. I ordered food because I didn't want you slaving in front of a stove after a hard day's work. Why don't you understand that? Why are you talking like this? Let's get married. Why do you want to be in this line of work? It's such a hard place for a woman."

Avani pretended not to hear.

"Can you stop that racket!" Indraneel yelled. over the clatter-bang of the utensils.

"I don't have a maid to do cook and clean. I am Avani *bai* here!" she retorted, flinging the last spoon into the steel draining basket.

She turned off the tap and turned, her eyes fixed intently on Indraneel's face. "Cast me in your next film, Indraneel. Then there will be no exploitation."

He was not prepared for this. His silence brought tears glistening to Avani's eyes.

"Anyway, I'm sleeping with the director," she added flippantly.

Drunk as he was Indraneel was completely serious. "You are so talented, Avani. Such a fine actress! You should work with Shyam Bengal or Rituparno Ghosh, who showcase your talent."

Avani cut in. "For all the credit you think you are giving me, you couldn't even think of two names. Rituparno Ghosh is dead; he could certainly cast me in his next ghost film! So I'm not good enough to be the heroine in your 100 crore films?"

In the complete silence that followed, Avani could feel her heart pounding in her chest. "I know why you wish to marry me – to look after your parents, like a maid. That's why you chose me – someone with no money, no connections. Your Chitra left you because she didn't want to be that person either," she commented bitterly.

"ENOUGH!" Indraneel yelled, the pent-up rage of the last two days finally exploding.

"Why Indraneel? Why may I not speak of your parents? You used their money to finance your films, didn't you? Well, you know what my friend? Even if I did marry you, I would never live in the same house as them."

It dawned on him that he had made a serious error of judgement.

"It's over between us, Indraneel. Over."

"You're calling it off? You really want to do that? Is that your decision?"

"Hell yes! Aman told me you were looking for someone who would adjust with your parents and live in the same house; not an actress...or at least a girl who would quit acting."

"So you're in touch with your ex-boyfriend?" asked Indraneel incredulously.

"Stop over-reacting," Avani snapped. "I've known him far longer than I've known you."

"When did you last see him?" Indraneel asked, fuming.

"It was he who took me to the hospital for the abortion."

A red mist descended over Indraneel eyes. "Why him Avani, why him? Why did you have to discuss such a private thing with him?" He could not get over her betrayal.

"He called when I was feeling low and I ended up telling him," Avani confessed.

Indraneel insisted on knowing more. "What did he say?"

Avani hesitated. "That he still loves me; that he never got over me."

Indraneel thought for a moment and then said quietly, "Assuming he does love you. Why Cooper Hospital, Avani? I could have taken you to Leelavati...I was at Cooper yesterday... it's such a filthy place!"

"It's always about money for you, isn't it Indraneel? You feel you can buy people. Well, just so that you know, Cooper has some of the best doctors. I really wonder what I saw in you? Anyway, it's over," Avani stated quietly.

"So you are getting back with Aman?"

Avani did not answer.

Indraneel dug into his trouser pocket for her apartment key and put it down on the kitchen table. He went into the bedroom and picked up his backpack and left the apartment, shutting the door softly behind him.

9

Numb with misery, Indraneel didn't remember leaving Avani's building. Loud honking by irate motorists brought him back to an awareness of his surroundings. He was drenched; he had been walking in a steady downpour. He looked around and realised he was about two kilometers from Avani's place. He must have been walking for about 25 minutes.

A cruising taxi slowed beside him. Indraneel peered inside; it was empty. He got in saying, "Cuffe Parade," in a muffled voice.

It was raining in sheets now, lashing Indraneel's face through the open window of the cab, but he remained unaware of it.

"Khidki band kar lo Saab... seat bheeg rahi hai [Close the window Sir…the seat is getting wet]." The cabbie said loudly, irritated by the man's thoughtlessness.

Indraneel wound up the window mechanically. 'What did I do wrong with Avani?' he wondered. Chitra had been a loud woman, interested only in comparing herself with her four sisters. She never tired of buying jewellery and clothes or going on holidays to exotic locations. She had little time for him, caught up in the rat race with her family. She didn't get along with his parents, but neither did she want to shift to another place; she loved the address. He was dismayed to find that she disapproved of Prabhu Da, and he had a specific aversion to the way she pronounced Shakespeare.

Chitra and Indraneel had nothing in common after their initial physical attraction burnt itself out. It was an arranged marriage and the proposal had come through a common friend. Chitra didn't understand his work, his drive or his passions; she made no attempt to find common ground. At first he had tried to understand and give her space, but nothing seemed to penetrate her narcissism. They were simply incompatible as people.

Though they lived together just under a year, it took an emotional toll on Indraneel. And the divorce dragged on, lost in legal wrangling over money, property and jewellery... After that bitter experience, he lost himself in his work. It helped. His film worked at the box office. The only woman he had had a relationship with after that had been Avani. It too, had been intense. After Chitra she had been like a breath of fresh air. From the same creative field, she understood his work and Indraneel respected her acting talent. They often discussed cinema. She gave herself to him so easily – physically, mentally and emotionally. He had loved her with all his heart. Not money-minded, she was free of societal pressures and drives. Indraneel had envisaged her as his wife.

The cab stopped at a signal. An auto-rickshaw stopped next to them, the film song *Kambakt Ishq* blaring loudly.

'We're the ones who put this rubbish on the streets to mock people's lives...my own life,' Indraneel thought despairingly. His head began hurting in earnest. He waited for the signal to turn green, willing time to move faster. The numbing effect of alcohol was fast receding and the gut-wrenching pain of his break-up with Avani was like a hot lance piercing his heart.

He did not know how he would face the future without her.

10

A sudden, searing pain caused Indraneel to look down. The still burning stub of his cigarette had touched his fingers. He realised he had been staring at the thick black clouds on the horizon through the floor-to-ceiling windows of his office.

He stubbed out the cigarette in the heavy crystal ashtray, already overflowing with butts, and poured what he guessed from the nearly empty decanter, to be his fourth drink of the evening. It was barely 7 pm.

It had been two months – 61 days to be precise – since his agonising break-up with Avani. He had simply told his mother that he had a lot of work to do and needed to stay at the office. His laundry got done and fresh clothes appeared miraculously, thanks to Lily, who asked no questions.

Fighting against the dark, twisting pain that threatened to swallow him, he worked doggedly on *Struggler*, wrapping up and finishing the post-production work. He had channelled the black energy of his failed relationship into the film, working like a man possessed by the devil. He expected his team to work with the same manic urge. They loved him but told everyone at the first opportunity they got that he was a pain to work with. His easy-going nature died and he became a simmering mass of volcanic rage about to explode. Though he never lost his temper, those around him could feel the barely controlled anger lying just below the surface.

Struggler premiered at IMAX, Wadala. It was well received and garnered critical acclaim. It also rocked the box office. For a film featuring rank outsiders, it grossed an astonishing 40 crores in the opening weekend. The media dubbed it a mega-hit. Shalini Shinde called to say the media was going all out to promote the genre. For Indraneel, nothing seemed real other than his grief. There was just one genre to his emotions – pain.

He went through the motions of promoting his film on auto-pilot. He did his best because he felt he owed it to his newcomers cast. He hated the thought of exploiting their talent for a pittance and then canning their work. They deserved the film to be promoted well after all the hard work they had put into it. Hindi films were sold to the audience much like colas and potato chips. Though he hated every minute of it, he did it all – promoting the film on TV channels and in different cities.

Finally it was behind him.

Indraneel spent his days and nights in the company of a whisky bottle. He drank, smoked, rarely slept and barely ate. Drunk and depressed, he replayed over and over again the ugly fight he had had with Avani, wondering what he could have done differently. Fantastic ideas floated into his alcohol soaked brain.

He was a mass of misery, incapable of any action. He just wanted to curl up and lie dormant. He could not face the pain. Clinically he explored different levels of pain – the sharp cut which draws blood; the crushing pain that does not allow one to breathe; the burning pain that incinerates the insides. He was now familiar with all these *avatars* of pain. Drink in hand, he went back to gazing sightlessly out of the windows, the seascape blurred behind a curtain of hot tears.

He heard the shrill ringing of the doorbell. Wiping his eyes roughly with the back of his hand, he took two steps towards the door and then decided to ignore the summons. But the person outside was persistent. The shrill ring sounded again and again.

Indraneel watched the second hand on the clock make its preordained journey four times. The four minutes of persistent ringing seemed like an eternity. It was followed by deafening silence. A strange quiet enveloped the apartment. Then Indraneel's cell phone began to ring. For a moment he wondered if it was Avani trying to reach him and hurried to pick it up. Arunodaya's name flashed on the screen. He thought of turning it off but on second thought pressed the green button.

"Open the bloody door!" shouted Arunodaya angrily.

Unable to take the volume emanating from the phone, Indraneel muttered, "Wait...I'm coming."

11

When Indraneel opened the door, Arunodaya walked in without a word. He paused, taking in the state of the room and then went over to the windows, pushing them open.

"Gawd Indraneel! This place is a smoke trap. I can barely see, let alone breathe. How many cigarettes have you smoked?" Arunodaya looked at the overflowing ashtray with concern.

Indraneel did not answer. He couldn't remember anyway. "Drink?" he asked.

"I think you've had my quota too..." responded his friend sarcastically. But worry nagged at him. "I'm famished. Got anything to eat?"

There was always a lot of food, he remembered and walked to the pantry to explore the contents of the fridge.

Before he could open the massive fridge door, Indraneel soft, slurred voice reached him. "No food...only liquids."

Arunodaya opened the fridge. Soda bottles and beer cans. "Indraneel, when was the last proper meal you ate?" he demanded.

"I don't know and I don't care," Indraneel slurred. "You know, Avani had a cute Garfield T-shirt with that quote... amazing huh?"

"What's so amazing?" Arunodaya asked irritably.

Indraneel continued reminiscing. "I miss the smell of her hair...I miss her perfume... Why Arunodaya? Why did she go back to Aman? I could have given her a much better life." He attempted to light a cigarette but failed, the flame and cigarette refusing to connect.

Arunodaya lit a cigarette and handed it to Indraneel. "Dude, you really need to ease up on the smoking."

But Indraneel was wrapped up in his own thoughts. "Beautiful Avani...she just left me," he lamented, taking a deep drag of his cigarette.

"Indraneel, this is your last drink. You are going to sleep after this," Arunodaya said firmly.

Indraneel reacted almost violently. "You know I'm scared of sleeping, Arunodaya. Every time I close my eyes I see Avani and Aman. Sleep is my torture chamber. I see them together...it's killing me," he whispered.

"Man...you're a mess," Arunodaya observed quietly. "Let's order some food."

He picked up the phone and called for some curd rice, the perfect recuperative. When he was done, he heard Indraneel sobbing in the bathroom. After a few minutes the sound faded away. Arunodaya did not speak; he knew his friend needed privacy to deal with himself. Soon he heard the sound of the shower. Indraneel finally emerged freshly showered, wearing shorts and a clean black T-shirt. He looked haggard, thin and unshaven, but more or less sober.

The intercom buzzed, announcing the arrival of their curd rice. Indraneel stood up to get his wallet, thrown carelessly onto his desk, but a wave of dizziness assaulted him.

Arunodaya steadied him, saying almost angrily, "You just sit down."

The doorbell rang. Arunodaya opened it, paid and collected the food.

"I don't want to eat anything," Indraneel muttered like a petulant child.

Ignoring him, Arunodaya fished around for a plate, served a portion of the curd rice and set it before Indraneel. "Eat!" he ordered.

There was silence as they glared at each other, then Indraneel meekly picked up the plate and began to eat. After two forkfuls he put the plate down. "I'm feeling sick...I can't eat."

Arunodaya fetched him a glass of iced water, saying kindly, "Sip the water slowly. The queasiness will settle."

Indraneel drank obediently. After a few moments of companionable silence, he picked up the plate again and ate a little more of the curd rice.

"I cannot live without her," Indraneel blurted suddenly, his voice breaking.

Arunodaya hated to see his friend so shattered but didn't know how to comfort him. He cursed Avani. He could have happily wrung her neck.

"She wasn't worth it, Indraneel," he said forcefully, lighting a cigarette.

"What do you mean?"

"You'll hate me for saying this, but she was caught up in her own ambitions."

"She's a good artist, Arunodaya... you know that."

"She was two-timing. Theatre and cinema don't mix."

"Oh shut up!" Indraneel exclaimed, reaching for a drink.

"At this rate you will kill yourself, you know. You'll drink yourself to death. It won't even be a quick process." Arunodaya snatched away the decanter.

He became pensive. After a while he said, "I think you need a change of scene. Why don't you go to Rishikesh, in the Himalayas? My sister Vaz's friend just returned from there, raving about the untouched beauty of the place."

"Is this the Reiki-dabbling friend of Vaz who dates wealthy men and falls in and out of love every season?"

"Whatever...but Rishikesh helped her. She says it's a divine place."

"Look, I don't like to use divinity as an emotional bandage," Indraneel said firmly, shaking his head in dismissal. "Besides, how can a change of scene, even an extreme change like visiting the Arctic Circle, help me? My misery is in my heart. You don't understand Arunodaya, it's gnawing at my soul and I'm a bleeding mess inside. I need her in my life to feel whole again. I cannot heal without her."

"Precisely!" Arunodaya asserted quickly. "Healing will happen in Rishikesh. There are divine vibrations there. And please forget your charitable impulse of sparing divinity for emotional purposes.

What the hell will you use divinity for if not to fix your wounded heart? Ma Ganga is there. Go, even as a sceptic, just go! Get out of Bombay for a while. Go to a place you don't know." Arunodaya held Indraneel's gaze, hoping for agreement, even if reluctant.

But Indraneel closed his eyes, rubbing his fingers over his forehead, trying to drain his emotional agony. "Huh..." he murmured.

"Trust me, you will feel less self-destructive once you have a break," Arunodaya urged.

Indraneel brushed him off. "I'm not going anywhere," he stated stubbornly, staring out at the ocean waves dashing with unnecessary force against the jagged rocks and then breaking into spray.

"Are you afraid you will forget the pain of a broken relationship? A Caligula kind of situation?" Arunodaya taunted.

Camus and Kafka, Kundera and Murakami, Tagore and Gorky – they had read them together and often laced their conversations with references to what they had read. Arunodaya remembered the intense agony Caligula had suffered at the demise of his beloved, in Camus' play.

"Caligula? Come on! It's an irrelevant comparison. Do you really think a small town by the Ganga can make me forget Avani?"

"It might...yes. Or do you prefer to wallow in pain? Does it make you feel good to waste a perfectly good life? It's nothing but sheer selfishness," Arunodaya told his friend. "Have you once thought of your parents in the past two months? Can you even imagine what they must be going through? We owe it to ourselves to move on. People in far worse circumstances pick up the pieces and get on with their lives. This kind of lamenting and pathos is a self-indulgence not many can afford. You are behaving like Avani is dead. Get real, Indraneel!"

Arunodaya walked over to his friend and gripped his upper arm. "She DUMPED you! She does not realise your worth. Take a break. Now tell me where you want to go."

Indraneel did not answer.

"You have to do this for me. Just for a week or so. You need a change. Please...for my sake, go on a holiday." Arunodaya was almost pleading.

Indraneel's heart melted. He had never seen the fiery Arunodaya like this. "I'll go wherever you want me to," he conceded blankly, his eyes full of tears.

Arunodaya called Lily and asked her to make arrangements for her boss to travel to Rishikesh.

12

The loud boarding announcement for his flight jolted Indraneel back to the present. He got on the bus which ferried passengers to the aircraft waiting on the tarmac. The man next to him wore a shirt and trousers made of the same faux silky material. He was using two cell phones simultaneously, giving instructions about the procurement and transporting of something which he repeatedly referred to as *maal* [goods].

The electronically operated door of the bus slid open and the passengers got off. The plane looked like a giant eagle. Indraneel smiled at the stewardess who stood with folded hands, saying, "Good afternoon, welcome aboard". He had an aisle seat and the passenger with the window seat boarded after him. He was a foreigner, carrying a backpack and wearing a green T-shirt with a picture of the Beatles, his dark glasses tucked onto his head.

"*Hari Aum* [The Lord is Absolute], brother!" the newcomer said with a warm smile, climbing over

Indraneel's knees and getting into the window seat with practised ease. "Madhusudan," he introduced himself.

Indraneel looked more closely at his neighbour – a carbon copy of Bruce Willis. "Indraneel," he responded pleasantly.

"We are on the plane at last," Madhusudan said with heartfelt relief, buckling his seatbelt. "You're going to Rishikesh, *Dev Bhoomi* [Land of the gods]? Pilgrimage?"

"*Dev Bhoomi*? I don't know. I'm going to Rishikesh though. But not exactly on a pilgrimage."

"Rishikesh is the land of the gods. It's called *Dev Bhoomi*," Madhusudan explained. "You start in Rishikesh and climb up the Himalayas – that's *Dev Bhoomi*, my dear. The land of gods! So you're going for river rafting?"

"No, not river rafting, just a few days off in a quiet place."

"Welcome, then!" Madhusudan shook hands.

"You're from America?" Indraneel asked.

"No, Canada. But I've lived in America."

Indraneel asked the light-eyed stewardess passing by for a pillow and blanket. The thing he needed most was rest. Not just rest for his body but something that would penetrate within and give him respite. He gave a big yawn.

"Brother, you look tired, almost drained. But don't worry, Mother Ganga will give you peace... right here!" Madhusudan pointed to his heart.

'A warm-hearted man,' Indraneel thought, dozing off.

The sounds and smells of snacks being served woke him. Two stewardesses offered sandwiches and patties. Indraneel felt a lot better though he had slept for just 15 minutes. Dreamily he looked out at the nacreous clouds, feeling a sense of ease, finally.

A passenger sitting across the aisle pointed to him and asked, "*Lafangey*?"

When people recognised him as the movie director, they usually just asked, 'Indraneel Barua, right?' Sometimes a few words were exchanged. But no one ever asked for an autograph, as they would with an actor. Indraneel smiled at his co-passenger before turning to the Canadian beside him.

"So, you've come to India before?" he asked casually.

"Well, I've spent half my life here for the past 30 years. I first came to Ananda Ashram in Rishikesh way back in 1981. That was when I met my Guru and was initiated by him. I found true love in Ananda Ashram." Madhusudan spoke with warmth and emotion.

"That's great! India sure does things to people," Indraneel replied in an off-handed fashion.

"So Indraneel, have you met any saints?" Madhusudan asked abruptly.

"No. My mother used to visit some when I was young, but I don't remember much. Some even came home, but I don't recall their names."

"So you are an initiate who's unaware," Madhusudan said, adjusting his seat.

"Unaware? Maybe."

"India is a generous place. It has given me so much." Madhusudan took a sip from the thermocol glass of water the stewardess had brought him some time ago. "I am reminded of the great Swami Vivekananda, who said: 'If you seek your own salvation, you will go to hell. It is the salvation of others that you must seek and even if you have to go to hell in working for others, that is worth more than to gain heaven by seeking your own salvation.'" He took a bite of his sandwich. "Being in the West is rather like going to hell – worldly, materialistic people, spiritual pigmies, money, power, sex and violence..."

"Well, the West has its own merits and we have our failings," Indraneel observed practically.

"Whatever the failings, spirituality is the greatest merit of India! When all's dark in the West, some Indian, a holy man, has to take the plunge. My Guru's Guru wished to go there and spread *naam* [the name]."

"*Naam*?" Indraneel asked without any real desire to know. One of his Punjabi cameramen had a ringtone on his phone that began with *Ek Onkar Satnaam* [Only the Absolute is the Truth]...

"*Naam* is the name of God. But I meant the *mahamantra* [supreme *mantra*]: *Hare Krishna Hare Krishna Krishna Krishna Hare Hare, Hare Ram Hare Ram Ram Ram Hare Hare.*"

Indraneel had another question. "So did your Guru visit you in Canada?"

"No, he didn't. But, by his grace, I have a beautiful place just an hour from Montreal forest. There's a mountain there with a crystal clear lake. I live according to my Guru's teachings – no smoking, no drinking, no meat."

"What about your family when you come to India?" Indraneel enquired, his curiosity about this unusual man finally awakened.

"No family. I live alone."

Indraneel was surprised. He knew many foreigners came to India in search of truth but he had never realized how much they actually absorbed.

The man sitting across the aisle seat was watching an action movie and showed his displeasure at Madhusudan's somewhat loud narration. But the foreigner was not bothered in the least.

"So what do you do in Rishikesh," Indraneel asked.

"Nothing specific, you know. Many foreigners have come to India and started on their spiritual journey after listening to me talk about my Guru. Who knows, even you may meet my Guru," Madhusudan said smiling.

The captain announced they would be landing shortly and that all passengers should fasten their seatbelts. Indraneel found Madhusudan interesting company; he had helped to distract his mind from thoughts of Avani.

On arrival they deplaned and walked to the terminal. There were no buses or aerobridges here. Indraneel was amused by the sudden drop in the pace of life.

The airport itself was small, though set in a scenic location. The surrounding mountains seemed to hold it in a protective embrace. Fat fluffy white clouds had parked themselves lazily on the hills; the air felt cool and fresh.

Madhusudan noted Indraneel's phone number, promising to take him to see Ganga *arati* [ritual offering of lit lamps]. Then he shook hands and hugged his new friend before parting ways. He waved from the taxi as he left.

There was something open and sweet about Madhusudan and Indraneel took an instant liking to him. The fact that he was not Indian and didn't know him as a film-maker, helped Indraneel feel less wary and more receptive to the large Canadian's friendly overtures.

13

The mobile phone rang as soon as Indraneel switched it on as he left the airport. It was Arunodaya.

"Indraneel, you are a classic guy...you leave for an unfamiliar destination without even confirming where you are going to stay!"

Indraneel laughed sheepishly. "Too much on my mind, *yaar*." He reiterated ruefully, "Far too much..."

"I will text you the address of the guest house Vaz has recommended. The cab driver will know the place," Arunodaya rattled off.

"What's the locality?"

"Muni-ki-reti."

"Muni-ki-reti..." Indraneel repeated. 'Strange name,' he thought, 'Sands of the Saints'.

The combination of fresh hill air and lack of sleep lulled Indraneel into deep slumber. The next thing he knew the driver was calling to him. "*Saab aap ki jagah aa gayi* [Sir, you've reached your place]."

Indraneel glanced at his watch. It had barely been a 25 minute cab ride but he felt strangely refreshed. He got out and pulled his strolley from the boot. Paying off the cabbie without even bothering to ask the amount, he walked into the guest house.

"Could you give me a room with a river view?" Indraneel asked the saffron-clad manager at Reception.

"River view? River view?" The man's laughter was touched with sarcasm.

"What's so funny?" Indraneel asked, irritated.

"There's no river here, gentleman! No river. There's only holy Gangaji," the manager informed Indraneel, ringing the bell on his table.

A *pahadi* [mountain] boy, whom the Manager called Mangal, appeared. "Which room, Swamiji?" he asked brightly.

"302. Gangaji-side," the portly Manager directed.

Indraneel regretted having shown irritation. 'Turns out the man's a Swamiji!' he thought wryly.

His room had a river view. It was only much later, when he took in the full panorama of the Ganga, that he realised what the Swamiji at Reception had tried to say – there was something unriverlike about this water body.

Indraneel looked at the fresh-faced *pahadi* boy who had picked up the keys from the Manager and shown him the room. He wore a soiled T-shirt with the intriguing message: *No Education. No Job. No Wife. Then fuck off.* Indraneel couldn't help but smile. Obviously the boy had no idea what his T-shirt said. The garment was clearly a hand-me-down from some guest.

The boy opened the balcony doors, saying simply, "Gangaji, Sir."

Dropping a ten rupee coin into the boy's hand, Indraneel told him he would call if he needed anything. He walked towards the open doors, stretching his tired body to remove the kinks in his stiff neck. He stopped in mid-motion, overwhelmed by his first sight of the Ganga. He was dumbstruck by the beauty of the river. She sparkled blue and green, glistening in the sunlight with a million diamond prisms. The sheer expanse blew him away. He had never expected anything like this.

Indraneel looked more closely to see the filth that had been so much written about, but there was nothing but a few marigold flowers floating along on the shining surface. The river appeared pristine. 'How come nobody talks about what a beautiful river the Ganga is,' he wondered. 'So much is written about the Nile and the Amazon...'

He ran to fetch his camera from his backpack and began taking pictures. After a few moments he realized he had not touched his camera for nearly three months. The familiar weight felt good in his hands. It was like finding an old friend.

Indraneel continued taking pictures as the quality of light changed. The prisms on the reflective surface of the Ganga kept changing. Finally, he put the camera down and simply gazed at the river, suddenly filled with an urge to touch the waters. He stood in silence, taking in the unfamiliar sights and sounds.

A solitary, saffron-clad man was offering something to the river. Laughter from a pilgrim group drifted across to him as he gazed at the suspension bridge spanning the water. From this distance the people on it looked like ants. Boats plied up and down, ferrying passengers.

The surroundings were alien to him and yet, somehow not at odds. Quite the contrary.

14

Indraneel had agreed to meet Madhusudan and go to see Ganga *arati* that evening. For the past week he had just slept. When awake, he felt an intense craving for alcohol. He knew Rishikesh had no bars except for some illegal taverns, so his drinking stopped cold turkey, overnight. But his smoking increased exponentially. He never stepped out of his room except to buy cigarettes from the *pan* stall opposite the guest house. He ate whatever food the boy Mangal brought to his room. His appetite increased slowly as the fresh, unpolluted air began to heal his much abused body.

Indraneel showered and walked over to the boat stand opposite Madras Café. Young girls were selling fish feed, flowers and lamps, calling out, '*Machhali ka khaanaa le lo... le lo! Machhali ka khaanaa le lo* [Buy food for the fish].' He was amused to see people buying the wheat flour balls to feed the fish in the Ganga.

He would have missed the boat but for the smiling flower girl who called out, "*Babuji!*" and informed him the boat was leaving. It was full of tourists, constantly taking pictures; a few from the Far East, though he couldn't tell whether they were Japanese, Korean or Filipino.

The motor thundered as the boat heaved off, moving smoothly towards the other bank. Indraneel leaned over the railing, running his fingers through the water lovingly, as he would have through Avani's soft hair. Despite it being a warm day, the water was surprisingly cold. Indraneel suddenly realised it came from a glacier. The man standing next to him scooped up some of the holy water in the cupped palm of his hand and placed it reverentially on his head, intoning, "*Ganga Maiyya ki jai* [Hail Mother Ganges]!"

A child leaned out of the boat and slapped the surface of the river with an open palm, splattering Indraneel's face. His mother saw this and reprimanded the child sharply. She pulled him onto her lap and smiled apologetically at Indraneel, who grinned at the child peering at him warily. He didn't bother wiping his wet face; the cool air blowing from the Ganga evaporated the moisture slowly.

He had always loved water, especially the rains. He would walk along Marine Drive in Bombay in the monsoon, listening to old Hindi film songs on his iPod....for the sheer joy of getting wet from the spray as the waves dashed against the sea wall. He had often stood at Worli Seaface, getting soaked by the giant waves, holding Avani's wet form close to him. He remembered her squealing with delight. The memory was so sharp he could almost taste the salty tang of the sea water on her lips. A fresh surge of despair filled his heart as he realised those happy moments were gone forever.

Indraneel could now see the steps of the Swargashram *ghaats* [pier], as well as a temple pillar to the right, and a clock tower further down-river. The boat ride had been short. They disembarked and walked toward Paramarth Niketan, through a narrow lane which housed several *ashrams* [hermitages], including the famous Gita Bhawan. There were also bookshops, eateries and stalls selling *puja* items such as creamy conches, beautifully carved marble idols of Ram, Sita and Hanuman, and *malas* [necklaces] of *rudraksha* beads, sandalwood and *sphatika* [crystal]. An endearing Westernised version of *Mahadeva Shambho, Shiva Shambho* (Praise Lord Shiva), played from a shop selling devotional music. Cows ambled along the streets, silently asking to be fed.

Indraneel was soon at the famous Ganga *arati* arena. He took off his sandals at the shoe stand and looked around. He smiled at Madhusudan's familiar figure towering over the crowd.

"*Hari Aum*! Welcome to Ganga *arati*," Madhusudan greeted him with a happy smile. "Let's get close to Gangaji and sit on the steps near the water."

Indraneel was glad he had come.

15

The *arati* took place on the steps of Paramarth Niketan *ghaat*. Half a dozen stepped rows led directly to the swiftly flowing water. An 18-foot high statue of Lord Shiva in meditation, sat on a platform in the river. The Lord sat on a tiger skin, sporting a crescent moon in his matted locks. The statue was well lit and one could sense the meditative poise by simply gazing at Him.

A short distance from the Ganga, a *yajna kunda* [sacred fire pit] had been installed, where children of the Paramarth Sanskrit School, clad in yellow *kurtas* and *dhotis* [traditional attire], sat. They looked charming in their glowing attire. Another group of students sat on a stage, ready to sing the *arati*, which began with the *Hanuman Chalisa* [invocation of Lord Hanuman]. Indraneel was familiar with what he thought of as its 'lyrics'. For the Ganga *arati*, hundreds of *ghee*-soaked wicks had been placed in a seven-tiered lamp. Once lit, the priest lifted the lamp to perform the *arati*.

Soon, other lamps were lit and waved before Mother Ganga. Everyone joined in the singing. The beat was so exhilarating that a couple of Romanian gypsies began to sway and then broke into a dance. The lamplight was reflected in the flowing water as the sun set.

"For me, there's no mother greater than Mother Ganga!" Madhusudan whispered into Indraneel's ear while moving to the beat.

It was all so beautiful. There were foreigners trying to capture the moment on their state-of-the-art cameras, iPads and iPhones. In the gentle breeze, hundreds of lit *diyas* [clay lamps] bobbed on the indigo waters, carried downstream, their tiny flames swaying in the breeze. 'Startling beauty in a single frame,' thought Indraneel.

In 15 minutes the entire river was punctuated with orange dots. Every *diya* carried a wish, made by the person who had lit it. Soon there were so many *diyas* of wishes floating around that the Ganga turned into a river of fire. It was a sight Indraneel found difficult to behold without emotion. Standing in this ancient spot he felt overwhelmed by the faith he saw all around him. So many people with hearts lifted in prayer! These ordinary rites of devotion, this coming together in an act of faith, these things touched him deeply. For the first time, Indraneel felt good to belong, though he was not a practising spiritualist.

"We who have seen Goddess Ganga with our own eyes are truly blessed!" Madhusudan said softly.

Indraneel was so caught in the moment that he made no attempt to take the pictures Arunodaya had requested him for. *Arati* over, the crowd dispersed and a great silence descended on the river.

"Can we sit here for a few minutes?" Indraneel asked.

"You can sit on the banks of the Ganga for a lifetime, my friend!" Madhusudan laughed.

What a joy it was to be here in the lap of the Himalayas and experience such peace, Indraneel thought, gazing at the hills beyond.

When they finally stood up to leave the *ghaats*, *Har Har Gange...Ganga Maiyya Ki Jai* [Hail Mother Ganges], echoed in Indraneel's mind.

"Come! Let me take you to Shaman's bookshop," Madhusudan suggested.

It was just a five minute walk away. In fact, they had passed it on their way to *arati*.

"Who is Shaman?" Indraneel asked, dodging an ambling cow that had appeared in his path.

"He is more than a friend," Madhusudan answered cryptically.

16

The bookshop was called Eldorado. It was rumoured that the Dalai Lama, Madonna and Ruskin Bond had all visited it. The signage, done in neat calligraphy on a rough wooden plank, hung suspended by short chains and swung carelessly in the breeze. The entrance was rather low and Indraneel had to bend to enter the store. Tinkling bells sounded the moment the door was pushed open, alerting Shaman, who usually sat reading at the counter. But he was not there now.

"*Hari Aum*, Payal! Is Shamanji here?" Madhusudan asked the girl at the counter.

"*Namaste* Madhusudanji! He is at prayers. Can I help you?" she asked with a smile that lit up her rather plain face.

Payal was a local girl with a pleasant demeanour, light eyes and a calm countenance. It was obvious she knew Madhusudan, who Indraneel rightly guessed to be a regular visitor. He was surprised that Shaman, the owner, was performing his prayers in the shop.

"We'll wait," Madhusudan told the girl.

Hunched over one of the tables sat an American. Madhusudan introduced him to Indraneel saying, "This is Michael, a researcher."

"Indraneel..."

"He's a film-maker," Madhusudan added, noticing Indraneel's reserve.

Michael merely nodded and went back to his reading. Indraneel looked around the mid-sized shop. It was brightly lit and the books were arranged neatly by genre: Yoga, Indian Literature, Classics, Poetry. The titles were sorted alphabetically... Ramakrishna, Osho, Vivekananda, Yogananda.... There was a range of new age books like *I Am That*, *Power of Now* etc. Indraneel noted there was a well-stocked children's section as well.

"Your friend has thoughtfully provided low stools so patrons can sit and browse as long as they want," Indraneel observed.

"Shaman doesn't mind if they read and don't buy. That is what makes this shop so special."

A thriving fortune bamboo plant and a Shri Yantra stood on the counter – the latter given to Shaman by his Guru. People dropped in all the time to chat. There were chairs around a table in the ante-room, where Shaman discussed all kinds of topics from politics to poverty, movies to *moksha*, with those who came.

When customers took a book from the shelf, he requested them to leave it on a table at the end of the room, not wanting to risk them putting it back in the wrong place. Shaman's life was free flowing and flexible but he sought order in his books. He didn't mind the extra effort he put into rearranging the books.

He also had a large cane basket near the entrance for people to leave their dripping umbrellas in the monsoon. On the counter he always had a cut glass vase of tube roses. Indraneel found their heady fragrance quite addictive. Shaman had put up a green felt soft board behind the billing counter for people to put up flyers and notices for free. There were notices about paying guest accommodations, as well as a quirky one which said someone was looking for authentic English muffins. Another said someone was looking for a companion to trek to the nearby Kunjapuri peak.

Indraneel liked the shop immediately; it wasn't like any other he had seen anywhere in the world. There was something intense about it, with a temple-like aura.

Indraneel's mind had calmed considerably after the Ganga *arati*. 'This is such a lovely place. There's so much calm and quiet in the people here,' he thought admiringly. He recalled with surprise that he hadn't thought of Avani in over two hours.

"Madhusudan..." Shaman emerged from within the shop and hugged the Canadian.

"I brought my new friend along to meet you, Shaman. This is Shamantak Srivastava, Indraneel."

Shaman folded his hands in a *namaste* and inclined his grizzled head. "Just call me Shaman," he said casually.

Indraneel returned the greeting in similar fashion.

Shaman was a man of medium height and wiry build, with piercing brown eyes. His salt-and-pepper hair was trimmed close to his head and he was clean-shaven. He had pronounced laughter lines which deepened every time he smiled. He was a Ph.D. from Harvard. He uniformly wore Kolhapuri *chappals*, jeans and a *kurta*, along with a large-faced watch on the inside of his right wrist.

When Shaman came into the shop in the mornings, sometimes as early as 7 am, even on dark wintry days, he just sat for some time, inhaling the fragrance of the new books that had just arrived from Delhi and were waiting to be sorted. In his ante-room he kept his own extensive collection of old books, which he read and re-read. He lent them only to close friends. Simply put, Shaman loved books. He dusted them with care and arranged them gently, almost reverentially.

"What brings you to Rishikesh, Indraneel?"

"Well, I'm taking a break."

"Breaks are good. Look at our friend Madhusudan here. He came here for a break and it has lasted 30 years!"

Indraneel noticed that Shaman was a sophisticated conversationalist.

"So Indraneel, what do you do?" Shaman asked with genuine interest.

"I am a film-maker."

"Oh, a creative man! Then this place will do you good."

"What will it do for me?"

Shaman caught the cynical note in Indraneel's voice. A little smile tugged at his mouth as he answered. "If you don't get caught up in shooting, like all those morons who are more interested in filming the river than in worshipping Gangaji, Rishikesh will blow your mind."

"How?" Indraneel was obviously sceptical.

"It will centre you. It will give you gravity. And it will give you levity. I repeat: It will centre you, give you gravity and levity."

"I don't understand." Indraneel wondered why it was necessary for Shaman to repeat his words. Nevertheless, they stuck in his mind: Centring. Gravity. Levity.

"You see, places like this have great inner energy – something centripetal that draws energy to its centre. Whoever comes here begins to look inwards. That's what Ganga and Himalaya, the twin magnets of spirituality, do to you." Shaman spoke slowly, pronouncing each word clearly. His words seem to come from some innate wisdom.

"But why do people make such a big deal about places like Rishikesh and Benares? Why do *sadhus* [ascetics] crowd there? God is everywhere, isn't He?" Indraneel asked glibly.

"Yes, God is everywhere, but the disposition to meet Him is not everywhere," Shaman answered shortly before adding, "People are interested in other things in other places, so the energy there is different. It is not centred but diffused in all directions. If you are interested in Hindi cinema, you go to Bombay. If you are seeking self-realization, you come here. There are mega malls of spirituality here. Why else would people come?"

"Maybe. But why here? Why not elsewhere?" Indraneel found it hard to accept the explanation.

"Why does iron get attracted to a magnet?" Shaman countered.

"Well, because of the magnet's properties."

"That's exactly how this works too. It follows the laws of nature. The inward energy of man is concentrated in the eastern and northern directions. In this world, our source of perception is light, and light comes from the East, when the sun rises. It comes from the North in the evening, when the North Star appears. These two directions are our natural compass points."

"I never thought of that. You explained it very well," Indraneel remarked thoughtfully.

"I'm wordy and garrulous. I might bore you if I say anymore," Shaman laughed.

"I'm not bored," Indraneel said seriously. "Tell me what's with the North?"

"You know a compass is set to absolute North? That's the benchmark. North in Sanskrit is *Uttar*, meaning 'answer'. So, all answers come from the North. *Yogis* face North to meditate, towards the holy men meditating in the northern mountains, who have the answers. And those answers come to us, too."

"Do they?" Indraneel asked uncertainly.

"Yes, they do," Shaman said with complete certainty. "Indraneel, do you pray?"

"Yes, but it's very basic. I recite the Ganesha prayer my granny taught me and I chant the *Hanuman Chalisa*. After that, I just talk to God for a few minutes."

"Great! Which direction do you face when you pray?"

"I don't really know. South?" Indraneel wasn't sure.

"Just try facing East in the mornings because East is *Purva*, meaning 'before' or 'first'. That's where one begins. And try North at night. Notice the difference," Shaman suggested.

There was no insistence in his words; Indraneel liked that.

"I will try," he said, trying to fight the growing urge to light a cigarette. But the desire was too strong. "Could we step out for a minute? If you don't mind, I'd like to smoke."

"Please yourself," answered Shaman affably.

Madhusudan nodded and they all went out to stand in the cool evening air. Indraneel offered the pack to the other two, who declined. He lit a cigarette, the butt glowing in the dark.

"Where are you going from here?" Shaman asked.

"To dinner. Madhusudan will guide me." Indraneel took another drag of his cigarette.

"I didn't mean right now. I meant where you will go from your present mental condition?"

"I don't understand." Indraneel was completely baffled by Shaman's words. He wondered if 'not getting Shaman' was becoming a pattern. Was this man a puzzle?

"If my guess is correct, you are a lost soul at the moment. Profound sorrow dwells in your eyes. Your face reflects pathos. You are not happy."

"I..." Indraneel wondered how Shaman could possibly have known, and how to obfuscate the issue.

"Don't bother, the details aren't important. The thing is you're not happy and that's not good if you want to centre yourself."

"I don't know if I want to centre myself," Indraneel protested. "You mentioned gravity and levity as well. I can make nothing of any of these things."

"You have a keen ear, Indraneel."

"You repeatedly drilled the words into me."

"Yes, sorry about that." Shaman was apologetic. "Listen, sorrow, grief and disenchantment are all good things if used well."

"What good can disenchantment do?" Indraneel had no real objection to trying this centreing Shaman recommended, if it could rid him of persistent thoughts of Avani.

"Well, the technical word for disenchantment is *vishaad*. It's a concept from the *Bhagavad Gita*. The very first chapter: *Arjuna Vishaad Yoga*. The *Gita* begins with Arjuna's disenchantment. Every quest begins with some sort of disenchantment, some disillusionment, some world-weariness. So that is good. The first chapter is about disillusionment. The Lord gives a sermon, disenchantment is dispelled, and there is enlightenment. You stand at the door of enlightenment, brother!" Shaman's words were affectionate.

Suddenly a gaggle of customers appeared, all foreigners. They greeted Shaman with '*Hari Aum*', spoken in a sing-song manner.

"You'll have to excuse me," Shaman apologised to Indraneel and Madhusudan. Waving, he walked back into the warm, inviting shop.

It was getting late anyway. Indraneel felt strangely drawn to Shaman. He experienced a sense of *déjà vu*, like he had met this person before.

"Shaman comes across as a knowledgeable man," he commented to Madhusudan as they walked along.

"Not knowledgeable, he is a plainclothes devotee, a closet *yogi*," Madhusudan remarked, adding to the growing enigma of the bookshop owner.

17

Two days had passed since the Ganga *arati* but Indraneel was still thinking about that evening spent with Madhusudan and Shaman as he walked out of the guest house at Ram Jhoola. They were normal people, he thought, English-speaking, modern and savvy. Yet there was something in them that Indraneel could not quite fathom. Why did people quit exciting lives to come here? What was this 'seeking' all about? Why did people actually cross the seven seas to visit India? Why?

Before they had parted, Madhusudan had told Indraneel that he would introduce him to Vedavati, a German lady who had lived in Rishikesh for 30 years.

"She fills the hours of solitude making devotional art," Madhusudan had mentioned.

The next day, Madhusudan showed Indraneel some marvellous oil paintings by Vedavati – a lovely image of the Mother Mary, one of Garuda, another of a *sadhu* with a *trishul*, etc. There was a simplicity to them which Indraneel loved. He had learnt to understand and appraise art from his mother; these paintings were good.

They were to meet Vedavati at six that evening and as Indraneel walked along, he spotted Madhusudan, wearing a yellow T-shirt with *Aum*, over white baggy trousers.

"*Chalo*! Let me take you to Vedavati," he suggested enthusiastically.

Indraneel was amused by the Canadian's local lingo. He had picked up Hindi really well. They took an auto-rickshaw to Seesham Jhaadi and then walked to the small lane leading to Vedavati Kutir.

Vedavati's original name was Viktoria Hoffmann. Her Guru had named her Vedavati. A disciple of Naam Yajnananda Maharaj, she was Madhusudan's Guru-sister.

They rang the bell. The door opened almost immediately. In the rapidly descending dusk stood Vedavati, a frail lady with a long blonde plait hanging over one shoulder. She was about 70 years old but appeared full of life. She greeted them with a high-pitched '*Hari Aum*'. Dressed all in white, her face was wreathed in smiles as she gracefully put her palms together in a formal *namaste*. One could see the Indian way of life had taken deep root in her, transforming her completely. She seemed glad to see them.

"I'm Indraneel…"

"Oh yes, Madhusudan told me about you."

Vedavati gestured for them to be seated. Indraneel noticed a pack of Toblerone chocolates on the table beside the water jug and smiled.

"What brings you to Rishikesh?" she asked.

"I'm on holiday…"

"Holidays are nice! You'll like the serene atmosphere here."

"Yes, it's a lovely place. I'm enjoying myself," Indraneel replied courteously, glancing around the house. It was lit like an inner temple. An aura of peace and piety pervaded the small but beautiful rooms.

"May I ask why your Guru named you Vedavati?" Indraneel asked hesitantly, not wishing to seem intrusive.

"Ha ha…that's an interesting question. Vedavati… You know, when I came to India for the first time and started going to Sivananda Ashram and Purna Prajna Ashram, I couldn't understand Sanskrit. So, whenever there was a Vedanta class, I understood nothing. I would just sit quietly like a mouse. But I loved the sound of Sanskrit; it felt like a divine song, some sort of prayer. Back then I didn't know Sanskrit was called *Devabhasha*, 'language of the gods'. Then a *sannyasi* [renunciate] at Vedanta class taught me Hindi, and some Sanskrit. That is how I started. I would ask my Guru many questions about the *Upanishads* and the *Bhagawad Gita*. One day, he laughingly said, 'Viktoria, you are a child of Saraswati. From now on I will call you Vedavati.'"

Indraneel loved her simplicity. She was such a genuine and warm-hearted person.

Vedavati spoke softly. Her English was not very good but she managed to convey the deep pull she felt towards Indian religion and spirituality. She told Indraneel about the Guru she and Madhusudan shared – Naam Yajnananda. Then she asked Indraneel a few questions about what he did and where he lived. She was most excited to hear that he was a film-maker.

"I must confess I have seen few movies, but *The Passion of Joan of Arc* – Carl Theodor Dreyer's silent, fascinating and forbidding masterpiece, is my favourite."

When Indraneel mentioned that he too loved it, she beamed with joy.

"Look at this, Madhu! Indraneel has seen the movie! I can't believe it!"

"The story of Joan of Arc, a 15th-century French peasant girl who heard voices telling her to lead a mission to throw out the English..." Indraneel related softly.

"Yessss...that's the one!"

The conversation meandered from Joan of Arc to Papa Ramdas, the saint who had an *ashram* in Kerala.

"Papa Ramdas has been a source of inspiration to me personally," Madhusudan told them.

"His writings go straight to the heart. He has a directness and candour that is self-evident and needs no argument," Vedavati agreed.

"I get what you're saying. Shaman calls it 'absence of intellectuality', which brings out the radiance of the soul-sun," Madhusudan observed.

"Hold on, hold on....absence of intellectuality which brings out the radiance of the soul-sun? That's pretty complex. This Shaman chap seems to be a genius, huh?" Indraneel remarked irreverently.

"Oh yeah, a genius! But isn't he much more than that, Madhu?" Vedavati turned to her Guru-brother.

"Yes, much more...."

"He's a saint!" Vedavati said with conviction.

It was time to leave. Indraneel would have loved to stay longer but Madhusudan had still to find someone to repair his laptop.

18

Indraneel wished to spend time with Shaman for reasons he himself did not quite understand. On the face of it Shaman was a knowledgeable man and there was a lot one could learn from him, but it was Shaman's enigmatic personality that drew Indraneel. He casually dropped by the shop. Shaman was standing outside and greeted him warmly.

"I was wondering if we could just chat," Indraneel said awkwardly.

Shaman nodded. "Sure, sure...but right now I am going to collect a package. Why don't we meet this evening at the German Bakery?"

Indraneel agreed, smiling.

"My pleasure." Shaman began to walk away but turned back to say, "Browse and read in the store if you feel like it."

Indraneel once again thanked him and entered the shop. The signature smell of tuberoses permeated the air. There were many interesting books in the shop; Indraneel browsed through a dozen and bought two before leaving for the guest house.

Indraneel always travelled with a collection of Oscar-winning films. He watched parts of two movies on his laptop that afternoon. He was to meet Shaman at the German Bakery near Lakshman Jhoola at 7 pm.

The auto-rickshaw dropped him close by, beyond which point he had to walk. There was a bite in the air, with autumn yielding reluctantly to winter. Indraneel asked a man hurrying by how to get to the German Bakery and was pointed in the right direction. He ran up the steps, panting with the effort. How out of shape he had become! He looked around but there was no sign of Shaman. There were just two people – a big Caucasian man, typing furiously into his Mac, and a young French girl, sitting in an impossible yoga posture, reading a book and occasionally sipping her tea.

Indraneel made his way to a corner table. The flooring was made of loose Ganga pebbles and the red and white tablecloths looked neat and clean. The café sat perched high on a natural cliff, overlooking the river, with a 180 degree view. It was close to the famous rope bridge and one could see people on it, jostling for space with scooters and trying to avoid the chattering monkeys which jumped about. When the monkeys smelt anything edible, they lunged for it and then dashed off. They were fearless and ferocious. Indraneel reached for his camera and took some pictures of the Ganga in the dying light.

The waiter came to ask if he was Indraneel. Surprised, he nodded.

"Shamanji asked you to try the hot lemon-honey-ginger, and said he would be at the table in five minutes."

Indraneel ordered the beverage and waited. Night had descended and a soft blackness enveloped everything outside. Suddenly the power went off. Some children who were playing below, squealed with excitement. Indraneel knew this was a common occurrence.

The waiter came to the table with a lit candle. As he looked at the melting wax near the burning wick, Indraneel remembered another occasion when the power had gone off. Avani and he had been to watch a play at the NCPA, and he had offered to drop her home since he was to pick up someone at the airport later that night. But the play had been so bad they had abandoned it at the intermission. Since they were close to his place, Indraneel asked Avani home for a drink. She agreed, so they drove to Cuffe Parade. His parents were away, attending a wedding in Jaipur, so it was just him and her.

Like his office, the large penthouse apartment offered a stunning view of the sea. Avani gasped and ran like a child to the huge floor-to-ceiling glass windows. Indraneel thought once again how beautiful she was in her flame-coloured silk sari and tiny gold blouse. He couldn't help being besotted though he was aware she was seeing someone else and he himself still legally married to Chitra, despite their separation.

Suddenly, there was a power outage and in an instant the glittering lights of Bombay were hidden under a cloak of darkness. One could see the little fishing boats with their lanterns bobbing up and down in the sea. The crescent moon came into its own. The twinkling lights seemed to have been transferred to the starry sky.

Avani stared in wonder. "Wow!" she whispered.

The building generator started up and the lights came back on. But Avani asked if they could turn them off for a little longer. Indraneel readily agreed and switched off the lights. Bringing in a perfumed pink candle, he set it in the polished brass candlestand, its small flame shedding a soft swaying light. He went to stand beside Avani at the window. The cool breeze made her hair fly. He touched the thick strands that blew across his face. They felt like fragrant silk.

Though he was immune to the view, having seen it all his life, her excitement was infectious. He watched her thinking how gorgeous she was.

Time passed in complete silence. In the darkness one could hear things more clearly and they had both caught the strains of the old English song, *Sealed with A Kiss* by Jason Donovan, from the floor below. Avani commented that it was one of her favourite songs.

"Dance?" Indraneel proposed.

She thought for a moment, then nodded, saying, "Why not?"

To an onlooker it must have seemed rather foolish – a couple dancing without either lights or music. And yet it had been magical for them both. It had been casual to begin with, her hands resting loosely on his shoulders while his circled her slender waist lightly. Her bare midriff felt like silk. After a few minutes he pulled her close and kissed her on the cheek. She did not resist. In fact, Indraneel felt her move imperceptibly closer. Emboldened, he kissed her on the lips.

The mainline power returned. Children within the building shrieked in excitement. The tender moment was broken and Indraneel gently released Avani. There was no awkwardness between them, nor did they refer to the incident.

When he dropped her off that night, Indraneel kissed Avani on the forehead. He had decided to pursue her. So what if she was seeing someone else? Thereafter, he discovered her plans discreetly through friends and tried to be at the same parties and plays, doing his best to make it seem coincidental. Prabhu Da being Avani's mentor helped.

Indraneel was not sure whether she had noticed what he was up to. He decided to offer her a position as Assistant Director since there wasn't much happening with her acting career, only offers for tacky Gujarati plays, which she turned down. He wanted to spend more time with her...

The lights came back on at the German Bakery. Indraneel saw Shaman come striding in like a king.

"Hi! Did I keep you waiting?"

"Not at all. As Madhusudan says, one can spend a lifetime watching the Ganga," Indraneel said, only half in jest.

"Yes, *teertha*...the sacred water flows..." Shaman said almost to himself.

A bull bellowed and ambled along in the darkness. Indraneel could see the lights on the other bank of the river. The Buddha Café and other eateries on the sloped terrain were illuminated.

"Thank you for suggesting the hot ginger-lemon-honey drink. The waiter gave me your message." Indraneel raised the glass that still had some of the sparkling honey-hued liquid.

"Did he? Great!" Shaman glanced around to locate the obliging waiter.

"By the way, what did you mean by *teertha*?" Indraneel asked curiously. "I thought *teertha* means a holy place?"

"Yes. Just *teertha* means 'sacred water' but *teertha kshetra* is 'holy spot'. It could be a river, ocean or mountain. The scriptures talk of seven towns as givers of *moksha*: Ayodhya, Mathura, Kashi etc. These places are supposed to be the seven doors to God."

"That's interesting. But why are they specifically the doors? Why isn't Bombay or New York a door to God?"

"They are *the* doors because things come in and go out here, as they do in your body. Your body too, is a Puri – a holy city. Did you know that?"

"No..."

"Well, two eyes, two ears, two nostrils and a mouth – these seven are the doors. The whole body is, in fact, a door, but these organs are especially open – things enter the body through them and go out. Unlike say hands or feet. So, while Bombay is a door, these are greater doors."

"What's so special about these places? I mean, isn't God everywhere? Why does one have to go to Benares to find Him?" Indraneel asked, glancing at the Ganga.

"You're right. It's just that at any given point in time there are more people looking for God in these places. And these people put together the subtle technologies of God-seeing. So it becomes easier for the keen ones to see. If you light a torch, even I can see if I'm on the same path as you. In places like Benares and Haridwar, such torches are well-lit in every corner. And that helps."

"I see what you mean, but what's stopping people from putting together God-seeing technologies in Bombay and New York?"

"The vibrations of those places are different. In Bombay and New York more people are likely to respond to the word 'gold' than 'God'. Here, there is already a field planted over centuries; you can't disturb it."

"You mentioned Haridwar. What vibration is there in Haridwar? Somehow I feel that places like Haridwar and Benares are places of death. I find them dark."

"I'm not surprised, Indraneel. Many people are blinded by the darkness of ignorance, as you are just now. There's a powerful *shakti* [energy] in Haridwar. There are two powerful *shakti* temples – Chandi and Manasa."

"I would like to go sometime, but not alone," Indraneel declared.

"When would you like to go?"

"I don't know. Sometime soon."

"What are you doing tomorrow?"

"Tomorrow? Well, nothing in particular..."

"We'll go tomorrow then," Shaman decided.

Before they parted, Shaman gave Indraneel a book on the life of Naam Yajnananda Maharaj and his doctrine. Indraneel was not keen on reading it but since sleep eluded him that night, he began to browse through the pages for want of anything else to do. It was a well written biography. Indraneel sat up reading till 1 am.

19

The next day, Indraneel and Shaman visited the two Devi temples in Haridwar. Both shrines were perched high in the hills, on opposite sides of the Ganga. At Haridwar, the Ganga enters the plains. Chandi Devi and Manasa Devi temples welcome the river to the plains, serving as her sentinels. Both temples are accessible by cable car.

Indraneel felt a new sense of freedom as they skimmed high over the treetops, with a panoramic view of the Ganga spread in all her glory as the plains received her. The silence in the glass cubicle was complete. It encased him in a private world of awe at the untamed beauty of nature. Though the ride was brief, it was enchanting. Shaman told him the idol of Chandi Devi had been established by Adi Shankara. Roughly hewn, it had a deep ochre colour and commanding eyes that seemed all-encompassing and all-knowing.

"It seems like She knows everything I want. I don't feel the need to vocalise my prayers. I just know she *knows it all*," Indraneel said to Shaman, feeling bewildered and overcome.

"Yes, she is the Mother Goddess. She knows it all. I'm glad you were willing to be childlike. An open heart and mind opens all doors." Shaman popped some *prasad* into his mouth.

Mansa Devi was located atop Bilwa Parvat in the Shivalik hills. The Goddess was said to have emerged from the mind of Sage Kashyapa, in response to his desire for a daughter. *Mansa* means 'wish'. It is believed the Goddess fulfils the wishes of all sincere devotees. Her form is finely crafted of shining white marble, beautifully embellished, and she has many faces.

Indraneel gazed at the infinite kindness in those eyes and experienced an overwhelming desire to pour out his troubled heart. After the *darshan* [viewing], he felt a strange emptiness, almost relief. So much had been going on in Indraneel's mind that the intensity of his thoughts and feelings sometimes made him feel he had lost himself somewhere along the way.

Standing before Ma Manasa, he had felt troubled. 'What do I ask from the Mother? Success in my film career? No, that is not in my mind at all. Avani? No, that is long past. What then? Ultimate truth? Am I being brainwashed by this guy, Shaman? Should I ask her to sort out the muddle of existence in my head?' he wondered frantically, gazing into those all-seeing eyes.

Though unsure of his own mind, Indraneel's heart felt lighter as he left the presence of the deity. Unbidden tears came to his eyes and he turned away, not wanting Shaman to see.

A priest was selling red threads under a *karpatra* tree; one could make a wish, tie the thread around the trunk of the ancient tree, and return to untie it once the wish had been granted.

Indraneel watched Shaman tie a thread and then asked curiously, "What could you possibly want, Shaman? A person like you tying a thread here? What did you wish for?"

"And what kind of person am I?" Shaman asked laughing. He did not wait to hear Indraneel's reply before adding, "I asked the Divine Mother to free me from all desires."

"I'm sorry; it was personal."

"Nothing personal, dear one. I feel like an atom in front of the Devi. In this stupendously vast universe, what is the value of a wish from an atom like me? Anyway, I've already told you what I wished for." Shaman was astonishingly candid.

Indraneel looked at the thousands of threads tied with complete faith, each carrying a prayer to Mansa Devi.

"Only She is real," Shaman said softly as they walked out of the temple precincts.

It was hot and dusty and the two of them felt tired but strangely satiated. A long tail of traffic inched forward along the crowded road. Between two towns they passed a small forest section known as Motichur Reserve. A mountain stream gurgled and tumbled over big, smooth boulders. Indraneel noticed the delicate arches of a quaint old bridge, now abandoned. Further on, there was a more modern bridge, spanning the stream. Their car crawled over the bridge and they had ample time to observe their surroundings.

The stream was framed by lush green cover on either side, so luxurious that sunlight did not seem to penetrate the canopy of trees. As Indraneel looked down, a doe emerged, hesitantly sniffing the air. Fascinated, his eyes remained glued to the elegant animal. Shaman had noticed her too. She had a beautiful, brown coat with white spots. A small fawn emerged from the trees, sticking close to his mother. The doe, confident there was no immediate danger, nudged the fawn to drink from the stream. As the fawn bent to the water, their car moved; the jam had cleared.

It seemed so strange to Indraneel to see wildlife so close, in their natural habitat. Shaman told him he had seen deer and elephants at Janaki *ghaat*, in Koyal Ghaati.

"It's a wonderful walk along the river, ending at the barrage. You must go there in the morning, take a dip in the river, and walk around," Shaman suggested.

Indraneel was excited by this piece of information. He had not visited the Rajaji National Park, though Arunodaya had been hounding him to do so from his first day in Rishikesh. He thought of going to Janaki *ghaat* the very next morning. He also wished to visit Naam Yajnananda Maharaj's *ashram*. It was Navaratri; Devi had been installed and was being worshipped over nine days at the *ashram*.

'I could walk around Janaki *ghaat* in the morning and then go to the *ashram*,' Indraneel thought. He told Shaman of the planned visit.

"If you are going, I'd like you to take some CDs of *Varakari* devotional music and incense sticks from Pandharpur to the *ashram* and give them to a devotee called Nagaraj," Shaman requested.

He had them in his sling bag and handed them over to Indraneel, who nodded in agreement.

20

After his walk along Janaki *ghaat*, Indraneel headed for Naam Yajnananda Maharaj's *ashram* for Devi *darshan*. He carried with him the CDs and incense sticks for Nagaraj. Getting on a *phatphatiya* (six-seater rickshaw with a motorbike engine), charging 10 rupees per passenger, he got off a little ahead of the actual lane.

"Just walk along the Ganga and you'll reach Ananda Ashram," a local told him.

Indraneel bathed in the waters of the Ganga and changed into fresh clothes. Then he walked to the *ashram*. It had a huge gate with a small and tasteful sign saying: Ananda Ashram. Established in 1956. As he entered, Indraneel felt a surge of peace and purity. Walking in he heard a rhythmic sound – a man was rubbing sandalwood on a rough stone. The deep fragrance hung in the air.

He saw the head cook instructing his assistants how he wanted the almonds cut for the evening *prasad*. There were many *kutirs* or individual rooms, all ensconced in silence. Indraneel peeped into one and found the inmates deep in meditation. Curling smoke from the *yajnakunda* and the unmistakable scent of wood, smoke and *ghee,* greeted him. A woman was sweeping the temple, singing the *Hare Krishna mahamantra* softly. Another woman repeated the words as she sat washing the large bronze lamps and *arati* plate. There was also a large patch of pumpkins, with gourds the size of oversized footballs, nestling amidst the green tendrils.

"I'm Indraneel Barua," he said, introducing himself to one of the young *sadhus*. "I came for Devi *darshan,* and to give this to Nagaraj."

The *sadhu* nodded and led him to where the huge Devi idol had been installed, clad in a red sari and astride a lion. Ganesha and Kartikeya stood beside her. At her feet were the two demons, their hearts pierced by her trident. Her commanding presence was majestic and the lustrous gaze of her large eyes intense and lifelike, even in their stillness.

Indraneel closed his eyes and prayed to Devi to remove the obstacles in his life. When he opened his eyes, the *sadhu* was no longer there. Another *sadhu* sat in a corner, reading from a text.

"Where can I meet Nagaraj?" Indraneel asked hesitantly, sorry to disturb the scripture reading.

The *sadhu* looked up. "Nagaraj? He must be in one of those rooms," he said, pointing south.

As Indraneel began to walk in the direction pointed out, another young priest brought him *prasad* [food offered to God and then distributed to devotees as a blessing], in a leaf-bowl. He thanked the priest and ate the *prasad*. It was delicious coconut fudge.

Nagaraj was sitting in a small room that looked like an office. "Welcome, welcome," he said in heavily accented English, offering Indraneel a seat. "I hear you are a film-maker and future *yogi* [seeker of enlightenment, following one of the eight prescribed paths]."

"A film-maker yes, but future *yogi*? Who told you that?"

"Shamanji. He's never wrong. His word is like Lord Ramachandra's arrow; it never misses the mark." Nagaraj laughed at his own joke.

Indraneel handed over the packets of incense and the CDs Shaman had sent. Nagaraj offered Indraneel black tea and told him a little about Swami Naam Yajnananda, between phone calls. He was organizing a million things in connection with the Navaratri *puja* at the *ashram*.

Indraneel sipped his black tea; it was not bad. Though Nagaraj insisted he stay a while, Indraneel did not want to be in the way on a busy day. On his way out, he saw three large baskets full of pink lotuses. An old *sadhu* sat counting them. Indraneel wondered why the blooms needed to be counted.

As if reading his mind, a lady devotee who was checking that the flowers were in pristine condition, told him they needed 108 perfect flowers for the *puja* later in the day. "One lotus is offered for each of the 108 names of Devi," she said.

21

The beautiful Devi seated on the big cat, and the lotuses, reminded him of his visit to the Mahalakshmi Temple in Mumbai. That day, Indraneel had finished earlier than anticipated. The day's shooting had been wrapped up by 4 pm.

Everything had gone well. He was getting into the car at Filmistan when he decided to call Avani and check what she was doing. He was pleasantly surprised to know that she too, had just finished a Gujarati voice-over at a dubbing studio close by.

"If you're free, could we meet up?" Indraneel suggested.

"Sure! Pick me up from Cinemax at Juhu." Avani's response had been direct and unhesitant.

When he got there, she was already waiting for him outside the building, in the process of removing the jacket she was wearing.

"It's like Siberia in there," she said, giving him a semi-hug as she got into the car. "Those dubbing studios are all freezing." She stuffed the jacket into her large shoulder bag. She was casually dressed in a pink sleeveless vest and snugly fitting jeans. Indraneel could not take his eyes off her as she reached into her bag for her dark glasses and put them on.

Avani suddenly became aware that Indraneel was watching her. "What are you staring at?" she asked with a half smile.

"You!" Indraneel replied unapologetically.

She blushed. "I think eyes on the road are safer for now!"

They chatted about their day at work.

When Indraneel asked where she would like to go, she replied, "Anywhere. A long drive perhaps?"

"In this traffic?" Indraneel pointed to the congested road which seemed to have every possible form of transport. There were cars of every description, lorries, tankers carrying chemicals, buses overflowing with people, autos, as well as vendors touting car chargers, and urchins selling roses and the evening newspaper.

"I don't mind the traffic," said Avani cheerfully. "In fact, it's the pulse of Bombay. I like even the horns and traffic fumes. I love the fact that the city never sleeps."

"Like Seattle?" Indraneel laughed.

"No, *not* like Seattle," Avani immediately retorted. "I meant that it's so different from Indore, where I grew up."

"Well then, a long and exciting stop-start drive is all yours."

Indraneel drove towards the city. He turned on the radio and the opening beats of *Churaa liya hai tumne jo dil ko* [You've stolen my heart], a Hindi film song, filled the car.

"I love this song," Avani smiled, humming to the infectious beat.

"Yes, I do too," Indraneel agreed. "Panchamda's music is so full of passion. That opening sound we heard, I read somewhere that it was created with a glass tumbler and steel spoon."

When they passed Bombay Scottish, Indraneel pointed it out to her saying, "That is the school I went to."

"Bombay Scottish? No wonder you are friends with half the film industry! Almost every other celebrity studied in your school."

It was almost 6pm when they drove past Mahalakshmi Temple's narrow entrance lane.

"You must have been to this temple many times?" Avani asked, taking it for granted.

Indraneel paused for moment and then said, "Actually no....I've never been inside."

"Whaaat? You mean you have *never* been to Mahalakshmi Temple?"

"No." Indraneel wished she wouldn't make such a big thing of it. Despite himself, he felt a little guilty.

Avani decided instantly that they would go to the temple right then.

"You get the yummiest *bhajjis* [batter-fried onions] there," she said, trying to tempt him.

"*Bhajjis*? You mean *pakodas* and stuff?"

"You heard me...*bhajjis*."

With great difficulty Indraneel managed a U-turn and drove into the narrow lane leading to the temple. It was surprisingly empty. They easily found a parking slot. There were many vendors selling *puja* baskets. Indraneel gave Avani a look that said 'You're the boss, I don't know these things'.

"I want a single lotus," she said quietly.

By the time Avani had fished out the money for the flower, Indraneel had already paid for it. She was surprised and smiled her thanks. They went up the stairs together. There were stalls selling garlands of tuberoses, incense sticks and *mithai* [sweets] for *prasad* [offering to the deity]. Popular Hindi songs, remixed with religious lyrics, played loudly. The effect was quite ludicrous. *Maiyyaa aajaa...* styled after the famous item number *Kaataa lagaa*, had them both in splits.

They reached the top of the stairs, mirth writ across their happy faces. Avani told him to leave his shoes in one corner. As they walked towards the golden idols, there was a reverent hush despite the noise outside. They could see the lapping sea waves just meters away. The three Devis stood with hands raised, blessing the city and people of Bombay.

"You know where Bombay gets its wealth? There's so much money here because of Ma Mahalakshmi," Avani stated with complete conviction.

"I thought Mumbai derived its name from Mumbadevi," Indraneel, the eternal sceptic, retorted.

"They are the same!" Avani declared, facing the deity. "Look! On either side are Durga and Saraswati." She closed her eyes and prayed for four long minutes.

Indraneel shut his eyes briefly, then opened them and just looked at the idols closely. They wore different coloured saris – red, green and yellow, and had *mehendi* [henna] designs etched on their open palms, lifted to bless their devotees. He wondered how a frozen bronze statue could exude maternal love.

Avani touched him on the shoulder and gestured they should move on. They were standing directly in front of the three deities. Avani took a 100 rupee note from her bag and put it on the plate that had a lamp on it. Indraneel wanted to put something in as well but Avani held his hand and said it was enough, from them both. The priest waved the flame in front of the faces of the goddesses, casting light on their smiling features, before handing them some *prasad*.

They walked out towards the sea and Avani guided Indraneel to a wall just behind the temple, which had several coins stuck on it. She fished out a coin and attempted to stick it on the wall as well, explaining to Indraneel that anyone who succeeded in doing so, was sure to become very wealthy. Unfortunately, the coin did not stick and fell into the slot from which dropped coins were collected by the temple authorities. Avani tried several times, but in vain. Indraneel gave her the coins he had, but alas they too, failed to stick.

Indraneel had one last coin. "This is the last one. Let's give it a shot together," he said.

They placed the two rupee coin on the wall, pressing hard with their thumbs. It stuck. Avani was elated and hugged Indraneel with the unadulterated joy of a child. He hugged her back.

With an arm around her waist, he asked, "Now, where are the *bhajjis*?"

"That's where we're heading to. I missed lunch and I'm very hungry," Avani answered happily.

Indraneel marvelled at her spontaneity and innocence as they walked down the steps leading to a small eatery with a tin roof. It had steel chairs and tables randomly scattered about. Apart from a few canoodling couples in the corners, the place was empty. It overlooked the sea and the setting sun had painted the water in blazing scarlet. They gazed at the unbridled beauty of sun and sea. There was a strange stillness all around.

'A daily occurrence but nobody in Bombay has the time to enjoy it,' thought Indraneel.

"*Sirf bhajji hai* [only *bhajjis* are available]," the bored waiter muttered routinely.

"*Do plate lao* [Give us two plates]," Indraneel said, holding up two fingers.

Suddenly they heard drumbeats in the distance. The quiet of the evening was shattered. As the minutes passed, the tempo and volume of the drumbeats increased. Indraneel and Avani turned towards the sea. Despite all the noise and fanfare, just a small Ganapati was brought for *visarjan* [idol immersion] by a large group of young boys, yelling at the top of their voices: *Ganapati Bappa morya* [Lord Ganapati, bless us]!

"But Ganapati *visarjan* is on the 19th isn't it?" Indraneel asked. "Today is the 14th."

Just then their *bhajjis* arrived. Piping hot, they were accompanied by a spicy chutney. Avani picked one up, blew on it, turning the small golden sphere to cool it.

"Today is Gauri – she leaves on the fifth day. Those who pray to Parvati as well as Ganesha, do *visarjan* on day five."

The rays of the setting sun fell on Avani's face. She looked beautiful and sensuous in the tight clingy vest. Her hair was tied back in a ponytail, drawing attention to her delicate neck.

They ate their delicious *bhajjis*, dipping them in the spicy chutney. More Ganeshas appeared. The sea looked like a crimson lake. The drums made conversation impossible. They paid and were about to leave when Indraneel saw some people whispering into the ears of the departing Ganapatis. Intrigued, he pulled at Avani's waist and asked what they were doing. She was surprised at the physical contact but showed no signs of discomfort. In fact, she rather liked it.

"People ask for their dearest wishes by whispering them into Ganapati's ears. In fact, they wait on the beaches so they can post their pleas into the ears of 21, 51 or perhaps 108 Ganeshas..."

Indraneel was so surprised he thought she was pulling his leg. Then he realised she was dead serious.

"Do *you* wish to say anything into Ganesha's ear?" she asked conspiratorially.

"I don't know... Could we take a closer look?"

Avani nodded. Leaving the car parked in the temple premises they walked to the rocky beach behind the temple. The *visarjans* were on in full swing. The loud drumbeats were hypnotic. There were Ganapatis of all sizes; some came in cars, others in tempos. Some were simply carried on people's heads. There was a crazed air of charged energy. Everyone was dancing. Shouts of *Ganapati Bappa Morya!* rose from a hundred throats.

As one group finished, another *visarjan* began. *Gulaal* [red powder], was scattered into the air, raising scarlet clouds. Indraneel saw a primordial and intense display of devotion. There was something deeply personal about it, something that took one beyond...

Indraneel held Avani close. She held onto his arm. Children danced around joyfully. Less noisy *aratis* were also performed for some of the Ganeshas and *prasad* was distributed.

Indraneel was surprised to find himself clapping to the famous *Jaya Dev Jaya Dev Jai Mangal Murati* [a song in praise of Lord Ganesha]. Avani accepted some *sheera* [an Indian sweet], in her joined palms. She gave some to Indraneel first and then raised the rest to her mouth.

They seemed to have crossed an invisible milestone in their relationship.

A large Ganesha, standing on a mouse, came in an open lorry. The idol was at least 15 feet high. The noise and cacophony of drumbeats reached an ear-deafening crescendo. The sound of ringing bells and blowing conches filled the air. The crowd jostled forward as everyone rushed to whisper something into Ganapati's large ears. Avani looked at Indraneel but he shook his head saying it would be a bad idea to go any closer. So they just sat and watched, arms around each other.

A fat eunuch, dressed in a glittering and garish orange sari, came to ask them for money, with the signature clapping of hands. Avani got a creepy feeling and moved closer to Indraneel. Unperturbed, he gave the eunuch 50 rupees. He blessed them saying, "*Tumhaari jodi salaamat rahe* [May you as a couple, stay protected]."

"Are we a *jodi*?" Indraneel asked Avani softly after the eunuch had left. She merely smiled.

The big Ganesha was inching its way to the water. Firecrackers were lit in his path. There was frenzied activity and the drumming was so loud they made sane thought impossible.

Indraneel bent close to Avani's ear. "I think it's time we left..."

She nodded. He helped her to her feet and they headed back to the car. The drumbeats mercifully faded into the distance.

22

There was something about Rishikesh that appealed deeply to Indraneel. He could not say exactly what it was but the place brought him peace. He enjoyed the leisurely pace of his life here; went on long walks and took hundreds of photos. Exercise in the pollution-free environment restored his appetite and helped him sleep better. The complete change of scene worked positively on him. There were no reminders of Avani here. This place did not carry the burden of memories, happy or sad.

Rishikesh had a considerable international tourist population who helped to define the town. There were also a large number of small, speciality restaurants serving different cuisines. Italian, Japanese and Iranian food was freely available.

Indraneel had always loved 'people watching'. Here, he had the opportunity to watch thousands, from diverse nations and social classes. It distracted his mind somewhat from his inner struggle. Rishikesh provided him with enough natural beauty to keep him engaged. The skies were a kaleidoscope of changing colours which fascinated him. He spent hours taking photographs with different filters in various light conditions.

Indraneel decided to stay on for a while without an agenda – just breathe and live.

23

Vedavati accompanied Indraneel to Shaman's shop one evening. He greeted them with a warm *'Hari Aum'* and offered them a choice of tea or coffee. They both declined. Vedavati mentioned she had a houseguest – Pierre Reine – a French author who had recently published *Descent of the Nagas*.

"Shaman, you might like to meet him. He is very knowledgeable. If you're interested, I will ask him about a convenient time and let you know."

"I have *Descent of the Nagas* here in the shop," Shaman said, pointing to the copies on display. "It is doing well, especially with the foreigners."

"I was introduced to Pierre in Paris, by a friend of mine. I think he had come to give an inter-faith talk, and to promote his book," Vedavati told him. "Although Pierre knows much and speaks much, somehow I cannot relate to his interpretations." She had, however, loved his book, which she read in the original French. *Descent of the Nagas* was a recent English translation.

Shaman pondered a moment. "It might be interesting. See when it would be convenient for him."

"Indraneel, you come too. Shaman, he can come?" Vedavati looked at Shaman, head on one side like a little sparrow.

"Of course, of course...authors and film-makers are more akin than booksellers and film-makers," Shaman responded laughing.

"You're hardly a bookseller, Shaman!" Vedavati chuckled.

"It's my bread and butter; I must own up to my profession."

On their way back, Vedavati spoke to Indraneel about Pierre, saying she found him a lively and observant person. Despite his deep knowledge, he had the air of being an unburdened soul. He lived a simple life and was interested in day-to-day things. He often closeted himself in his room for hours, a day, a week. Perhaps he read or wrote in solitude.

"Every day," Vedavati told Indraneel, "he leaves for the other side of Ganga and mingles with the hobo *sadhus* there."

"Why the hobos?" Indraneel enquired.

Vedavati did not know. She had tried to direct Pierre to the more established *sadhus* who had distinguished themselves and become *mahatmas* [great souls], but Pierre remained sceptical about them. The great souls who presided over the larger spiritual institutions in Rishikesh held no interest for him. He considered them to be hypocrites, for they had a roof over their head and many luxuries, including cars and air conditioners. That, he thought, was not how a *sadhu* ought to live.

Vedavati had tried, feebly, to tell him that these *mahatmas* had undergone many hardships in their years of austerity and it did not matter if they enjoyed a little luxury now. What mattered was that they had found spiritual illumination. But Pierre disagreed. The *sadhus* on the road were his kind. Not being argumentative by nature, Vedavati had not pursued the matter.

A few days later, Shaman and Indraneel met the author at Vedavati's house. Indraneel arrived first and she offered him a seat on the terrace, where she had arranged the chairs so as to avoid being in the direct sun.

"We'll wait for Shaman and Pierre. Sit comfortably," she said. "I'm catching up on some things in the house so I'll be back in a while."

Indraneel sat looking at the huge *neem* tree outside. Shaman and Pierre arrived almost simultaneously. Vedavati carried in a jug of watermelon juice, which she offered to everyone, making introductions at the same time.

"Shaman, since you handle so many books, I'd like to ask what you think of the *vaani* [voice] of saints as opposed to other writings?" Pierre asked.

"There's something utterly limiting in the writings of authors who are full of themselves," Shaman replied in a no-nonsense manner. "Noble saints, on the other hand, effaced themselves, bending before the fount of eternal knowledge. Therefore, when they write, God speaks." He named Tulasidas, Kalidas, Kabir and Surdas. "They laid their work at God's feet. They waited for God to inspire their words. Their writing is life-transforming as opposed to just intellectually exciting."

Shaman sipped his watermelon juice, waiting for Pierre's response to his direct words.

"You say Kabir is one of them, but Kabir was not self-effacing. He indulged in self-glorification. At the end of his verses he says, *Kahat Kabir* [Says Kabir], identifying the work with his name. He did not surrender authorship the way you say," Pierre said rather acerbically.

"No, that is just a manner of speaking. Kabir does not use his name for..."

"But he propagated himself," Pierre insisted.

"You have missed the point. Kabir referred to himself...why?" Shaman asked.

"To glorify himself; it's obvious," Pierre stated.

"Absolutely not! He could have used 'I' instead or '*Kabir kahat*'. But he did not. His was a subtle third person usage which comes when one has evolved beyond the sense of I. This kind of third person referral is common in Hindu tradition." Shaman would have liked to explain further but he let it go, sensing Pierre's mind was closed on the subject.

The conversation turned to Indian authors writing in English. Pierre felt there was a lot of violence in Indian writing. Indraneel disagreed silently. Perhaps the Frenchman had picked up books with communal violence as their theme? But he was well-read and had studied the *Upanishads* and *Puranas* [ancient Indian scriptural texts]. On Amazon, his profile said: 'An interesting author on the spirituality scene, he has travelled the world in search of spiritual masters and experiences; studied Taoism, Shinto, Babism, Kabbalah, Sufism, Buddhism and Vedanta; and published books about his explorations.'

Pierre mentioned that he visited India almost every year. "They have made it difficult for us foreigners at the visa office, though. The new rules make it hard. But I can't protest; it's mutual I guess. We don't make it easy for Indians to come to France, so they return the courtesy."

Pierre was surprised to learn it was almost impossible for authors in India to live by their writing alone. The meagre incomes simply did not sustain the cost of living. They were forced to look for alternative occupations and moonlight as ghost writers.

"Have you written about your experiences with the *sadhus* in *Descent of the Nagas*? That's an interesting title, by the way," Indraneel enquired, genuinely curious.

"No, no...it is a work of fiction. You'll find my Guru there, but the rest is fictionalised. I have added what sells – sex and spice."

"I have now lost interest in the book," stated Shaman.

Indraneel and Vedavati felt embarrassed by Shaman's forthright comment, but Shaman seemed unmoved.

"With a title like that, I was able to attract all seekers and then waylay them with a pot-boiler," Pierre said frankly.

"I don't care to peddle cheap literature in the name of spirituality," remarked Shaman.

"Come on, we are talking of fiction here," said Pierre, shrugging his shoulders.

"I wish you had written sincerely about your Guru, his *ashram* and his teachings, and not an exploitative treatise like *Deception about the Nagas*."

"*Descent of the Nagas*, not *Deception about...*" Pierre corrected.

"I know. I choose my words deliberately," said Shaman.

But Pierre refused to be provoked. "By the way, my Guru was unconventional. He had no *ashram*; he lived on the roads, in anonymity. I had to find him and hang around streets, in back alleys, anywhere but in an *ashram*. I invite you to forget these *ashrams* and come with me to the other side of the river, beyond Paramarth Niketan, where the real *sadhus* live."

"They smoke weed and live like beggars," Shaman stated unequivocally.

"But they are the real *sadhus*. They smoke weed, yes, but they are free souls. They share whatever they get by way of alms. There's great fellow-feeling there. Not like the pompous *sadhus* who discriminate." Pierre named a few.

"If I can be candid, I would say..."

"Let it be, Shaman. Let's have some herbal tea," Vedavati said, interrupting unceremoniously.

But Pierre was not averse to candid talk. "Go on... let's have some verbal tea as well," he suggested laughing.

"I realised the shallowness of a foreigner's perception of Indian spirituality a long time ago." Shaman addressed Pierre directly. "You draw conclusions on face value. To you, beggars and *fakirs* [religious mendicants] on the road, dressed in ochre robes, are the same as the *mahatmas* and heads of spiritual orders. Spirituality is only saffron deep? One has to look beyond appearances. These beggars are NOT *sadhus*; sense-enjoyment and *sadhuhood* don't go hand-in-hand. I'm terribly disappointed."

Pierre chose not to argue. Instead, he began to speak about non-dualism. He seemed to have little or no respect for other schools of thought. He denounced the heads of various orders saying he did not believe in them because they availed of cars and air-conditioning and had a cushioned life. Shaman pointed out they were beyond these comforts and should not be judged hastily, but Pierre's scepticism was too deep rooted to be removed.

When the discussion turned to Yogananda Paramahansa's *Autobiography of a Yogi*, Pierre aired his discomfort. "I don't like that book. It's too full of miracles on every page. Too many to be credible. Why try to impress the reader? Spirituality does not need miracles. They just put me off. Why should any holy man talk of miracles? Isn't life itself a miracle? Sunrise is a miracle, sunset is a miracle. The blowing wind is a miracle. Every aspect of life is a miracle. All this miracle-mongering seems phony and a sham to me. *Autobiography of a Yogi* is not for me. In fact, such books lead people away from true spirituality."

"You are right in saying that *Autobiography of a Yogi* is not for you. It is clearly beyond you, Pierre. You cannot understand it with your aptitude."

"Oh, come on...." Pierre laughed.

"Yes, I am coming on alright. These miracles are proof of something beyond common experience, beyond you...way beyond." Shaman rose to leave.

"Are you going?" Vedavati asked.

"No offence, dearest, but I can't talk to this man. He is welcome to his views, in my absence. By the way, your Naga potboiler will no longer be seen in my store. Bye Indraneel...see you around."

Indraneel waved. He had been a silent auditor to the exchange between the two men. He did not feel he knew enough on the subject to contribute anything but inanities.

Surprisingly Pierre was not upset by Shaman's comments. This amazed both Vedavati and Indraneel, both of whom were feeling rather uncomfortable with the impoliteness Shaman practised in the name of candidness.

"He is an honest man. I like him," Pierre announced.

24

It was Avani...Avani...everywhere! The image of her eating a *kala khatta* [dark and sour] ice ball and closing her eyes as the icy mixture hit her mouth; the look of awe on her face as she gazed at the baby chick she held in her palm for a shoot, refused to go away. Avani sleeping, happy and contented as a trusting baby, with her head on his shoulder, her gorgeous hair spread out...

Indraneel tossed and turned the whole night. Memories of Avani kept intruding every time he closed his eyes. The brutality of her betrayal was only enhanced by the crystal clarity of his memories. He had no respite from them, no matter what he did to distract himself. He had not slept through the night in months. His nerves felt frayed. His memories were like the serrated edge of a knife, poking his heart, keeping his wounds raw.

He felt so tortured that he stopped trying to sleep and changed out of his shorts and went down to the Ganga. Seated beside the flowing waters, he let the deluge of his past assault him; he no longer had the strength to fight.

Something was happening on the distant horizon. The dark, pre-dawn was illuminated by small flares, like matches being struck on a deserted beach. Slowly, these flares turned into tongues of flame, licking the sky. The silence was punctuated by deep rumblings that seemed to shake the hills.

Indraneel ran to his room. Fetching his camera, he began taking pictures. The intensity of the light increased, becoming sharper, longer and brighter; it seemed to violently tear away the gentle blush of dawn. The sky was now awash with dashes of violet light. The clouds were dark and low. The lightning, greedy and bold, reached down to touch the frothy Ganga. Thunder roared, keeping tempo with the streaks of lightning.

Indraneel took scores of pictures...awed by the raw beauty and play of the elements. He gazed through the shutter of his camera at the unbridled celestial energy around him. Then it began to rain in large drops. The view blurred behind a curtain of water. Though he was getting wet, Indraneel minded neither the wet nor the cold. He put the camera back into its protective cover. Tucking it into the crook of his arm, he began walking along the *ghaat*, his churning mind oblivious to the rain.

He saw a familiar figure step out of the Ganga. It was Shaman.

Towelling himself dry, Shaman greeted Indraneel saying, "You look like a drowned rat!"

"Shaman! You here?"

It stopped raining abruptly. There was complete stillness, in sharp contrast to the primordial sounds earlier. Indraneel looked at the skies in surprise. The rain had just disappeared.

"This is Rishikesh weather! Temperamental, like a bewitching mistress! Beautiful but ever-changing." Shaman donned his jeans and *kurta*.

"There's a *ghaat* near you, so why do you come here for your Ganga bath?" Indraneel asked.

"The Ganga feels different every day and at every *ghaat*. And I'm a greedy guy; I don't want to let anything go." Shaman made a grabbing gesture.

The pink light of daybreak slowly spread across the skies. The clouds moved away, the infant sun playing peek-a-boo and edging them with diamond-shine. The Ganga shimmered like a golden ribbon in the pale light. A new day was beginning in all its pristine glory.

"Why are you up so early?" Shaman asked.

"Memories..." Indraneel murmured.

Shaman did not ask for details.

"I haven't been too well recently. Lots of things weighing on my mind...like..." Indraneel hesitated.

"There's no need to bare your Khalil Gibran heart to me. I know it's about some woman... The remedy for the likes of you, and anyone in trouble, is *japa* [repetition of *mantra*]."

"How do you know what's weighing on my mind?" Indraneel asked curiously.

"Because I read a lot of Sherlock Holmes," Shaman laughed.

Indraneel did not like the way Shaman laughed and made light of his situation, but he had exactly read his mind.

"Come on, don't hate me for treating your situation lightly. It is far kinder than saying, I understand; your problem is one of human existence. Because it isn't! And *japa* is the answer."

"I wish I could convince myself," Indraneel said softly.

"I know it's difficult." Shaman's sympathy was genuine.

"Shaman, how can *japa* help to free my mind?"

"Memories form a mental loop. Your mind is currently being used by memories. Instead, if you give your mind some other work, it will focus in that direction."

"Will you teach me *japa*, whatever that is?" Indraneel's voice was a blend of despair and desperation.

"The pleasure is all mine! I'll teach you exactly what *japa* is – an ancient Hindu science – *Mantra Yoga*. I would be happy to set you on that course."

"What do I have to do?"

"Easy now...not so fast, buddy! Meet me at Vashishtha Gufa at 6 am the day after tomorrow. Carry an *asana* [meditation mat] and I will teach you the *japa* of the Guru *mantra*. It's an universal *mantra* in which *Gu* stands for darkness and *Ru* for light. Guru is a principle. The largest planet is Guru; scripture is Guru; the *Ajna Chakra* between the eyebrows, which grants discrimination, is also Guru."

"What about the person one calls Guru?"

"Well, s/he is Guru too. They are all manifestations of the same Guru energy," said Shaman, placing a hand on Indraneel's shoulder.

"And where's Vashishtha Gufa?"

"It's here in Rishikesh, not in Mauritius. I'll pick you up."

Indraneel nodded and said nothing more. It was clear to him that he needed this *japa*. He'd put up with all of Shaman's tantrums and ways if it would help him to find peace.

25

Indraneel had been trying Vedavati's number for what seemed like the millionth time, but she was not picking up her phone. He felt almost worried, remembering the frail German woman. 'I hope she hasn't had a fall', he thought.

He decided to call one last time; if she didn't answer, he would go and check on her. But before he could press redial, the phone in his hand rang. He was greatly relieved to see it was Vedavati returning his calls. She apologized, explaining the phone had been on charge in another room and it was her prayer time.

"I chant the *Shiva Mahimna stotra* [devotional verse in praise of Lord Shiva] every evening," she told him.

She was touched by his concern when Indraneel said he had been most worried.

"I'm looking for a woollen prayer mat. Could you guide me as to where I can buy one in Rishikesh?" he then asked.

There was a pause. Vedavati muttered something in German and then said abruptly, "Come home..."

Vedavati was not fluent in English so Indraneel was not sure if she had understood what he was looking for. "A woollen prayer mat..."

"Yes, of course. A woollen *asana*...right?"

"Yes. Shaman is going to teach me to do *japa* tomorrow."

"Oooolaalaa..." Vedavati exclaimed. "You come home," she reiterated, laughing.

Indraneel decided to walk to her house as it was a pleasant evening. On the way as he passed the flower bazaar. On impulse he bought a bunch of tuberoses. When he gave them to Vedavati, she smiled in delight and immediately placed them at the altar she had made for Mother Mary and her Guru, Naam Yajnananda.

A strange combination, Indraneel mused with a small smile. But they seemed comfortable sharing the same dais. Different people seemed to belong to the same genre of peace here. Indraneel looked closely at the picture of her Guru, the Master who had lured her to India, the one who had exerted such a magnetic pull that she kept coming back. Forty years later, the magic still lived. The eyes of the Master were kind and gentle but seemed to hold a well of wisdom. Half his gaunt face was covered by a white beard and moustache, his head crowned by a twist of plaited and matted hair.

Vedavati's whole house was now permeated with the sweet fragrance of the tuberoses. In her quaint accent she asked Indraneel if he'd like some tea or coffee.

"Black coffee, if possible."

"Of course, it's possible," she assured him. "Gimme a minute."

Vedavati called out to her house help, Bhama. The house was impeccably clean. Though small and cramped, it had undeniable comfort and warmth. Bhama came in with the coffee in a fragile porcelain cup, along with a plate of cookies which he offered with great aplomb.

As Indraneel sipped his coffee, Vedavati returned with a prayer mat in her hand. It was blood red with yellow tassels, almost like a thick mini-carpet.

"This is brand new. You can have it if you like. But we can go and buy another one if you prefer," she offered.

Indraneel dusted his hands of cookie crumbs and took the mat in his hands. The tag said pure wool. He was satisfied; it had been Shaman's only specification. He folded his hands, thanking Vedavati for her kindness.

"You are very lucky," she told him. "Shaman does not offer to teach *japa* to everyone. You must be special... He gives divine advice, you know. Last year I had migraines for a month or so and he meditated and asked me to go to the Hanuman Mandir of Anasuya Ma and read *Ramacharitmanas* [popular version of the *Ramayana*] there. I became well."

"Anasuya Ma?"

"Yes. Haven't you heard of her? She is famous here. Very pure. Very divine. She has seen Ma Ganga."

"You mean the river?"

"No, not the river-goddess Ganga. Anasuya Ma has had *darshan* of Ma Ganga. Her Hanuman temple is very powerful. In fact, she is in town. I'm going there next week."

Something made Indraneel ask at once, "Can I come with you?"

"Of course...of course....we'll go together. I'll let you know when I go. I have to ask another friend, who also wants to come."

Indraneel thanked Vedavati for her hospitality, the *asana*, and the offer to take him to Hanuman Mandir.

She came to see him off and he turned to wave good-bye.

26

Indraneel arrived at Vedavati's place at 10 am. She was outside, waiting for him in a cab. As he hopped in, she informed him that the friend she was bringing along was a German lady whom she had known for many years. When she introduced her to Indraneel, she mentioned her name was Yashoda.

"Who named you?" Indraneel asked from the front seat of the cab, his curiosity piqued.

"My Guru," Yashoda replied in a sing-song voice.

Everyone seemed to have a Guru in Rishikesh, Indraneel mused. It almost seemed to be a compulsory accessory.

It took them 15 minutes to get to the temple. The cabbie insisted on waiting and taking them back. They were 10 minutes early. Both ladies wished to visit the ancient Hanuman Mandir, almost hidden from view. A short dark alley abruptly ended at the massive gates of the temple. The dark and ill-lit alley perennially reeked of urine. A small door, cut into the main gate, similar to those found in prison entrances, allowed people access. The main gate was too large to be operated by a single person.

Once one entered the temple gates there was complete silence, almost a sense of desolation. The grass was overgrown and the smell of over-ripe fruit hung in the air. There was a huge population of airborne insects and crawling creatures. A giant *peepul* tree spread its branches over the domed temple, rather like the hood of Kalindi. Something fluttered above. Startled, Indraneel looked up. It was a kite, snared in the tree's lower branches. He noticed thousands of dark shapes festooned on almost every branch.

"Bats," said Vedavati, unperturbed.

Despite it being an open courtyard, a dank smell pervaded the space. Leaving their footwear outside, Indraneel followed Yashoda into the temple, somewhat tentatively. It was an intricately carved, ancient stone structure. The floor of the main temple felt cold. The bright mid-day sun was blotted out and darkness enveloped them. It was as if one had entered a great womb.

Indraneel stood still till his eyes adjusted to the sudden darkness. As he grew accustomed, he saw the massive stone figure of Hanuman, carved on the wall in front of him. He went forward to have a closer look. His footsteps echoed strangely in the cavernous space. Hanuman was depicted in mid-flight, the Sanjeevani mountain held aloft in one hand. The image covered the wall from end to end. Just two oil lamps threw eerie shadows all around. The entire domed ceiling was covered with frescos depicting scenes from the *Ramayana*, but due to the poor light, much of it was lost in shadow.

The unnatural quiet was unnerving. But the silence was not empty. It was a restrained noiselessness, as if someone was consciously holding his breath. Despite being so large, the place felt suffocating. It was an austere temple. No flowers adorned Hanumanji, perhaps because it would require a tall ladder to reach the head of the idol. Instead, a framed photograph stood at the base of the huge carving, festooned with a garland of orange marigolds. A small brass bowl of *sindoor* [vermillion] stood beside it, for anyone who wished to take a *tika* [holy mark on the forehead].

Indraneel walked towards one of the lamps to get a better look and almost banged his head on the large, ornate brass bell which hung suspended from the ceiling. It must have weighed over 100 kilos, he estimated. He didn't dare ring the bell because in that enclosed space the reverberation of that mighty bell would have been deafening.

He quietly prostrated himself in front of the Lord. The two ladies did the same, and then led him to the verandah. The dazzling sunlight almost blinded them after the near total darkness of the temple. Blinking, they slowly opened their eyes and dropped their shielding hands.

The verandah was where people waited to meet Anasuya Ma. The premises was well maintained. There were both Indians as well as foreigners in the queue which wound its way upstairs to where Anasuya Ma was giving *darshan*. Vedavati, Yashoda and Indraneel joined the line. Batches of ten were allowed in at a time.

Vedavati told Indraneel about Anasuya Ma's Ganga *darshan*. "She was bathing at the Ganga *ghaat* here... along with two other ladies...I forget their names. Anasuya Ma suddenly saw a young and beautiful woman with extraordinary radiance. She drew the attention of the other ladies to this being. The lady they beheld looked divine. She was bejewelled and bedecked with all the traditional marks of a Hindu married woman – red *bindi* [dot on the forehead]...*sindoor*...lots of bangles, toe-rings... She walked towards the river gracefully, her upper body uncovered. To Anasuya Ma, this was an unusual sight. The apparition walked past them, waded into the waters of the Ganga and simply disappeared...

Anasuya Ma knew she had had *darshan* of Mother Ganga."

Indraneel was absorbed in the story. Who were these souls, he wondered? They were surely not made of common clay? He was glad he had come; he was finding something deep within himself here. He was in Rishikesh because of Arunodaya. A wave of gratitude towards his friend washed over him.

In another 10 minutes it was their turn to go up. On the terrace, Anasuya Ma sat in a chair. She was an old lady but her face was smooth and unlined. Her eyes exuded kindness and compassion. She was dressed in a white saree, drawn over her head; her long hair tied in a neat bun. Devoid of any ornamentation, she was a starkly simple and unassuming soul.

After the two ladies had sought her blessing, Indraneel bowed at Anasuya Ma's feet.

"Ma, bless me so that I gain something to cherish forever in Rishikesh," he said.

"Ask that of your Guru and you will have it. Everything happens due to Guru's grace. I seek from my Guru, you seek from your Guru," Anasuya Ma replied, looking at him intently.

"I have no Guru, I am not initiated, and I don't know when it will happen," Indraneel said softly, loth to disturb the peace that permeated the place.

Anasuya Ma seemed pleased. She folded her hands and asked in a soft, kind voice, "Where are you from?"

"I came from Mumbai, for a holiday."

"You have come to Rishikesh. What a great opportunity you have opened for yourself. God bless you! You will find your Guru here soon, by the grace of Ganga Maiyya. He will give you the Krishna *mantra*."

Indraneel tore himself away from her feet reluctantly. They were each given an orange and a banana as *prasad*. Indraneel's mind kept returning to Anasuya Ma words: 'You will find your Guru here soon, by the grace of Ganga Maiyya. He will give you the *Krishna mantra*...'

*Who was h*e? Indraneel couldn't stop wondering.

27

Indraneel woke before the alarm rang. He felt a strange tension grip his body and experienced a sharp sense of anticipation. He quickly showered and waited for Shaman's call, though it was barely 5 am. Shaman had said he would pick him up at 6.

Indraneel placed the red *asana* under his room key so he wouldn't forget to take it. He looked at his watch for the tenth time; it was barely 5:10 am. Restlessness grated against his sense of wellbeing. He went to the balcony and watched the swiftly flowing Ganga. He remembered Vedavati saying Anasuya Ma had had *darshan* of Gangaji... He smiled; he just could not fathom that. 'She saw Ma Ganga, for real...while I see just plain water. Wow!' he thought.

His cell phone rang; it was Shaman.

"Although I said six, I'm ready. So if you are ready too, I could come in ten minutes."

"I'm ready," Indraneel said quietly, his heart thudding in his chest. What had he let himself in for?

He put the *asana* into a plastic bag, locked his room and stepped out. Within a couple of minutes Shaman appeared. They drove in sombre silence. Shaman had picked up on Indraneel's mood. After they crossed Lakshman Jhoola, the curvaceous ascent began. The Ganga was now far below – a green-blue ribbon which seemed to have fallen between the mountains. Vast powder-white beaches adorned her sides. They passed Shivapuri. Many rafting companies had pitched their tents on the pristine beaches.

The sun was now peeping over the mountains. Dawn... Indraneel and Shaman gazed at the spectacular sunrise; how the waters of the Ganga changed from aquamarine to a hesitant pink. It was so sudden it seemed unreal. As if responding to an unspoken request, Shaman pulled the car over to the side of the road. Indraneel jumped out and took a lot of pictures on his phone. Shaman smiled and watched.

When Indraneel returned to the car, he broke the silence, gasping almost breathlessly, "Shaman! I've never seen anything quite so beautiful. Thanks for coming early."

Shaman merely nodded.

"It looks photoshopped!" Indraneel exclaimed as he checked the pictures he had taken.

"Seatbelt..." Shaman's lips quirked into a smile at Indraneel's enthusiasm. "I love the dawn," he said. "It symbolizes the tremendous, untapped potential of the day; its myriad possibilities. One can get a lot done in the morning hours. You can do more between 4 am and 10 am than in the other 18 hours of the day."

"I agree. I'm an exception in the film industry because I do most of my shoots in the morning," Indraneel responded.

They saw a signboard indicating Vashishtha Gufa.

Indraneel got out of the car and looked around. "But there's nothing here..."

"We have to walk down," Shaman replied, pointing to a narrow pathway cut into the hillside. "Indraneel, there are many *gufas* or caves in the Himalayas...Ganesh Gufa, Vyasa Gufa, Uddalaka Gufa...but this is one of the most important." Shaman said as he walked down. "Vashishtha was one of the *Saptarshis*, the seven sages who were the first beings Lord Brahma created from his will power. He was Sri Ram's Guru and family *pundit* [priest]. This great being meditated in the cave we are about to enter."

Suddenly they heard sound of hooves. Shaman stepped to one side but Indraneel was caught unawares and almost crushed by a stampeding pack of asses rushing towards the road.

Once the animals had gone past, Indraneel turned to Shaman. "You could have warned me."

"I thought you were smarter than someone who would be crushed by asses!" Shaman laughed at his city-bred friend. "It's their daily path, so they just run up to the road."

They slowly descended some uneven steps. An *ashram* stood on one side – a long, low, nondescript building, with a large cowshed opposite. A peeling signboard pointed towards the cave. When Indraneel indicated the board, Shaman merely said, "Later," and walked on. Indraneel followed Shaman to the Ganga. She appeared completely different here. Indraneel remembered Shaman saying that Gangaji was different at every *ghaat*... It was so true! Huge boulders stood along her banks and she flowed over them with the exuberance of a child.

The pervading stillness made the place appear to have been in a freeze-frame for centuries. Nature's canvas stretched to the horizon and no manmade structures marred its rhythm. The water was emerald green and clear, revealing its deepest secrets. One could clearly see the huge sunken stones, nearly spherical in shape, along the riverbed. Indraneel climbed a boulder with great difficulty; it was smooth and gave no foothold. Centuries of water erosion had made the rocks into large, smooth marbles.

Shaman saluted the water, sprinkled some on his head, and then sipped a few drops before stepping into the river. Indraneel copied his actions.

Shaman told Indraneel to place his *asana* on a narrow strip of sand and then proceeded to instruct him on the techniques of *japa*.

"Wash your hands in the holy waters and come here. It is these hands which are going to lead you to salvation." Shaman looked at his open palms.

Indraneel did as he was instructed and then sat down on the *asana*. Shaman showed him how to sit in a relaxed posture, with his back straight. Then he placed his palms close to his chest, the right palm on top to keep count of units, and the left beneath, to keep count of tens.

"You start your *japa* on the central digit of the ring finger, known as *Anamika* or 'nameless', in Sanskrit. The vein of this finger is directly linked to the human heart," Shaman said.

"This is too damn scientific!" Indraneel exclaimed.

"Yeah, it is. This is called *japa* with a *karamala*, a rosary on the palm."

"But why on the palm? I have seen people carrying *malas*; isn't that better?"

"*Japa* on the fingers is preferred because the ancient *rishis* discovered that the different phalanges of the fingers are high energy centres which get activated when pressed with the tip of the thumb, during *japa*. This, in turn, sends currents to the whole matrix of *kundalini* [spiritual] energy coursing through the *chakras* [junctions of the subtle energy channels]."

"You mean, like a switchboard?"

"Yes. Like buttons on a control panel which can operate diverse electrical devices like fans, lights, fridge, microwave etc. in different locations, the human palm serves as an activator of spiritual energy."

Indraneel was impressed. "This is systematic."

Shaman finished explaining the procedure of doing *japa* on the palm and asked Indraneel to try it.

Indraneel was reluctant, afraid he would make a mistake and Shaman would reprimand him. But after some initial resistance, he tried and got it right the very first time.

"You were born to do this," Shaman remarked.

Shaman's words sent a wave of relief surging through Indraneel.

Shaman then took him to Vashishtha Gufa. The cave extended about 60 feet into the hillside, opening into a space big enough to seat eight people. It grew darker with every step taken into the cave. A silence too deep for words made Indraneel shudder involuntarily. Soon, a strong yet unknown feeling of comfort greeted them. Shaman walked in quietly, Indraneel following.

Indraneel felt the cool ground beneath his feet. He stumbled and touched the side of the cave for support, withdrawing his hand instantly, terrified by the uncertainty of what he might have touched in the darkness. He inched ahead. Then a soft and gentle light gave form to the dark formlessness. An oil lamp stood at the end of the cave. Ah! How much shape and form even a small lamp can give to darkness, Indraneel marvelled. He could now see the Shivalinga, before which the lamp burned.

Shaman sat down and gestured to Indraneel to do the same. He silenced Indraneel's impulse to speak with a finger on his lips. Quietly, he slipped into *japa*.

Indraneel didn't know what to do. He could feel the tremendous spiritual vibrations of the place. He looked around for a minute and then began doing *japa* the way he had been taught.

When he opened his eyes he found Shaman still rapt, sage-like. Once again Indraneel plunged into the newfound *japa* practice. He was interested, excited and happy. When done, he once again opened his eyes. He realised that Shaman's *japa* would take a long time, so he walked carefully out of the cave and sat in the open. While he sat outside the cave, three groups went in, stayed a short while, and then left.

A *sadhu* walked up to Indraneel; without exchanging pleasantries he said, "Swami Purushottamanandji Maharaj came wandering round the Himalayas to this cave, early in 1928. It was all jungle then. He lived inside the *gufa*, meditating for 30 years."

"It's a big cave," Indraneel commented, uncertain what response was expected of him.

"It is said this cave used to extend another 20 kms, to a place called Ghanta Karna Mandir, up in the Himalayas. A few years ago, the passage was closed. I hope you felt the blessings in the form of vibrations here?"

"Very much...very much..." Indraneel was still bemused by what he had so clearly felt.

Shaman walked out of the cave, saw the saint and greeted him.

"Shaman Maharaj...Shaman Maharaj!" the *sadhu* exclaimed joyfully.

Speaking a few words to the *sadhu*, Shaman walked on to the river and sat down quietly on a boulder. Indraneel followed.

"Tell me Shaman Maharaj, who are you? Every saint seems to know you."

"They also know every dog who has hung around long enough," Shaman retorted.

"You're a scam; you're always hiding something behind your cool façade," Indraneel said in a forthright manner.

"That's professionalism!" Shaman laughed.

Indraneel was not satisfied but he let it go. "I felt very good in there and I did some *japa*."

"Good! There are *siddhas* [adepts] who have been performing austerities at this place in the subtle body for thousands of years. Some yogis can see those beings. Some adepts hear the loud chanting of scriptures and the sounds of the *damaru* [small drum carried by Lord Shiva], *mridanga* [a large two-sided drum], and other instruments, coming from the mountain above the *gufa*." Shaman spoke softly.

The *sadhu* brought them cups of tea. They drank the hot brew and then climbed back the way they had come, passing a large group of foreigners going down to the cave. Shaman greeted them with "*Hari Aum!*"

Back in the car they said nothing to each other.

28

Indraneel walked along the *ghaats* near Ram Jhoola; it was late evening. People reverently placed lit lamps on the flowing waters of the Ganga, gazing at the bobbing flames as long as the eye could see, their prayers and longings mirrored in their faces.

Indraneel had tried to do *japa*, but each time his mind kept looping back to the pain of his separation. He wondered if he should call Shaman and speak to him about it. He genuinely wished to rid himself of the weight of this suffering; to be just himself and not share his mind with an entity from his past.

As Indraneel made his way back to his room he saw Shaman sitting just a few inches from the flowing Ganga, on the last stone step. He was immersed in *japa*, a picture of deep and solemn peace. Indraneel took it as a sign and decided to speak to him about his own inability to do *japa*. But he did not want to disturb Shaman, so he sat a little distance away, dipping his fingers into the river. Icy cold, the waters were moving swiftly, the current strong. He could feel the steady pull on his fingers and shivered.

The quiet of night settled over the town. Lights were switched off; the boat service ended for the day; *panipuri* and *aloo tikki* [potato snack] vendors wound up their businesses and tourists returned to their rooms.

Suddenly there was the loud barking of a dog and the grunting of a pig. The pair came hurtling out of nowhere onto the *ghaat*, close to where Shaman sat immersed in *japa*. The bristles on the pig's back were raised angrily. Barely a few inches away from the water, they were circling each other, the dogs' fangs bared and the pig's body quivering. Indraneel stood up to warn his friend but Shaman was oblivious to what was happening around him.

A motley crowd gathered to watch the animals fight. Some said the dog would win while others felt the pig had the upper hand. Indraneel was caught between watching the animal conflict and awe at the complete concentration of Shaman's mind. The pig suddenly charged at the dog, who lost his balance and fell into the river. He was swept away for a few meters, but recovered to swim back to the bank. He stood some distance away, still barking at the pig. But the fight was over. The pig ambled away. The drama done, the crowd melted away.

Indraneel watched Shaman, awed and amazed. It had been over 45 minutes since he had first spotted him at the water's edge and the man had not moved a muscle.

Further down the *ghaat*, a young girl was being taught to ride a bicycle by an older girl. The learner, unable to get her balance, fell over repeatedly. They giggled over their lack of progress. Indraneel was caught by their joyful innocence. When the child briefly achieved balance, he clapped and flashed a thumbs-up sign.

Indraneel heard Shaman call out to him. "*Hari Aum*! What are you doing here? I wouldn't have seen you if I had not heard you clap." He sounded pleased.

Indraneel walked over to where Shaman stood. Without preamble, he said, "Shaman, the dog and pig almost bumped into you, yet you just sat oblivious through it all."

"What dog and pig?" Shaman asked, puzzled.

Indraneel told him about the sensational fight that had taken place just a few minutes ago. "You didn't even know! How does one manage that kind of insulation from the world?"

"Well, one doesn't have to bother about the world. Just focus on what you have got to do. Keep repeating the *mantra*...that's all." Shaman walked up the steps of the *ghaat*.

Indraneel hurried behind. "But Shaman, I am unable to do that. Memories plague me. The moment I close my eyes the same demons raise their heads and I am unable to continue."

Shaman didn't answer immediately. Then he asked, "Dinner?"

Indraneel was not interested in eating. "Dinner is not important. Shaman, how do you do it?"

"Do what? And by the way, dinner *is* important to me. Are you joining me or not?" Seeing Indraneel still preoccupied, he added with a smile, "I am paying."

"Okay dinner...but Shaman, please don't joke. Tell me how you can sit still like that. I can't keep my mind quiet for two minutes." Indraneel was in deadly earnest.

"Come, we'll talk over dinner," Shaman said cordially as he led Indraneel towards the steps of Madras Café.

It was a small place with just six tables, rather like an ethnic boutique restaurant. On entering, one could see an old black and white photograph of Swami Sivananda eating a meal at the Café. Indraneel found the face of the saint strangely riveting. Specialty items on the menu were written on the wall: Himalayan Health Pulav, Hot Lemon Ginger Honey, Herbal Tea…

Indraneel had been told that though the place did not make the best *dosas* [South Indian lentil curry] in the world, it served a generous helping of nostalgia and old world charm along with the simple food it offered. The aroma of *sambar* (South Indian lentil curry), filled the air. Three of the tables were occupied by foreigners eating some of the simple, southern goodies.

Shaman walked to a corner table. The waiter greeted him, bending low to say, *Hari Aum*. He placed menu cards on the table and filled their glasses with water. Indraneel studied the menu but remained undecided.

"Let me order for us if you don't mind," Shaman suggested.

"Sure."

"The usual," Shaman told the waiter, who smiled, nodded, and walked away.

"Don't worry about the dark memories which keep appearing in your mind. Keep doing *japa*; that will still the mind," said Shaman, inaugurating their discussion.

"I have tried to do that, but the more I turn my mind to *japa*, the more my mind is invaded with thoughts and memories. I am distracted and cannot get to a point of peace," Indraneel complained.

The waiter brought them two glasses of hot lemon-ginger and said the Himalayan *pulav* and salad would soon arrive.

Shaman looked into Indraneel's cheerless eyes for a few moments. "Buddha used the term *kapichitta*, 'monkey mind', to describe the mind. It's okay if the mind is distracted; it's a monkey-mind anyway. Be a witness and treat your thoughts like strangers. They'll go away." Shaman trickled a spoon of honey into his glass of hot lemon-ginger.

"But I thought the whole point of meditation was to still the mind and not have thoughts?"

A Japanese couple entered the café and waved to Shaman. He waved in return, saying something in Japanese before turning back to Indraneel.

"Our thoughts have no outlet, no way of exiting our system."

"But we can forget?" Indraneel asked hopefully.

"That's a bluff. No one forgets. We just forget things for the time being; they go down to the bottom of our consciousness. But they're there all the same."

"That's new..."

"Sure, it's new to you, but well known to all yogis."

"I remember a lecture on YouTube that said thoughts are baggage," remarked Indraneel thoughtfully.

"Yes. We need to drop that baggage. But every garbage bin we throw it into, pours it into another bin. It just gets stored somewhere else within us."

The food arrived. The steaming hot *pulav* [vegetable rice] with cashews and pepper, mint and pomegranate, was light and delicious. Indraneel ate hungrily, Shaman lazily.

"You're saying we can't rid ourselves of thoughts? So where does that leave us?" Indraneel enquired, unwilling to accept there was no escape.

"Meditative consciousness is our way. It's a furnace which incinerates undesirable thoughts, feelings and stubborn impressions. Meditation brings things hidden in the subconscious depths of the mind to the conscious level. It's like an ambush in which they are exterminated."

Indraneel pushed his empty plate away. There was a sudden silence in the Café; nobody seemed to be speaking. Indraneel could hear Shaman's voice with startling clarity.

"Crazy stuff comes up during meditation; things I wouldn't normally think of, or even want to think of."

"Thoughts of sex? Violence?"

"Yeah...things that make me feel ashamed. Anger, resentment, acrimony...is that cause for concern?"

"Nope...you've got nothing to worry about. Meditate more intensely. It is like a heating knob – the more the heat, the faster the cleaning."

The waiter cleared the table and Shaman gestured for the bill. It came promptly.

"Thank you for sorting this out for me. I was going to discontinue my *japa* and mediation because I felt I was getting nowhere with all these thoughts messing up my head."

"I'm glad we had this conversation then."

"Thank you, Shamanji...." Indraneel said as they rose.

"Shamanji?"

"I don't know...the 'ji' just slipped out. You're so knowledgeable, so evolved. I mean, you're high up there. It feels odd to just call you Shaman."

"Ha ha! So you think I'm a Guru or something?"

"Exactly! That's what you are. I wonder why you run a bookstore? You should be teaching."

"Thank you! I know what I should be doing."

"What is that?"

"Exactly what I *am* doing!"

"Sure!" Indraneel muttered as they walked out of Madras Café. There was no arguing with Shaman.

29

Following his long conversation with Shaman, Indraneel felt he had a clearer idea about how the *japa* principle worked. It took a long time for him to fall asleep that night, his mind abuzz with new information.

Strangely enough, he was up before the break of dawn. He opened the balcony door and saw a picture of unmoving greyness. The mist on the Ganga seemed frozen into place. Daylight increased gradually and shadowy outlines began to assume shape. He noticed an old man, standing facing East. He was chest deep in the chilly waters of the river, his long, matted hair floating behind him, his eyes closed in deep meditation, his palms joined high above his head as he prayed. He stood ramrod straight. As the sun illuminated the cosmos, Indraneel could see the *vaishnava tilak* [sacred mark indicating a devotee of Lord Vishnu] on the man's forehead, the *tulasi malas* [necklaces of Holy Basil] round his neck, his gnarled fingers and emaciated body.

Instinctively, Indraneel offered a mental *pranaam* [respectful salutation] to the yogi. Inspired from some place within, he too, decided to bathe in the Ganga before starting the *japa* ritual again.

Indraneel had some urgent emails to send and by the time he went down to the river, the old man had left. The sun was out and pink light shone above the eastern hills. Indraneel took a quick dip and changed into fresh clothes. Spotting a large rock just a few steps into the river, he waded over to it. Spreading his red *asana* there, he sat facing east and began his *japa*, repeating "Guru... Guru... Guru..."

As the light increased, Indraneel remembered Shaman's words... 'From darkness to light!' Within minutes of starting *japa*, the familiar memories descended on him once again. They were like circling bees, angry and buzzing with negative energy. But this time he did not fight even the most painful images. He knew they would be incinerated like paper thrown into a flaming bonfire. He continued to repeat, "Guru... Guru..." till the sun's heat became uncomfortable. Then he folded his *asana* and waded back to the bank. Picking up his wet clothes, he returned to his room.

Before going to the German Bakery for breakfast, Indraneel decided to do *japa* again. He experienced a strange freedom as he patted the *asana* down. He remembered Shaman telling him the *asana* would be the only thing to be cremated along with his mortal remains. The *japa* practice was soothing, almost like he had found a personal exorcist.

As he walked up the steps of the German Bakery, Indraneel realised he was still muttering *Guru, Guru* under his breath. He was glad it had happened subconsciously and repeated it consciously now. It made him feel lighter. He recalled Shaman quoting the great Naam Yajnananda Maharaj: *Whenever in doubt or anguish, just keep repeating Guru, Guru, Guru...* Even in the auto-rickshaw, Indraneel continued chanting under his breath.

He felt less burdened.

30

One day, when Shaman locked up the shop at lunch time, the weather was so good that he decided to go for a walk along the *ghaats* with

Indraneel. As they reached Triveni *ghaat*, Indraneel spotted a man having his head shaved. Afterwards, the man sat for a *puja*.

"What is the significance of shaving the head?" Indraneel asked. "Isn't it a meaningless ritual?"

Shaman scoffed at the question. "India is a great country, Indraneel. Rituals are not superstitions; they are scientific manipulations of the body-mind complex."

Indraneel stopped walking in order to listen more attentively.

"In our culture, when someone dies, the surviving sons shave their heads. At *upanayana* or initiation to learning, the head is shaved. When one takes up *sannyasa* [renunciation], again the hair is shorn."

"Why?" Indraneel asked curiously.

"Because there's something special about hair. It is dead tissue, like nails. When clipped, it does not hurt. But it's not really dead. In fact, after one dies, the hair and nails continue to grow for a while."

"Really?"

"Yes, it's true. It means that these parts of the human body have a vibration that goes beyond death. Hair is called 'occult bondage'. It carries the subtle impressions of the before-life and after-life. Shaving the head removes all those impressions; it actually brings about a transformation in being. That's why, even in jails, the first thing they do is to shave off all the hair," Shaman explained.

"This is some learning for me, Shaman!" Indraneel was completely fascinated. "I've seen many people with shaved heads, following deaths in the family, but I've never paused to understand why. This is most interesting."

"Scientific," Shaman corrected.

31

Indraneel and Shaman were returning from tea and cookies in Madhusudan's room, when Shaman received a call from Ananda Ashram.

"There has been a freak accident at the *ashram*. Nagaraj fell in the bathroom, injured his head and is bleeding profusely," Niranjan, the *ashram* priest, communicated this somewhat breathlessly.

Shaman immediately responded by saying he would be there shortly. Both men hurried to the ashram. There, the *sannyasis* helped Nagaraj into a car. The small towel on his head was drenched with blood. In shock, Nagaraj sat slumped in the back seat. In minutes they reached Nirmal Hospital. The doctor at Emergency cleaned the wound and put in some stitches. As a precaution, he took a head X-ray.

"Nagaraj was lucky; nothing serious happened," the doctor told Shaman and Indraneel, who were waiting outside the ER. "You can take him home but he needs to be carefully observed for nausea or double vision."

When they saw Nagaraj again, he had a big white bandage on his head but appeared to be in good spirits. Both Indraneel and Shaman decided to spend the night at the *ashram* so they could keep an eye on Nagaraj. They occupied twin cots in the same room. Indraneel fell asleep almost as soon as his head touched the pillow. Later, when he turned over, he could hear the steady sound of rain. It was dark and chilly and he tucked his bedsheet around him, seeking warmth in its heavy folds.

As he was drifting off into slumber again, he smelt the unmistakable fragrance of incense. Shaman was awake, at his prayers. Indraneel glanced at his phone; it was 3:30 am. 'What a man! What's he doing up this early?' he wondered. Turning to a more comfortable position, Indraneel tried to go back to sleep.

The fragrance of *agarbatti* [incense] filled him with an unfamiliar but deep sense of wellbeing, serenity and security. Memories from the distant past welled up in his mind. Another dawn…another day…many years ago. Eight years old, he had woken in the semi-darkness of his grandmother's room, to the sound of cascading water. His grandmother was having a bath in the adjacent bathroom. She rose every day at 4 am. Then, as now, Indraneel had tried to go back to sleep, pulling the covers over his head to ward off the early morning chill. The fragrance of incense wafted over him. He knew his grandmother had begun her prayers. It meant that all was well in his child-world. She would pray for him and everything would be fine...

Indraneel woke to find Shaman had already left the room; he usually went to the Ganga Mandir to meditate in the early morning. Indraneel looked out of the window at the Ganga. The river once again brought back memories of his Ganga-loving grandmother. A plump lady, she was always dressed in starched white saris and smelt fresh and nice. Years later, Indraneel identified the perfume as Chanel 5. A great devotee of Nathji, she believed in Vallabha's teachings and chanted the *Narmada Ashtakam* [religious verse in praise of the river Narmada].

In her *puja* [prayer] room, there were baskets of flowers – mounds of creamy white jasmine, crimson hibiscus, golden *champaks* [magnolias] and generous quantities of green *tulsi* [Holy Basil]. As a child, Indraneel often awoke to the heady fragrance of these flowers. The spotlessly clean *puja* room was made entirely of milky white marble and contained a large silver *mandir* [altar]. In it stood the most beautiful, three-foot tall Radha-Krishna, on red velvet. Krishna had his flute to his mouth, with Radharani close to him – a picture of divine bliss. The image remained etched in his mind.

His grandmother made *malas* and offered them to Radha-Krishna. Although she was old, her fingers were nimble as she worked her way through the flowers, weaving them together effortlessly while singing the *Hare Krishna Mahamantra*, which Indraneel still remembered with perfect clarity:

> *Hare Krishna Hare Krishna Krishna Krishna Hare Hare, Hare Ram Hare Ram Ram Ram Hare Hare.*

He often wished she would sing the *kirtan* [devotional song] more softly; it disturbed his sleep, despite the fact that she had a sweet, girlish voice. By the end of the *puja* her idols wore garlands of four colours. She scattered delicate, orange-stemmed Parijata flowers on the red velvet cloth at the feet of the idols. The possibility that God did not physically exist never occurred to Indraneel.

His grandmother had gifted him a Balakrishna as a child, which he still cherished. She too, had a Balakrishna which she placed on a silver plate. She would bathe the idol in tepid water in summer and warm water in winter, dipping her fingers into the silver vessel to check the temperature. If she felt the water was too cold, she would call out to Indoo, the maid, to get some warm water from Small Gomati in the kitchen.

His grandmother also asked young Indraneel to run errands for her *puja*. He didn't like leaving his warm bed so early in the morning but he loved his grandmother and so went to do her bidding. She would then make him sit down next to her. Sleepy though he was, Indraneel would be enraptured by the way she spooned warm water over the Lord. With each spoonful she addressed the Lord by a different name...Krishna, Madhava, Keshava, Mukunda, Govinda... She would then wipe the idol dry with a clean white cloth and dressed Him in colourful silken attire and ornaments, before placing the crown with its peacock feather on His head. Then she applied fresh sandal paste to his tiny hands and feet, and with her ring finger, placed a dot on his forehead. She would give Indraneel *kismis* [raisins] and cashew nuts, while offering Toblerone chocolates to the Lord. Indraneel loved those chocolates but hated the *kismis*, but the pure affection on his grandmother's face when she looked at him, made him feel like a king.

He returned to the present... To his surprise, Nagaraj was up and about, doing his chores. The white bandage on his head was a comical sight. Indraneel walked to the *ghaat* behind Ananda Ashram for a morning bath. The Ganga was getting colder by the day, though winter had yet to arrive in its full majesty.

Despite his injury, Nagaraj offered Indraneel a cup of tea on his return, saying in a loud voice, "Only Baba saved me! Imagine, I had such a fall, hurt my head so badly, and look at me today! Nothing... I am fine! It's all his grace!"

Vedavati and Madhusudan rushed to the *ashram* as soon as they heard about Nagaraj's injury, and were glad to see him recovered. They sat chatting about Naam Yajnananda Maharaj over cups of piping hot tea, while Indraneel listened with great interest.

It was *navami* [ninth day of the lunar calendar]. The others asked Indraneel if he would be staying on at the *ashram* till evening. If he did, he could join the *naam* procession being organised.

"I cannot stay, but Indraneel, the *naam* procession is an interesting thing to be part of," Shaman said.

Indraneel was still thinking of his grandmother chanting the *Mahamantra*: *Hare Krishna Hare Krishna Krishna Krishna Hare Hare, Hare Ram Hare Ram Ram Ram Hare Hare*. He longed to hear it again, for her sake. So that evening, he joined the band of *naam* singers going around the temple with harmonium, *khol* and *kartals*, dancing to the tune of the *Mahamantra*. It was a delight to be a part of the *Naam Parikrama* [circumambulation while singing the Lord's name], passing through the streets of Rishikesh. Children tapped their feet to the rhythm, pilgrims stopped to bow, others joined in.

Indraneel walked behind the procession going to the Durga Puja Devi *mandap* [decorated tent] in the *ashram*. He noticed Naam Yajnananda Maharaj's cut-out in silhouette – it looked so real! A shiver passed through him. Who was he? Why was he drawn to him? Later, back in his room, Indraneel thought about the cut-out for a long time...it was like a past life connection.

That night Vedavati called Nagaraj to enquire how he was. Then she said, "Indraneel was in a different mood today. He did not speak...he was very quiet."

"He is a gem Shaman has discovered; *naam* will polish him," Nagaraj told her complacently.

32

When Indraneel woke, he could still feel the resonance of the *Naam Parikrama* moving in slow, ever-tightening, concentric circles in his head. The sound of the singing and ecstatic beating of the *khol* [a drum from West Bengal], refused to leave his subconscious.

He made his way to the balcony to watch the ever-changing, mesmerising Ganga. A large crowd of people were watching something with great interest. He looked in the same direction, wondering what was causing the commotion. A large elephant was frolicking in the water like a child!

Indraneel ran to get his camera and began taking pictures. The elephant turned and tossed on the sand beside the Ganga, blowing great jets of water onto itself through its trunk. Morning walkers, tea vendors, priests, beggars, and schoolchildren, all stood pointing at the elephant, gleefully shouting, "*Haathi*! *Haathi* [elephant]!"

Indraneel went down to the *ghaat*. One teenager saw his camera and requested him to take a picture of her with the elephant in the background. "*Facebook profile picture mein lagaaoongi* [Will use it as my profile picture on Facebook]," she told him. Indraneel smiled and took a few pictures of the girl as she posed with nonchalant ease, a little away from the others.

He heard a voice say sardonically, "Catching them rather young, aren't we?"

It was Shaman, climbing the steps of the *ghaat*. Indraneel quickly took down the email ID of the girl and promised to send her the pictures. Then he almost ran to meet Shaman, the only one uninterested in the playful antics of the elephant.

When Indraneel pointed to the playful creature, Shaman responded by saying, "If you peeked into my shower, you would find me having a bath. This is the elephant's space... obviously he is doing his daily stuff here."

Indraneel laughed at the languid comment, realizing it was true. Rishikesh was located amidst dense jungle – elephant territory.

"Shaman, I missed you at the *parikrama* last night. The *naam* singing refuses to leave me. I got up with its lingering sounds in my head this morning."

Shaman gestured to the young girl whose pictures Indraneel had taken. "I know all about lingering sounds and fragrances."

"No, Shaman..." Indraneel did not wish to make light of this. "On a serious note, there is something about *naam*...it struck a chord in me... I can't explain it... Tell me, what's special about *naam*?" Indraneel was eager to know.

Shaman listened and then, turning, caught the eye of the tea vendor, gesturing for two teas.

Indraneel saw the exchange. "I will get the teas."

Shaman walked ahead to where the quiet of the morning was still unbroken and sat down on the *ghaat* steps. Indraneel spotted him and came over, holding two small earthen pots of hot tea, the steam wafting over his face.

"I have been hearing about *naam*, but I wanted to ask you. What is this *naam*?"

Shaman took a sip. "Very simply, the practice of repeating any of God's names is *naam*. To chant the name of God is a universal practice in all religions. If you repeat Ram, Ram, Ram...or Durga, Durga, Durga, or Hari, Hari, Hari...you are doing *naam*."

"My grandmother would talk to me about sage Narada moving around chanting *Narayana, Narayana* [one of Vishnu's many names]... Is that *naam* too?"

"Yes. Narada chanted *naam* as did others like Kabir, Namadeva, Nanak..." Shaman assumed a lotus posture, looking like a sage about to deliver a sermon.

"But what they sing in Ananda Ashram – isn't that *naam*?"

"Yes. *Hare Krishna Hare Krishna Krishna Krishna Hare Hare, Hare Ram Hare Ram Ram Ram Hare Hare,* repeated together as one unit is also *naam*. It is called *Tarak Brahma Naam* [name of the Lord that liberates], and is by far the best among the *naams*."

Indraneel remembered the street singers who chanted *naam* with their neck-hugging Tulasi *malas,* copies of the *Gita* in hand. "It's a practice of the Hare Krishna Order, right? I've seen those guys singing in the streets."

"No. The *Mahamantra* is universal. It was popularised by ISKCON, but that doesn't mean it's exclusive to that Order. Just as Ram *naam* chanting is universal, the Hare Krishna *Mahamantra* is universal as well. It does not belong to any particular Order," Shaman said firmly.

"But many people find it boring and silly to keep chanting one name, one *mantra*." Indraneel spoke candidly.

"You think it's boring and silly? *You*?"

"I never said *I* found it boring or silly. I said many people do. I'm voicing a general sentiment. Can you deny it?" Indraneel evaded Shaman's sharp gaze.

"You're mistaken. You speak of the views of some half-educated people. The fact is that most people find *naam* interesting, intoxicating and fulfilling. As for it being boring, does breathing bore you?"

"Well, I don't even know I'm breathing."

"Correct. So, unknown to yourself, your life is a big bore. The point is that life *is* monotonous; the life force is monotonous. *Naam* is an antidote to that monotony. It tackles sameness with sameness It is spiritual homeopathy, *similia similibus curentur* (Let like be cured by like)." Shaman almost tripped over his words in his haste to explain.

"Sounds logical, but frankly I don't get it. What's the philosophy, the possibility? Does *naam* have any philosophy?"

"Of course!" Shaman assured him. "Repetition of the Lord's name is a simple practice based on the philosophy that names or words have mystic potential in the form of sound energy. By repetition and tapping into this sound energy, one can actually manifest the God to whom one is praying."

"Does that mean that if you keep saying Durga, Durga, Durga...Mother Durga will appear? Or that Lord Krishna will actually descend?" Indraneel the die-hard sceptic asked.

"That's exactly how it is. You can bring God before you by just repeating His name." Shaman spoke with the complete confidence of one who had actually experienced this phenomenon. "Actually, according to this deep theory, the truth of an object and its name are linked."

Indraneel still had his doubts. "One can argue that different civilisations have different languages. How can different words represent the same reality and work as a magnet?"

"You're right, there *are* different words. But all the names used for a particular object have a sonic unity." Shaman pushed his empty cup aside. "*Ma* in Hindi, *Amma* in Tamil, *Mother* in English, *Mère* in French, *Mater* in Latin... they all have the same sound frequency."

"What about Sanskrit?"

"It's *Mata* in Sanskrit. In advanced languages like Sanskrit, known as *Devabhasha*, the sonic realization is more direct, more intense."

Indraneel had also finished his tea. "So chanting *naam* is an easy way out?"

"It's an accessible, simple, joyous and incomparable means of reaching God. It's not an easy way out, but a practical way."

"You seem to laud *naam* with no hesitation," Indraneel said, quizzically raising an eyebrow.

Shaman smiled. "Aha! I wish I could laud it as much as it deserves. The best part about this practice is that it can be done anytime, anywhere. There are no don'ts, no restrictions. It is quick to bear fruit. All one has to do is to keep listening to the *Mahamantra* and keep chanting it."

"I must confess I am coming round to your way of thinking – a *naam* convert." Indraneel gazed at the river, hoping to find some answers in its rippling waters.

Shaman nodded. "Shall I give you the challenge that Naam Yajnananda Maharaj gave me?"

"What's that?"

"He said: 'I don't ask you to believe blindly – sing *naam* seriously for one hour in the morning and one hour in the evening for one month – you will yourself realize the greatness of *naam*.'"

"One hour in the morning and one hour in the evening? That seems like a lot. I don't think I can."

"It's your choice. If you can't manage two hours, try less."

"Alright," Indraneel agreed, somewhat doubtfully.

The tea vendor came to collect the cups. He bowed to Shaman before he left. The hustle of people on the *ghaat* had increased. The news of the frolicking elephant had spread and everyone seemed to be talking about it. A young *sannyasi,* intent on bathing, walked down the steps and gestured to Shaman, as if seeking permission.

"Aao Maharaj...Gangaji aapaki dubaki ki pratikshaa mein hai [Come revered Sir...Ganga is waiting for you to take a dip]," Shaman responded. Then he turned to Indraneel and continued. *"Mahamantra* listening and chanting is all-encompassing – a complete solution in itself. Chant *naam,* the *mantra: Hare Krishna Hare Krishna Krishna Krishna Hare Hare, Hare Ram Hare Ram Ram Ram Hare Hare,* with or without reverence, with or without faith, standing or sitting, walking or eating, in happiness or in sorrow, in confusion or in clarity."

Indraneel felt an unusual depth in Shaman's words. His words seemed to be coming from afar: 'Chant *naam* i.e. *Hare Krishna Hare Krishna Krishna Krishna Hare Hare, Hare Ram Hare Ram Ram Ram Hare Hare.'*

33

Indraneel sat in Buddha Café near Lakshman Jhoola, waiting for his hot lemon-ginger tea. He began chanting the *Mahamantra*. He was finding it difficult to do it for two hours. With time and practice, he hoped to do it without difficulty.

That morning Indraneel had received a couriered package from Arunodaya. It was a thick envelope. Now, as he sat at the café, Indraneel opened it but the stiff paper refused to budge. He gently blew into the envelope and then tugged at the heavy white paper, coaxing it out without damaging the document. On white parchment, in the most exquisite calligraphy in green ink, was a poem titled *10 October 1964 – An Account Of Light In His Eyes*. Indraneel put it aside to read once he had had his tea.

The delightfully hot tea arrived and he sipped on it, looking down at the Ganga absently. Suddenly he saw a great buzz of activity. People were setting up reflectors while others were hauling heavy lights. They seemed to be setting up for a shoot. A large van arrived. As people alighted from it, he thought that many of them looked familiar. Buddha Café stood on a cliff overlooking Lakshman Jhoola, a fair distance below.

Pulling out his heavy camera, Indraneel focused his long range lens on the crew. The small figures leapt into sharp focus in the view finder. He smiled as he recognized Dhurandhar Banerjee, the Assistant Director of his first film, sitting in the chair labelled Director. Indraneel rose, paid for the tea and walked down the steep steps towards the *jhoola*.

Even before he reached the filming site, a couple of boys from the crew, smoking on the sidewalk, recognized him and ran to touch his feet.

"*Sir...aap yahaan* [Sir, you here]?" they exclaimed in chorus. One of them made a call from his phone. There was chaos at the site as everyone came running to where Indraneel stood, smiling.

Dhurandhar hugged him, saying happily, "Da, good to see you!"

Indraneel was overwhelmed by the spontaneous outpouring of affection. He saw a *chaiwala* [tea vendor] on a cycle and ordered a round of tea for everyone. The spot boy appeared magically, to hold an umbrella over his head. Indraneel felt embarrassed. They all walked back to the shoot, the umbrella held over Indraneel's head. To them he was royalty in the film world of Bollywood.

Once seated on the folding chairs, Dhurandhar offered Indraneel a Benson and Hedges cigarette. He declined, but told Dhurandhar to go ahead.

"What are you shooting here, man?" Indraneel asked.

"An ad commercial for mineral water, Da," Dhurandhar chuckled. "Pure water from the Ganga springs!"

"What's the brand?"

"Amrit Ganga."

"Jesus Christ!" Indraneel was amazed by the tackiness of the ad.

"Amrit Ganga!" Dhurandhar repeated. They laughed at this most uncreative name. "What brings you here, Da?"

It was Indraneel's turn to explain. "If you're asking why I was at that café, the answer is I came to read a poem Arunodaya sent me."

"Arunodaya? That guy's doing great stuff in theatre? The poem sounds interesting. Let's go for it, if you don't mind sharing it with us."

Indraneel began to rummage in his bag for the envelope. Suddenly the skies darkened and fat raindrops began to fall. The crew ran with tarpaulins to protect their precious camera. Everyone knew the drill.

Indraneel knew how unpredictable the weather in Rishikesh could be and said to Dhurandhar, "It's always like this here. Temperamental weather." He recalled Shaman saying Rishikesh weather was like a 'temperamental mistress'.

"Tell Madam Mihika to wait at the hotel...we will call once the weather clears," Dhurandhar told one of his assistants.

It began to rain heavily, with loud thunder rolling across the heavens. The boys hurriedly shifted the fragile equipment to the safety of the van. Indraneel suggested they go to Buddha Café till the weather cleared.

Dhurandhar looked at the sky woefully and then at Indraneel. "So we pack up?" It was barely 11 am.

"Even if it clears after an hour, you can still get more than five hours of clear daylight, so don't announce a pack-up," Indraneel advised as they began walking up the steep *ghaat* steps to Buddha Café, umbrellas held over their heads. He turned around to call out, "Once you guys safeguard the stuff, join us at Buddha Café. *Sab ko bolo* [Tell everyone]."

There were just two foreigners in the café – a girl and a man. They sat sketching and smoking. Dhurandhar and Indraneel sat down in a corner, away from the artists.

Indraneel gestured to the waiter. "We need 20 teas and some mixed *pakodas*." He turned to Dhurandhar. "You have about 20 people with you, right?"

"Nineteen, including the driver," Dhurandhar replied. "Da, you always had a great instinct for the numbers working on a unit," he said admiringly.

34

"Let's read the poem," suggested Indraneel.

As soon as the manager realised Indraneel was going to read something, he ordered the waiter to join five tables and arrange them in a semi-circle. Everyone sat down and the reading began.

'10 OCTOBER 1964: GURU DUTT ~
AN ACCOUNT OF 'LIGHT' IN HIS EYES

There first appeared a wrinkle on the forehead,
And the eyes constricted;
The second wrinkle spread a little lower,
And the eyes became intense,
With an overpowering expression.

The third wrinkle slowly appeared,
Making the forehead look
More wide, more expansive than before.
This time, the two dark, black eyes
Suffused, with a stillness that seemed eternal.

They were cold but affectionate;
Uncomplaining but compulsive;
And it was from within this,
A kindling glow flickered,
And lit the entire depth of far-focussed darkness.

Perhaps, a meteor passed by;
Some shooting star,
That sparkled just at the opportune moment,
Fired by the brightness of a fierce existence,
Intent upon a purpose.

Just for a moment, the entire illumination,
Of the distant stars lighted the two eyes,
And the eyelids fell,
The cameraman said 'cut';
And silence came upon, lasting forever.'

"Wow!" Dhurandhar exclaimed. "What an image! *The cameraman said 'cut'; And the silence came upon, lasting forever...*superb!"

Indraneel had read the lines slowly. He noticed that several people outside their group had joined in to listen. Teas and *pakodas* arrived and he read the rest of the poem without a break, repeating the lines he felt were important and needed to be underlined.

'*The two dark, black eyes,*
Rested a little while
On this thing, and then the other,
Until they could drink in the images,
And the light of this whole wide world.

These two dark, black eyes had in them,
The wide-angle lens,
Which had learnt to grasp.
No picture was quite irrelevant,
No picture without a theme.

Two dark, black eyes,
Rested every time on the picture,
As if they could
Forever trap the panorama outside-
They had an unceasing desire to see.

They didn't see many things frittering;
They saw a few things with such great intent,
That the unseen found a way,
In the realm of the focus.
The organs internalized.

With these two dark, black eyes,
It was not just the recording of the scene;
But becoming,
They became what they saw
And they believed.

These innocent, young and ambitious eyes,
They were in themselves a spectacle.
The spectacle, which,
Even a great drama of manifold accomplishments
Couldn't recreate.

Then one day,
The two dark, black eyes looked
Into the mirror at their own self;
And said, 'I am the art.'

For a long time
The two dark, black eyes
Passed through many a studio,
Many a theatre,
And many a colourful place.

The two dark, black eyes said:
'I am the art,'
And communicated with the art
In other eyes,
Hoping to cure the need.

Once, they became the eyes of a defeated poet
And the poem was the eyes.
They said a lot while being a defeated poet
Accursed of misery,
And three hours they blazed on the screen.

Often times blank,
Sometimes grief-stricken, sometimes merry.
But the merry moments of the eyes were few to be.

When these two dark, black eyes
Prepared themselves for the screen,
They didn't just show
Enactment within the deep centre of the pupils;
They loved.

And they felt,
They cared,
And they touched;
They were you and me
Entirely.

The two dark, black eyes
Once met another two dark eyes;
Beautiful, adorned,
With wonderful arch of the brows,
There was 'the art' in these other eyes.

The two dark, black eyes saw it with certainty.
Often, the two dark, black eyes
Met with their reflection in the feminine charm
Of those arched brows,
And the wonderful world within.

One day,
The two dark, black eyes said to the pair;
'You are my art, I love you.' 'Yes, they said it:
'You are my art, I love you.'

Some haziness had come over
In the other pair of beautiful eyes;
For they didn't at all see anything,
So the two dark, black eyes
Said it over and over.

'You are my art. I love you.'
And always the other eyes couldn't see.
Remorseful and sad,
One day the two dark, black eyes
Wept from inside.

Without dropping a tear,
For even the weeping was unfathomable,
But in which part
Of the interior of the eyes
They wept?

The two dark, black eyes
As they passed thirties,
Saw more life and more misery,
The art was in the eye,
And so was the misery.

The two dark, black eyes
Glimmered in the beams of light,
Shone from the rays of the sun,
Danced with the strings of melody,
Winked in the face of the camera;

They penetrated in other eyes,
To bring alive the real life in them.
The next three hours on the screen,
Mirrored the essence of their agony
Frame by frame.

The helplessness in them,
The innocence in them,
The love in them,
Passed into the next
Three hours on the screen.

The dark, black eyes saw art once again,
And said to the other pair of eyes:
'You are my art, I love you.'
And once again,
The same unfathomable blurring occurred.

After a long day's work,
The two dark, black eyes,
Now aged by growing years
But still young with emotion,
Paused…

They paused to see, if
The other eyes showed,
The light of appreciation
Or at least understanding,
And they saw nothing.

The two dark, black eyes
Once stood facing the camera and asked:
'Am I becoming blind?
Is the water in me drying up?'

Perhaps, the light
These two dark, black eyes
Wanted to see
Really existed,
But couldn't be fathomed.

Or perhaps, the hope,
Of these fond dark, black eyes
Had flared up,
But couldn't be brought to sight.

There first appeared a wrinkle on the forehead,
And the eyes constricted;
The second wrinkle spread over a little lower,
And the eyes became intense,
With an overpowering expression.

The third wrinkle slowly appeared,
Making the forehead look
More wide, and more expansive than before,
This time, the two dark, black eyes
Suffused, with a stillness that seemed eternal.

They were cold but affectionate;
Uncomplaining but compulsive;
And it was from within this,
A kindling glow flickered,
And lit the entire depth of far-focussed darkness.

Perhaps, a meteor passed by;
Some shooting star,
That sparkled just at the opportune moment,
Fired by the brightness of a fierce existence,
Intent upon a purpose.

Just for a moment, the entire illumination,
Of the distant stars lighted the two eyes,
And the eyelids fell down,
The cameraman said 'cut';
And the silence came upon, lasting forever.

The light in his eyes
Bade farewell to the world…
Two dark, black eyes,
Which often lived and shone amidst the darkness,
Froze introvertly.

Guru Dutt committed suicide on 10th October 1964.'

Indraneel, who had not even sipped his tea, now reached for his cup and gulped down the tepid beverage. No one spoke for some time. *Guru Dutt committed suicide on 10th October 1964.* The words sent a chill through the group.

"This is not a poem, it's a film," Dhurandhar commented.

"I think so too. It's as subtle and transcendental as the black and white imagery that Murthy, Gurudutt's cameraman, captured," the group's senior cameraman commented.

"Arunodaya wrote this?" Dhurandhar asked softly.

"No, not Arunodaya. It's from a book called *Sagarika Anusagarika. Echoes of Nine Rivers,*" Indraneel replied.

"Never heard of it."

"The writer was a boutique poet and the book is dead…out of print," Indraneel clarified.

"Da, I love this poem, it captures the essence of Guru Dutt – his inner self, its yearnings. It's simple and profound. You know, the other day they screened *Kagaz Ke Phool* at Bhavans in Mumbai and Prabhu Da talked about Guru Dutt and this film."

"It's my favourite movie," Indraneel said quietly.

"Incidentally, Prabhu Da mentioned you several times in his talk, saying you had gone to the Himalayas to be brainwashed by *sadhus*. Anyway, what is your take on *Kagaz Ke Phool*, Da?" Dhurandhar gestured to the waiter to turn the fan away; the papers Indraneel had been reading from were flying.

"I had no 'take' on it the first time I saw it. It simply overwhelmed me! The intensity of the language, music, characters, cinematography, and the aesthetic play of light...everything was piercingly deep. I was held captive!"

"Yes, it's that deep a film; it sucks you in," Dhurandhar conceded.

"It portrays the transience of it all. The unreal *Kagaz Ke Phool* still ignites passion, attraction and the uncontrollable desire to engage with them. It's only when you get closer and surrender to them that you realize that they lack the *rasa* [juice], the essence, the fragrance of real flowers! They are *maya* [illusion]!" Indraneel spoke passionately.

"*Bichade sabhi baari baari...* [We lose everything again and again...], " Dhurandhar interjected.

Indraneel nodded. "Success, love, relationships – everything is transient. Everyone leaves you one by one. Eventually one is left alone. That is what Guru Dutt was trying to say."

"But Da, don't you think he was too pessimistic?"

"No. He was right in painting these pictures. I feel all of it is true. But why could he not see that failure is also as transient as success? That's my point. The *Gita* tells us to rise above both, success and failure, and let not our minds be affected by either. If Guru Dutt could have believed this, he would have been alive to experience the success of his movie a couple of decades later." Indraneel banged the table with his open palm, thinking of the enormous talent lost by Dutt's premature demise.

"Wow! I don't know whether the Himalayan *sadhus* have brainwashed you or not, but you've certainly picked up an edge, Da! Here you are talking about the *Gita* and analysing Guru Dutt... that's fundoo stuff, I swear," commented Dhurandhar, half in fun, half in wonder.

"O shut up! You know the scene in the film...the moment when Guru Dutt and Waheeda Rehman withdraw from their mortal forms. There is a beautiful play of light and shadow as they merge into eternity, beyond separation. *Waqt ne kiya kyaa hasiin sitam* [Look what time has done my love]…" Indraneel sang the first line of the famous song.

"What a flight of imagination for Kaifi Azmi and Burman Da. Waheeda and Guru Dutt's acting and the song and its picturization are frozen in my mind forever," Dhurandhar remarked.

"I think Guru Dutt showed the human capacity to go beyond the limitations of the body, the world," Indraneel commented seriously. "That the film failed at the box office was because the world was not ready for it. The intoxication of political freedom and rising aspirations fuelled by the Nehruvian brand of socialism, heading toward industrialization, mechanization and automation, ignored the impact of all this on humanity. Large-scale migrations from the villages to the cities in search of jobs began to show the dehumanization of people, their vision and behaviour. A narrow vision of the self developed, along with a lack of loyalty, commitment, love and care – all part of material progress, success and enrichment. Guru Dutt's *Kagaz ke Phool* was a looking glass. He anticipated this future and depicted it in all its stark and fierce reality. But the time was not right. Two decades later, when the world saw the truth, Guru Dutt was recognized as a visionary."

"What you just said is wonderful and enlightening," a newcomer observed. He was a man in his sixties, and he had quietly listened to the whole poem and followed the conversation.

"Thanks...are you a Guru Dutt fan?" Indraneel asked.

"Die-hard fan," the man immediately responded. "And when it comes to *Kagaz Ke Phool*, don't you think he knew, right at the outset, what he was depicting? It follows from the very title."

Indraneel nodded. The man had a point.

"*Maya* [illusion]...that's what he showed," Dhurandhar pitched in.

"Yes, *maya*. Unfortunately he didn't live to see *mahamaya*," commented Indraneel reflectively.

"What's that?" Dhurandhar asked, taken aback by the spiritual depth of Indraneel's discourse.

"The truth behind the illusion," Indraneel answered.

"I don't think Guru Dutt believed in God," the cameraman reminded them.

"It doesn't matter whether he believed in God or not. With every Guru Dutt film, one sees the shadows of pain and sorrow that attend all things beautiful. He takes us to the depths of sorrow and then transcends, leading us beyond darkness." Indraneel was amused by his own words. He felt the breeze of the Ganga clearing his mind. He seemed to have grown more lucid and articulate. "Think of the way he took his own life. He first made a film in which a film director commits suicide, then put together the same set and committed suicide himself."

"Sure, it was premeditated. Fatal artistry!" Dhurandhar agreed.

"He needed aesthetics, even in death...integrity with his work. He merged into his Art. If done in light rather than in darkness, the act would have been glorified as sacrifice," Indraneel concluded as he paid the bill.

The group rose and left the café, still chatting about the poem. Indraneel waved to Dhurandhar and then walked back to his room. A couple of stupid questions bothered him: Why was there a 'Guru' in Dutt's name? And why had Arunodaya sent just this poem? Why was the Guru thing following him everywhere?

He had no answers.

35

Indraneel realised that a love of *naam* was developing steadily in his heart, like a growing flame. His grandmother had always sung her melodious *naam* in the early mornings and he had come to associate it with the serenity of dawn and the fragrance of incense. Today was auspicious *Ekadashi* (eleventh day of the lunar calendar), Madhusudan had told him. Indraneel decided to join the *naam* session.

He put on a lemon yellow flannel shirt and jeans and set out for the *ashram*. There was a steady clatter of auto-rickshaws, most of them on their first run of the day, each chock-a-block with school children. It was a lovely sight. Some people were walking their dogs. The dogs-in-residence wore special sweaters in Rishikesh during the winter. This stringed belly-apron, widely available in town, looked cute. Indraneel was amused at the way the cows roamed the streets without fear. He nudged one away as he turned into the narrow lane leading to the *ashram*.

Mitali Sen, a classical singer from Delhi, sat in the Guru Mandir, singing *naam*. Indraneel took a seat. He could see the huge *bilwa* (Aegle Marmelos) tree through the window; two red and yellow birds of unknown species sat perched on it. He mused over the contrast of this tree with the one next to it, which was almost leafless; no birds sat on it. Behind the trees he could see the expanse of the Ganga.

Mitali was a fair, portly lady with long hair, dressed in a burgundy coloured Mysore silk saree. She sang with great devotion. Within half an hour the Guru Mandir was full. Mitali first sang the haunting strains of *naam* in raga Ramakali and then switched to Asavari. The beat of the *tabla* [drums], quickened. Indraneel clapped, keeping time. He knew this *raga* [Indian classical melodic scale]. It was along the lines of Manna Dey's *Umariya Ghatati Jaye* [Life keeps waning] from the film, *Mother India*.

The priest brought in a large copper plate of cut fruit – blood red pomegranates, pears, oranges, bananas, dates and sugar candy. He closed the curtains as he entered the sanctum and offered the *prasad* to the Guru's idol. *Naam* singing continued in the hall.

Mid-song, Mitali broke into a bout of coughing and got up to get some water. Indraneel instinctively picked up the tune, singing softly. Before long he found himself the lead singer, with the whole group echoing him. He mentally rendered thanks to Rehan, his music director. Being in films had helped. Here he was, singing *naam* to filmi tunes.

When Mitali returned and took up the music, a *sannyasi* thrust some brass *karataals* [miniature cymbals], into Indraneel's hands, gesturing for him to play. Indraneel didn't know how. 'Should I risk it? What if my *karataals* is so out of beat that it derails the whole rhythm of the *kirtan*?' he thought, feeling lost.

He had often seen people singing *bhajans* to the accompaniment of these little cymbals, even in Bombay's local trains. He had even tried playing the *karataals* on one occasion, in Rehan's music studio. Rehan had been his music director for all three of his films. During the long music recordings that went on night after night, Rehan had educated Indraneel about various musical instruments.

Indraneel now struck the famous 1-2-3 rhythm commonly used in *kirtans*. He missed the beat. A *mridanga*, *harmonium* and various other instruments were playing in concert, and their harmony was undone by Indraneel's *karataals*. Discordant notes invaded the beautiful rhythm that had thus far pervaded the temple. It disturbed Mitali, and she responded by pumping the harmonium loudly. But Indraneel just could not get the rhythm. He should have stopped playing, but alas, he created a cacophony instead.

Mitali's husband, sitting in the enraptured audience, shot angry glances at Indraneel and then loudly admonished, "Maharaj...STOP! You will bring the devil down with your notes."

Indraneel heard, 'Get out!' in his tone. It was too embarrassing to bear. Putting the *karataals* down on the floor, he rose to his feet. Not lifting his head, he left the *ashram* and rushed into the street. Mr. Sen's words and his own pathetic attempts at playing the *kartaal* besieged his mind.

"These things happen." Shaman tapped him on the shoulder. He had apparently followed Indraneel out. "Don't take those words to heart, he has no patience...he doesn't know the divine rhythm. Eternal music is made when a discordant note marries a harmonious one!"

Indraneel felt somewhat consoled by these words but he could not shed his sadness.

"Want me to drop you back?" asked Shaman, pointing to his car, parked a little way ahead.

"No thanks, I'll manage," replied Indraneel, still feeling bogged down by humiliation.

"Alright, suit yourself. But don't worry about it. Just keep walking the Path."

Shaman's words reiterated in Indraneel's mind the larger truth, that aid comes to us from on high; one just has to keep going. He walked back towards his room, thinking about Rehan's studio and the evening he had tried playing *karataals* for the first time. He decided to call the music director.

"*Yaar, karataals kaise bajaate hain* [Buddy, how does one play *karataals*]?" Indraneel asked directly.

"What? *Karataals*? Where the hell are you and what the hell are you doing?" Rehan asked, completely at sea.

"I'm in Rishikesh. Just tell me how to play *karataals*," Indraneel repeated.

"Indie, it's difficult to explain these things on the phone. But you can play 1-2-3. Usually most *kirtans* are in eight *maatraas* [beats], but listen to it and decide whether you want to do a three-beat cycle or a four-beat. Clap to get the beat."

"Thanks Rehan," Indraneel responded automatically, feeling disheartened by the lack of specifics.

"Welcome, bro! Does it help?"

"Nope, but that's okay." Indraneel hung up.

36

Indraneel was deeply frustrated at not being able to coax a rhythm from the *karataals*. In his hands they just seemed like two brass disks making loud dissonant noises. The people around him were able to do it so easily, but they were unable to explain how exactly it was done. 'Just watch and follow,' they would say.

'How the hell does one get it? It seems impossible. I just can't get it! Perhaps the easiest things are the most difficult to teach. How would I teach someone to swallow; how would he understand?'

Feeling forlorn, Indraneel walked along the Ganga, anxious thoughts playing in his mind. He was unable to put the insult behind him. 'I just *have* to learn *karataals*,' he told himself. 'But who will teach me?' He smiled wryly, remembering Shaman saying, 'God will provide at each step, my boy! Pin or elephant, God will provide it on the way. Just keep walking the Path.'

'Am I walking the Path?' Indraneel wondered. He was so engrossed in his thoughts that he did not realise till much later that he had lost his way. Rishikesh was a small place, he rationalised. If he retraced his steps, he would get back onto the right path. It was getting cold, the sun playing hide-and-seek with the clouds as the evening shadows lengthened. Indraneel reached down to zip up his thick black fleece jacket against the chill.

At dawn and dusk, he had noticed there was always a lot of activity in the bird world. Either they were waking up and chirping or they were winding down and chirping. The crickets too, began their calls, quietly at first and then with authority, as the birds shut shop for the day.

Indraneel loved the bite of winter. He took a deep breath of the clean, crisp, unpolluted air and walked on slowly, savouring the sights. He could see lazy tendrils of smoke from the *chillams* [clay smoking pipes] of some mendicants sitting on the wayside. They greeted him with, '*Bum Bum Bhole* [Hail Lord Shiva].' For some reason he responded with '*Hari Aum*', and then walked on.

Indraneel heard the faint strains of Hare Krishna *naam* being sung but when he looked around, he could see no one. He walked on. The tender singing became clearer and more haunting. He looked around in earnest now. It was almost dark. On the banks of the Ganga, a girl of about seven was singing *naam* in the voice of an angel. It struck him that she was using a small pair of *karataals* like they were extensions of her small palms. The others sitting with her, swayed to her singing; rolling joints and saying 'Hari Aum' from behind puffs of blue smoke. From their matted hair and dirty saffron clothing, they appeared to be mendicants. Indraneel was reminded of the French author, Pierre, and Shaman's comments about the underbelly of Hinduism.

Indraneel felt drawn to the girl's singing. As he drew closer, he saw there were two women and five men in the group, all in an equally inebriated state. He sat on a rock close by, listening to the *naam* sung to the accompaniment of the gurgling waters of the Ganga. He moved closer for a better look. The young girl's eyes were closed in devotion. One of the men in the group saw Indraneel and gestured to him to come and sit near him.

Indraneel sat down, putting his phone on recording mode. Soon, lost in the waves of delicate melody, he began to sway. The man next to him offered him a drag of his *chillam*. Indraneel refused, smiling politely. He felt high on life. As the tempo picked up, the girl's hands became a flurry of movement with her *karataals*. The two women of the group stood up and began to dance, not with synchronized steps, but moving with joy, their hands thrown into the air with abandon, keeping up with the tempo of the singing. Indraneel closed his eyes and gave in to the mystic intensity of the moment.

When he felt heat near his feet, Indraneel opened his eyes and found the group had built a small fire. The singing had stopped. One of the women was helping the girl to drink from a glass of water. In that instant Indraneel realised the girl was blind. He casually introduced himself to the group.

"*Kaunse ashram mein aaye ho, Baba* [Which ashram are you visiting, Sir]?" one of the group asked.

"Ananda Ashram. Muni-ki-Reti."

The group, still intoxicated, didn't really care. Indraneel went close to the young girl. Though blind, she perceived the presence of a stranger.

"*Kaun hai* [Who's there]?" she asked in a frightened voice.

Indraneel introduced himself as a traveller and told her that she sang beautifully. The girl remained silent, though a trace of happiness was apparent at the compliment.

"*Kya chaahiye* [What do you want]?"she asked warily

"*Kuch nahin* [Nothing at all]!" he replied immediately. He told her he had been passing and stopped when he heard her sing. He also told her he had recorded her voice and played the recording back for her. Although excited, she was unable to understand how he had done it, and remarked that her voice sounded very different. It was evident she had never heard herself before.

Indraneel took some chewing gum from his pocket and closed her hand over it. She opened her fist carefully, feeling the seams of the packing with her small fingers, and then popped the gum into her mouth. She relaxed visibly.

Indraneel asked what her name was. The woman preparing to cook answered on the child's behalf: "Meera! We found her abandoned near Manikarnika Ghaat in Varanasi. She has been with us since then. She was born blind."

"We took her to quite a few doctors," one of the others added.

"She must have been thrown out like *kachara* [rubbish] when the family realized she was blind," another remarked, putting some more sticks on the fire.

Indraneel felt deeply moved. 'What a world this is!' he thought. Taking out his camera he took a picture of Meera. She was a fair, frail child, with delicate elfin features. The old frock and threadbare sweater she wore made her look even more vulnerable. She shivered as the cold gusts of wind hit them. Indraneel unzipped his fleece jacket and wrapped it around the girl.

The group informed him they were travelling to Dwaraka the following day. Indraneel tried to light a cigarette but was unable to do so in the wind. One of the bearded men picked up a burning twig from the fire and lighted the cigarette for him. They just sat in companionable silence, the girl playing with her *karataals*. Indraneel watched, fascinated. Unerringly, she played the rhythm of every filmy tune the women sang. There was a lot of laughter.

Indraneel was assailed by an idea. He asked Meera if she would teach him to play the *karataals*.

She looked confused. *"Kaise sikhaayen* [How to teach]?" she asked but then quickly decided to hold his hands and play. That way he could follow the movements on his own.

She came over to Indraneel, who lifted her onto his lap; she handed him the small *karataals*. Through gestures, he learnt the correct way to hold them. She clasped his hands and began to sing a simple *naam* tune, directing Indraneel's hands in bringing the two *karataals* together in slow rhythmic union.

Lo and behold, there were beats, not noise! Indraneel felt as pleased as a child on his birthday. Meera continued this for five minutes and then removed her hands, asking Indraneel to play on his own. To his utter astonishment, he could! It was a little patchy but he soon got the hang of it. He felt elated! The child sat comfortably in his lap, singing as he played. She corrected him twice. The skill had been transferred to him almost organically.

Just then Indraneel's phone rang. It was Shaman, demanding to know where the hell he was. He realized he had forgotten their 8 pm appointment. Hurriedly, he bid goodbye to Meera, handing over all the chewing gum he had in his pockets. He gave the group leader the 5,000 rupees he had on him, telling him that Meera was special; they needed to take good care of her.

Then he literally broke into a run, in search of an auto-rickshaw.

37

From time to time Indraneel received calls from his friends, asking about his return. Especially Arunodaya, who felt let down that Indraneel had not been present for the opening of his play, though he had promised. Indraneel had got tickets for the opening night but somehow he just couldn't bring himself to leave Rishikesh. He had asked Lily to cancel the tickets and send a gigantic bouquet of flowers to Prithvi Theatre instead.

Arunodaya was livid at receiving the flowers. He had called Indraneel late at night. "I'm not a woman you can placate with expensive hot house flowers," he had thundered.

Indraneel stayed in touch with his mother, calling her regularly. She never once asked him to return. She only wanted to know if he was happy, whether he was eating on time. She sensed unerringly that her son needed this time away.

Rishikesh, with its unique mix of forests, the Ganga and the Himalayas, acted like a balm on Indraneel's troubled mind and seeking soul. But over time it became more – he began to experience a deep sense of comfort, like being enveloped in the soft folds of a quilt on a cold day. He loved Rishikesh and began to feel it was his home. It didn't seem like he had arrived for the first time just a couple of months ago. He now felt inextricably linked to the people here – to Madhusudan, Vedavati, and especially Shaman. Indraneel experienced a sense of homecoming in this small Himalayan town. He knew he could spend the rest of his living years just gazing at the Ganga and trekking the hills.

The days passed. Indraneel didn't even realise it was Diwali.

38

L eafing through a guide book on Rishikesh, Indraneel came across a piece on the famous temple, Neelkanth. The fact that getting there involved a trek through a forest, drew his interest. He made preparations and then began the trek through dense jungle to the Shivji temple located high on a hill, singing *naam* as he made his way up.

The place was practically deserted and Indraneel had a marvellous *darshan*. He knew from his reading that the temple was crowded only during the *kaavad* season, when people from all over the country congregated here in the month of *Sawan*, to offer water to Shivji.

Indraneel felt happy after his trek, but also ravenously hungry. Back in town, he made his way through the market near Madras Café and saw the *aloo tikki* vendor doing his usual brisk business. The appetizing aroma of the frying *tikki*s drew him like a magnet and he ordered two plates without the *masala* [spice].

As he waited for his order, there was a sudden downpour. The crowd around the vendor scattered. Indraneel took fragile shelter under the tarpaulin of the *tikki* cart. The vendor muttered and cursed the rain under his breath, for ruining business. Everyone ran helter-skelter, hurrying to save themselves from getting wet; children squealed as the cold drops fell from above.

Indraneel saw a beautiful, slender woman running for shelter from the rain. She too, noticed him standing under the tarpaulin. As their eyes met, she recognized Indraneel in a flash and a delighted smile spread over her face. She changed direction and ran over, hugging him in spontaneous joy.

"Indraneel!" she gasped, out of breath.

It was a cinematic moment, frozen in time. Avani! Indraneel had her in his arms before he realized what was happening. Avani was in his arms! She still smelt as divine and felt as good to hold as he remembered. A familiar tingle of awareness ran through his body. Slowly, he released her. Holding her shoulders Indraneel looked at her closely.

"You here? How come?" he asked gently.

Avani was feeling rather embarrassed and flustered that she had almost thrown herself at him. She looked away from his gaze and shook out the moisture from her long hair.

Before she could answer, the *tikki* vendor said, "*Sirji, aapki tikki ready hai* [Sir, your patty is ready]."

Indraneel looked at Avani and asked if she wanted a *tikki*.

She nodded, adding, "But it's very fattening."

Indraneel laughed. "Look at you....slender as a reed."

"You know how the camera adds pounds," she replied.

Indraneel felt almost irritated. Some of the joy at seeing her again so unexpectedly evaporated.

"Do you want it or not?" he asked impatiently.

Avani read his mind. "I'll have one; don't get angry." With a gesture of familiarity she placed her index finger on his forehead. "Now remove those frown lines."

Indraneel didn't answer, he just asked the *tikki* vendor to make another plate. Avani pulled out a rubber band from her bag, gathered up her thick hair and tied it into a bun. Indraneel watched. She looked beautiful in the light of the petromax lamp. She was wearing a long white crinkle-cotton skirt with mirrorwork and a turquoise blue raw-silk sleeveless top which left her midriff exposed. On her hand was the charms bracelet he had given her. It made Indraneel happy to see her wearing it.

There was a loud clap of thunder and it began to rain more heavily.

"My room is round the corner; we can eat there," Indraneel suggested

Avani nodded in agreement. He paid for the *tikkis* and they quickly made their way, walking under the eaves of the houses to avoid getting wet.

"I am here for the International Yoga Camp," Avani mentioned. "I've been here for three days. I leave the day after. I thought I'd explore the place a bit first. And what are *you* doing here?"

"I live here," answered Indraneel. "Watch your step, there are some puppies here," he cautioned.

"Oh, they're so cute!" Avani exclaimed as they stepped past the huddle of fat, cuddly black puppies. "What do you mean you live here?" she queried, looking back at him.

"Just that: I am living here," Indraneel answered. "Now we need to dash across the road. My room is there." He gestured to the building on the other side. "But how are you going to run in those heels?" he asked, pointing to her six-inch silver stilettos.

Avani looked at him for a moment and then laughed. "Watch me!" She quickly dashed across the road through the lashing rain.

39

They entered the building laughing like kids.

"So Indraneel, am I capable of running in heels or not?" Avani asked, giggling like a teenager.

Indraneel did an elaborate *pranaam*, bowing low. As they walked in, he spotted the *pahadi* boy, Mangal, and asked him to get two plates and two spoons.

But Mangal was not listening to Indraneel, he was staring at Avani in open-mouthed wonder. Finally he gathered his wits. "*Aap Shakuntala hai na* [You are Shakuntala, aren't you]?"

Indraneel interjected, "*Nahi...yeh madam Avani hain* [No, this is Madam Avani]."

But Avani smiled and nodded at Mangal. He told her he was an avid viewer of her television serial, *Anokha Rishta* [Unique Relationship]. *"Aap bahut sundar hain* [You are very beautiful]." Mangal gazed at her in wide-eyed admiration.

"Thank you." Avani was happy to be noticed, even in Rishikesh.

Indraneel could see Mangal had a serious crush on Avani. As he opened his room door, she explained that she was working in a teleserial which had become a big hit with great TRPs. The character she played was called Shakuntala.

The pieces fell into place for Indraneel. "Oh okay... but didn't you always say you would never act in teleserials?" he asked as he switched on the lights and put the room key on the table.

Avani went to the window, looking out at the rain. Lightning streaked across the cloud-laden sky.

"People change, circumstances change," she said in a serious voice. "But some things don't, Indraneel," she added with a laugh, making an effort to make light of her earlier comment. "See, I'm still wearing the bracelet you gave me." She held up her hand so he could see the bracelet dangling on her slim wrist.

Before he could react, Avani changed the subject, asking once again, "What *are* you doing in Rishikesh?"

Indraneel contemplated telling her that he had nearly died of a broken heart when she left him and that Rishikesh had helped him join the living again, but changed his mind. He merely said, "I just needed a break after *Struggler*; it has become an extended holiday."

"Ohhh... Till your film was released I knew pretty much everything that was happening with you. There were so many interviews with you during the film's promotion. But after that I heard nothing. In fact, there was some vague talk that you were doing a carpentry course in some exotic place." Avani thought for a moment biting her lip. "I think it was Budapest..."

"Whaaat! Budapest?" Indraneel was genuinely amused.

Avani twisted the little teddy bears on her bracelet. Eyes downcast, she murmured "Even Arunodaya and Prabhu Da never said a word about you. It felt like..." she paused, "they were hiding you."

Indraneel sat on the bed, listening without interrupting.

"Not that I asked them directly," Avani clarified as she turned to look at him. "It was almost as if you fell off the face of the earth!"

"I didn't, however, fall off the face of the earth, even if I could!" Indraneel smiled wryly.

"But you were not checking Facebook or WhatsApp. Now that is falling off the face of the earth!" Avani shrugged her slim shoulders. Her cell phone rang. "One moment, I need to take this call," she said hurriedly.

It was her friend from yoga camp, telling her the *ashram* gates would shut at 8 pm sharp that evening. Avani glanced at her watch anxiously. It was already 7:45 pm.

"A problem?" Indraneel asked.

"Curfew time…" Avani explained.

"Which *ashram* it is?"

"Brahmananda."

Indraneel said he knew a short cut and they left hastily. Thankfully it had stopped raining.

"Can we meet tomorrow?" Avani suggested as they ran through the narrow lanes.

"No yoga tomorrow?" Indraneel asked, deftly dodging a cow on the road.

"I'll skip it," Avani answered blithely, expertly jumping over a giant puddle. She held her long white skirt high in one hand, her slender and shapely legs exposed, her beautiful face flushed from all the running. She was completely unaware of how lovely she looked.

'What an exquisite creature!' Indraneel thought.

They were nearly at the *ashram* gates. A thin man with a tuft of hair sticking up on top of his head sat muttering loudly to no one in particular, "*Aath baje gate bund* [Gate closes at 8]. If God Himself comes, I will say 'Come tomorrow!'"

Indraneel glanced at his watch; they still had three minutes. "So what time tomorrow?"

"Eleven, I think. I'll attend the morning session and skip the rest…"

"Alright. Good night."

Avani gave him a quick hug, saying goodbye.

Indraneel suddenly thought of something. "Where? Your place or mine?"

"Now that's a suggestive comment!" Avani giggled.

Confused for a second, Indraneel smiled at his own words. "What I meant was… "

"I know what you meant," Avani laughed.

The gateman, still muttering *"Aath baje gate bund,"* began to pull the heavy black gates closed, their hinges creaking in protest.

"Pick me up here. Don't forget I want my *aloo tikki*; I missed eating it today…"Avani turned and ran into the *ashram*, waving as she went.

40

It was nearly 11 am. As he walked towards Brahmananda Ashram, Indraneel caught sight of Avani before she saw him. She was standing under a *parijata* tree, wearing a pair of tight, low-waisted blue jeans that moulded her figure. The jeans had faded to almost white in some places and were ripped artistically in others. She wore a soft-knit purple and pink cropped top with full sleeves that tapered to her wrists. It had a deep boat neck and clung to her curves. A thin gold chain glittered round her neck, just above her collar bone. Lipstick the same pink as her knit-top accentuated her perfect mouth. A pair of well-worn sneakers completed the look.

Avani's luxurious hair blew in the light breeze and she tucked the wayward curls behind her ears impatiently as she waited for him. Her beauty stuck Indraneel in the gut like a powerful fist. He could never get over how gorgeous she was.

Avani looked at her phone yet again. When she looked up and finally saw him, her whole face lit up. Running to meet him, she hugged Indraneel exclaiming, "You look so good!" She casually ran her hand over his flat stomach, remarking, "Washboard abs!"

Indraneel removed her hand gently. "You are embarrassing me."

But Avani persisted. "Indraneel, I know you. You are getting tickled, not embarrassed."

Indraneel laughed self-consciously. "Yeah sure, I'm ticklish."

Avani looked at him closely. "Seriously Indraneel, are you exercising a lot? Is there a gym close by you go to?"

Indraneel shook his head. "No, I don't exercise. But I walk a lot. That's all."

"Whatever it is, Indraneel, you're looking fit and healthy." A minute later she turned to him and said, "I'm hungry! The yoga session was at 5 am and I haven't eaten anything. Just a glass of milk."

"Would you like an early lunch?" Indraneel suggested.

"That sounds good."

As they walked Indraneel commented casually, "You've grown your hair. It's way past your waist now."

Avani halted. "You don't like it, Indraneel?"

"No no! I love it. It suits you. You have gorgeous hair," he responded immediately, touching her mane gently. "It's like silk."

Avani smiled. "Silk?"

"I always told you that," he reminded her.

"To tell you the truth, it's a pain having such long hair. But I need it for my role. Otherwise, using hair extensions every day takes another 30 minutes to get ready for the shoot."

Indraneel flagged down an auto-rickshaw. It was full but the driver said they could get into the front. Indraneel glanced at Avani to see if she was agreeable. She nodded in response to the unspoken question. So Indraneel got in next to the driver and Avani squeezed in next to him, beside the open door. Since there was a great deal of noise and chatter in the rickshaw, conversation was out of the question.

It was a rough ride on bad roads and they were tossed about like popcorn.

"Man! He is driving like an insane Michael Schumacher being chased by hounds from hell," Avani yelled into Indraneel's ear.

He laughed, trying hard not to fall onto Avani. She took his arm and placed it over her shoulder. Indraneel looked at her questioningly, but didn't resist.

She said impishly, "At this rate I may fall out. You need to hold me."

Indraneel smiled, relaxed, and held her comfortably. Finally the bone-jarring ride ended and they got out thankfully, and walked towards a hotel called Divine Ganga. The restaurant was almost empty. It was too early for the lunch crowd. There was just an elderly American gentleman finishing his coffee. The restaurant had an unrestricted view of the Ganga and deep forests on the far bank. It was stunning.

Avani shrieked in delight. "It's so crowded near the yoga camp. This is simply divine! Indraneel, please take some pictures of me."

"I don't have my camera," he pointed out.

"The phone will do."

The waiter came and Indraneel asked for five minutes. They went out onto the balcony which skirted the restaurant and he took some pictures. Avani looked pretty even in the phone camera lens. She posed with the ease of the professional actress. Indraneel remembered a hundred occasions in the past when she had posed for him. He turned her face to a more flattering angle so that he got the right light. Touching her was so easy, he realized. There was no awkwardness between them at all.

He got some great pictures of her with Ma Ganga in the background. Like a child, Avani wanted to see every picture. She insisted he delete those in which she felt she looked fat.

As he watched her walk back into the restaurant, Indraneel commented, "You look like you've been poured into your jeans. How did you get into them?"

Avani laughed. "Come on, Indraneel. You know they are stretch jeans – Calvin Klein."

"I know they are Calvin Klein."

Avani was surprised. "How do you know?" she asked curiously.

"Your top is short and the label clearly visible."

"Indraneel! Are you ogling me?" she giggled.

He didn't reply, just smiled. It was close to the truth.

"Perhaps I'll model for CK one day," Avani said wistfully.

They were now seated. "Have you seen the Calvin Klein ads?" Indraneel asked. "They have fairly explicit sexual overtones."

Avani merely laughed, tossing her hair back with one hand. "Then it must be fun to shoot those ads!" she said.

The waiter returned with the menus.

"Indraneel, you order for me, like always."

He ordered all her favourite things – *palak kofta, missi roti, boondi raita, pudina rice*, and the waiter left.

Avani gazed at Indraneel, her eyes moist. "You haven't forgotten my favourites," she said softly. There was a brief silence before she asked, "Shall I tell you something funny?"

Indraneel nodded.

"I went home for a few days, three months ago, wearing these jeans," she gestured to her legs. "When I was packing to return, I couldn't find them. I looked everywhere. Then I asked my mother. She said she had thrown them away because they were torn. I was horrified, and so relieved to hear she hadn't chucked the garbage out yet. Otherwise I would have had to fish through the community muck to find my jeans!"

Indraneel was genuinely amused by this graphic description of her plight.

"That's not all! My grandmother gave me 500 rupees saying, '*Beta*, I know things are bad for you...you are wearing rags. Buy something nice for yourself.' Seriously Indraneel, you know it's considered inauspicious to wear torn clothes and now we are paying top dollar for ripped jeans."

Indraneel was still laughing when their food arrived. Avani ate hungrily but declined dessert. Indraneel helped himself to a hearty helping of *rabdi* and *malpua* [traditional Indian sweets].

Avani watched him in awe, gesturing to the high calorie sweets. "How do you manage to stay so fit after eating such food?"

Indraneel finished, drank some water and then said in a flat voice, "Metabolism." He sat back. "Avani what would you like to do now?"

Avani thought for a moment. "You decide. I have no idea about Rishikesh."

The restaurant was getting crowded, so Indraneel paid the bill saying, "Let's get out of here first."

They walked to the *ghaats*. It was a day clad in soft clouds, with a gentle breeze. The *ghaats* were nearly empty but for some couples sitting on the steps, seeking privacy.

Avani looked around. "Indraneel, how long have you been here?"

Indraneel was evasive. "A couple of months I guess."

"How do you spend your time here? I mean it's a beautiful place but what do you *do* the whole day?"

Indraneel just smiled. Finally he broke his silence. "I just walk around. I spend hours just watching Gangaji, and I sing Hare Krishna *naam*."

Avani's eyes flew open in wide-eyed astonishment. "You sing Hare Krishna *naam*? The stuff they sing at the Juhu ISKCON temple?"

"Yes. In fact, I try to sing for more than two hours a day."

"You joined ISKCON?" she asked, amazed.

"No. You don't have to join ISKCON to sing the *Mahamantra*...it's sung all over the country."

"For two hours?" Avani said incredulously. She was truly aghast. "But doesn't it bore you?"

"Initially it was hard but now I enjoy it. In fact, I wonder how I spent so many years without it."

Avani was not convinced. "But *why*, Indraneel? Why do it? Have you joined some cult? Are you doing drugs?" she asked seriously.

Indraneel chuckled. "No Avani, I'm not into any groupie thing. Hare Krishna *naam* fills me with peace and I really need that."

Avani simply could not understand. "So how long are you planning to stay here?" she asked finally, trying for normalcy.

Indraneel swallowed and thought for a bit before answering desultorily, "No plans, Avani; just taking each day as it comes."

Avani was more confused than ever. "What about films? You have such a passion for making films. How will you make films sitting here? Don't you miss Bombay? Your friends? Arunodaya? Prabhu Da? What about your parents? Do they know what you are doing?"

"I don't know what I have a passion for," he replied. "Or if I will ever make films again. I just have no idea what the future holds for me. I only know I am happy here and I am living in the present."

Listening to him Avani became contemplative. She nodded her head murmuring, "Hmmmm…"

They walked on in silence. After a few minutes she asked, "Smoke?"

Indraneel looked at her in surprise. "You've started smoking?"

Avani shrugged. "I'm not a regular smoker but I carry a pack."

"But you always lectured me about it." Indraneel protested, still surprised.

"I had to do it for my role and I sort of liked the image. See Indraneel, I'm a small town girl and I desperately need to fit in. Sometimes the cigarette in my hand helps."

Indraneel was not convinced.

"You wouldn't understand," she said with a sigh.

Indraneel wanted to hug her and tell her that she was great; she didn't need these gimmicks. Instead, he said, "Avani, I quit smoking because you hated the habit."

They walked on in silence. Further down the *ghaats* they could see a small *mela* [fair] in progress. Children were laughing in delight on the giant wheel.

Avani's face lit up. "Can we go there?"

Indraneel raised his eyebrows. "You want to ride a giant wheel?"

She nodded enthusiastically. So they went to the *mela*. Before long they were seated in the giant wheel. As it turned they became suspended high in the air, their box swaying in the breeze.

Avani hid her face in Indraneel's shoulder, saying in a small voice, "I'm scared…"

Before he could reply, the giant wheel spun between heaven and earth in rapid succession, at a speed which made their stomachs heave, leaving them breathless with laughter. Slowly the wheel stopped. As each box emptied, Avani straightened up from Indraneel's arms and noticed that her short chain had got caught in his shirt button.

"Wait! Don't pull. Open it slowly," he advised.

Avani began to giggle. "Open your shirt?"

Indraneel laughed too. "The chain silly, not my shirt!"

Asking him to keep still, Avani tried to disentangle the chain. "This situation is quite filmy, *na*?" she remarked.

"Mostly films are inspired by real life," Indraneel remarked. If he moved, his mouth would brush against her delicate ear; Avani was that close. He felt disturbed. Suddenly the chain came free. Phew! He sighed silently, relieved.

They got off the giant wheel and sauntered about the *mela*. They heard whispers of *'Woh Shakuntala hai kya* [Is that Shakuntala]?'

Avani pulled out a pair of huge wrap-around dark glasses from her shoulder bag and put them on. "Don't want to create a scene here," she explained.

As they walked they could hear the gurgling Ganga hopping on and off the rocks. Suddenly there was a distant clap of thunder.

Indraneel looked heavenwards. "Looks like some serious rain is coming our way."

Oblivious to the threat of rain Avani bought some cotton candy and handed one stick to Indraneel. "Remember us eating this on Chowpatty?"

As he licked the pink fluff, Avani commented, "You look ridiculous with a pink mouth. Maybe I should take a picture." She pulled her phone out of her bag.

Indraneel took the phone away from her hand and held it high above her head. Avani jumped to get it but there was no way she could jump that high.

"Damn! Today of all days I'm not wearing heels," she lamented.

Jumping up again, her short top moved up, revealing her tiny waist. Indraneel noticed she had pierced her navel. He handed her phone back and held her still to look more closely.

"Now you're embarrassing me," Avani protested.

"Did it hurt? The piercing, I mean…" His voice held more concern than curiosity.

Avani felt somewhat shaken by his close scrutiny. "A little. I was bored one day on a shoot in Goa. It was an impulse thing."

A light drizzle began. "Shall we go to my place?" Indraneel suggested.

She nodded. They got into an empty auto-rickshaw and went back to his room.

41

When they arrived at Reception, Indraneel asked Mangal to buy some *aloo tikki* without *masala* [spice] and bring it to the room, along with two plates, spoons and a bottle of water.

Climbing up the stairs, he unlocked the door and they entered. Indraneel walked over to the balcony door and opened it. It was raining in sheets now. He asked Avani if she wanted to use the restroom but she shook her head. They watched the falling rain in silence, each lost in their own thoughts.

Finally, Avani turned to Indraneel, unabashed longing in her voice. "It was a wonderful day, *na*? I had such a good time."

The doorbell rang. Indraneel went to open the door and Mangal came in with bottled water, two plates, two spoons, and the paper-wrapped *aloo tikkis* – all of which he placed noisily on the table, and then left reluctantly, gaping at Avani until Indraneel closed the door.

It was still raining heavily. Indraneel opened the rough newspaper packets and served the *tikkis* on the plates – two for himself and one for Avani. She slipped off her shoes and sat crossed-legged on the single bed, the plate held in her lap.

Indraneel sat on the other side of the bed, his long legs planted on the floor, and blew on the *tikkis*.

"Eat quickly. It won't taste as nice once it's cold."

Avani toyed with her food; she wasn't really interested in eating. Indraneel..." she began. "I want to tell you something. I wanted so much to call you; within two days of your leaving my apartment. But I didn't have the guts to do it. I didn't know how you'd react."

Indraneel stopped chewing and listened to her intently.

"I dialled your number several times but cut the call before it went through. I made a huge mistake by breaking up with you, and an even bigger mistake by terminating the life of our baby."

Indraneel was caught off-guard. The mention of the baby gave him a sharp pang.

Avani put her plate aside and crawled over the bed to where he sat. Taking his free hand between her own, she said urgently, "Let's get back together Indraneel! There has been no one but you." There was a catch in her voice. "The year I spent with you was the happiest for me. You treated me with so much love and sensitivity, you made me feel like a princess. Above all, Indraneel, you showed me, a girl from nowhere, so much respect." Tears rolled freely down her cheeks.

Indraneel disengaged his hand from hers and bent to put his plate on the floor.

Avani was now sobbing openly, her pretty features crumpled like a crushed flower. "Is there someone else?" she asked between sobs.

Indraneel knelt on the floor and held her hands in his. "Avani, there is no one else. But I just cannot go back to being with you," he told her gently.

"Why, Indraneel? Why?" Avani cried like a baby, her slender body wracked by the force of her sobs. Freeing her hands she hugged him tight. "Please give it one more chance, Indraneel! I love you..." she whispered into the crook of his neck.

He could feel her hot tears on his skin. Indraneel's heart ached to see her weep. "Avani sweetie... don't cry... The man you love no longer exists...the Indraneel you see now has changed. I can't go back to where we left off. I'm sorry. Please stop crying."

But the tears continued to well in her beautiful eyes, now red and swollen. He kissed her on her forehead, saying with complete sincerity, "The time I spent with you was infinitely precious. I cherish those memories."

"Why memories, Indraneel, when you can have the real me?" she asked in desperate appeal.

Indraneel tried once again to explain. "Please understand darling, I cannot go back. I have changed too much. I'm not the same person. I have changed irrevocably."

"Why are you being so stubborn, Indraneel?" Avani asked, breaking down once again.

To his shock, Indraneel suddenly realized he no longer had any awareness of her as a woman –

a woman he had once wanted with an almost desperate, suicidal craving. Now, in his arms, she just felt like a child who needed to be comforted.

He slowly stood up and walked to the balcony door. The rain fell in torrents.

"We can't undo the past Avani...but it's over..." He looked at the crying woman, feeling pity. He reflected that only a couple of months ago this would have been a dream moment for him. He would have done anything to have had Avani back in his life. But now, there was just no connect. He liked her as a person, a friend, and wished her well. All his bitterness was gone. He was free of her.

Indraneel walked back to the bed where Avani still sat crying like her heart would break. Seeing him come towards her, she got off the bed and hugged him again.

"It's the will of God I met you here. Marry me, Indraneel," she begged. "We always had such good chemistry." She rained small kisses on his face.

Indraneel placed two fingers on her lips to stop her from kissing him. "Avani, it's over between us. I can't go back." Before she could say anything more, he clarified, "There is no other woman in my life. But there is no going back for us."

Still Avani persisted. "Indraneel, I know I hurt you very deeply and I'm sorry. Please forgive me. Let's start afresh."

Indraneel wiped her tears with the cuff of his full-sleeved shirt, cursing himself for not having tissues handy. "Avani, forget a future with me. Right now I don't even know where I am headed. I'm at a crossroads," he said with complete sincerity.

Her cell phone rang in her bag. Avani made no attempt to reach it. Indraneel handed her the handbag and urged her to answer. She obediently wiped her eyes, controlled herself, and answered the call. It was her friend from the yoga camp. Indraneel understood from Avani's responses that her friend was asking how she would get back in this rain. Avani told her friend she would see her in the morning and then hung up.

Indraneel firmly told her it was not a good idea for her to spend the night in his room.

"But why, Indraneel? Are you afraid I'll seduce you?" Avani asked with a rueful laugh.

Indraneel did not answer, merely saying he would arrange for her to be dropped back.

The rain stopped abruptly. Indraneel called Bhuwan, a rickshaw driver, on his cell phone. The man said he was parked just down the road and would be at the building in a few minutes.

Indraneel told Avani to wash her face, but she refused. He opened the small wall cupboard, pulled out a fresh hanky and wiped Avani's tears gently, like she was a small child. He even wiped her nose.

Avani held onto his hand. "Indraneel, you're a good man. I'll wait for you." Fresh tears welled in her eyes.

Indraneel shook his head firmly. "No, Avani. Don't make this any more difficult. Don't wait for me. Move on."

It slowly registered on Avani that the Indraneel she knew had somehow faded away. She pleaded no more.

They walked down to the auto-rickshaw, Avani holding his arm as they negotiated the steep steps. She turned to say good-bye.

"One last kiss, Indraneel?" Before he could answer, she had stretched up on her toes and kissed him on the mouth.

Indraneel felt nothing.

Avani now truly knew it was over. She felt deeply unhappy but the vacuum she had felt after he left had somehow disappeared. She now felt a sense of closure, almost a release.

As she got into the auto-rickshaw, Indraneel gave Avani an affectionate look. "Take care of yourself."

"You too, Indraneel!" she called as the rickshaw trundled off through the rain.

Indraneel returned to his room without glancing back, a strange sense of lightness filled his being. He felt free; no longer holding onto what was not to be.

42

Extended *naam* sessions had made Indraneel's throat a little sore. He had begun to walk the long stretches along the Ganga, singing *naam* and consciously listening to the murmuring waters. Sometimes, at night, he actually felt Ma Ganga was whispering something to him. He almost laughed aloud thinking how the imagination could create such powerful suggestions.

It was Diwali. Shaman told Indraneel that on Diwali night the citizens of Ayodhya had illuminated the entire city with earthen lamps to celebrate Lord Rama's return to his capital following his victory over Ravan in Lanka. Rishikesh too, was lit up. That it was also a new moon night was forgotten. Every house was liberally garlanded with fairy lights. Though there was nothing aesthetic in the way the lights were strung or in the choice of colours, the spontaneity was endearing. The town looked like a radiant bride, full of joyful anticipation, waiting for the *baaraat* [groom's procession] to arrive.

As the evening light faded rapidly, numerous women stood waist deep in the cold Ganga waters, setting afloat their lighted *diyas*. Another group sat readying the *diyas* and handing them on large trays to the women in the water.

'I too, would like to offer lamps to Gangaji.... on my birthday perhaps.' The thought lodged in Indraneel's mind.

The gentle singing of the women came to his ears as soft humming. They stood in the Ganga, oblivious to the freezing cold. Their utter devotion was deeply touching. At other places along the *ghaats*, children were lighting fireworks. The sky occasionally exploded into myriad coloured diamonds. Colour splashed across the sky, creating stunning spectacles which faded just as dramatically into nothingness and smoke. In those moments the sky above and the river below seemed like reflections of a thousand sunbursts. Mother Ganga was a river of flame.

'Deepavali in Rishikesh is truly a sight – even for the Gods, peering from the heavens above,' Indraneel thought as he stood on the banks of the Ganga and gazed at the sky.

43

From his balcony Indraneel noticed a band of white men with shaven heads, singing *naam* on the *ghaats*. He remembered Shaman's words about the occult bondage of hair and ran his fingers through his own long curly locks. 'My hair is binding me to my past,' he thought suddenly. Nothing was more precious to him at that moment than freedom.

Indraneel quickly dressed, locked his room and sought out the nearest barber, asking him to shave off his hair.

"You have beautiful hair. Are you sure you want me to shave it all?" the barber asked.

"Let it all go..." Indraneel muttered.

The job was done in five minutes. He saw the clippings on the floor and felt happy. There was a strange sense of release as he gazed at himself in the mirror. He was unrecognizable, even to himself; he looked ten years younger.

As Indraneel walked back to his room with the cold air blowing on his bald head, he felt convinced he had made a new beginning.

44

Indraneel's phone started buzzing from early morning. He felt very different on this, his 39th birthday. There were numerous calls and text messages – from his parents, Arunodaya, Prabhu Da, the *Struggler* crew, fellow directors, aspiring actors, as well as some bigwigs of the film industry. He remembered Avani, but did not really miss her.

Indraneel thought of Shaman's suggestions for his birthday – offering fruits at Ananda Ashram and lighting ten lamps on Gangaji. Fruits and lamps were simple enough, concluded Indraneel. He called Nagaraj and spoke to him about the fruits. Nagaraj offered to go to the market with him and then take the fruits to the *ashram*.

Indraneel spent the morning in reflection. It was the first time he had been quite alone on his birthday. Questions about his life rose to his mind, questions he never would have asked himself: Who am I? What am I doing on this planet? Am I happy?

His parents had called to bless him, but he felt like an orphan. 'I need an anchor,' he thought. 'Surely there's more to life than making films, money and a name. There's peace and light on the other shore; the right to be free, to the supreme wisdom that is my heritage. Do I need a Guru? Yes, yes, yes!' For some strange reason, tears welled in his eyes, making tracks down his almost gaunt cheeks.

Indraneel called Shaman and had a long chat about his predicament.

"You are ready for the next level of existence... the animal is dead, the man is born," said Shaman.

Curiously, Arunodaya had used exactly the same words. He too, had said that Indraneel was ready for 'the next level'.

Just as he finished his call to Shaman, the doorbell rang. A bored young boy from Reception said a courier had come for him. Indraneel was surprised; he was not expecting anything from anyone. He went down. Before signing, he turned over the envelope to see who had sent it – Prabhu Da.

Indraneel was both surprised and pleased Prabhu Da had sent something. He carefully tore off the strip of tape along the envelope flap as he started towards his room. Curiosity gripped him. He opened the envelope to find a rough draft of Prabhu Da's new play, *Why Does it Not Rain Whisky*? Indraneel felt excited. He set it by his bed to read that night, without disturbance.

As he walked to the *ghaats* in the evening, Indraneel saw Madhusudan come out of a net café.

Before he could greet him, Madhusudan looked up and exclaimed in surprise, "Shaved your hair!" He touched Indraneel's head lightly. "You look like a monk," he declared.

Indraneel smiled. "I needed to change."

Madhusudan nodded vigorously in agreement. "Yes, change is good!"

Indraneel hesitantly asked if Madhusudan would accompany him to the *ghaat* to float some lamps. Perhaps it was an odd request. But Madhusudan readily agreed. They walked to the *ghaat*, peering through the rapidly descending dusk. It was 6.15 pm. Indraneel found a lone lamp-seller sitting in a corner and asked the woman to place the lamps in a wicker basket she had, and give him a matchbox as well. The woman obliged, adding some extra camphor in case the breeze played spoilsport.

Thus armed, they went hunting for the ideal spot to float the lamps. Madhusudan found a spot where the steps gently ended in the flowing Ganga and squatted on the last step. Indraneel tried to light the first lamp but the breeze and growing darkness hampered his efforts. Finally he got it right.

He asked Madhusudan to set them on Gangaji gently. It was a beautiful sight. Indraneel's lamps floated along the buoyant waters. Two... three... four... five lamps. It became easier to do. Indraneel took his time floating the sixth and seventh lamps, knowing the comforting task was coming to an end. He asked Madhusudan to light the remaining lamps but his friend smiled and walked away, leaving the lamp job to Indraneel.

Madhusudan played with the *ghaat* dogs. A fat one with winter fur let Madhusudan scratch him under his chin, in doggy heaven. Indraneel called to him and he came away reluctantly, watching the lamps being carried away on the gentle current. Indraneel reminded him it was getting late.

"Come, I want to introduce you," Madhusudan said.

"To whom?" Indraneel looked around surprised.

"To the *ghaat*-dog, of course! Come! He is very cute. It is an honour to meet him."

Ghaat-dog? That was a fine term! When Indraneel was introduced, the dog's complete indifference and meditative stance on the Ganga *ghaat* made him appear to be the *mahant* [head] of a monastery.

Indraneel returned the lamp basket and the two men walked back to the road, negotiating the throng. Indraneel wanted to get back to his room and read the play Prabhu Da had sent.

45

Indraneel got up to go to the restroom at 3.30 am and was unable to fall asleep thereafter. He chanted the *Mahamantra* for an hour. His stomach grumbled, reminding him he had skipped dinner the previous night. Hungry, he foraged through his bag and found a small bar of Mars chocolate. It had a red sticker on it. Though tempted, he put it away.

Restless, he decided to distract himself. He donned an old red sweater with a hood and made his way out into the early morning darkness. It was 5 am. As he walked towards Triveni Ghaat, all was silent except for the occasional barking of the street dogs. A heavy grey mist rolled off the Ganga, reducing visibility. A motley group of men stood near a small bonfire made from cardboard and refuse. As a thin mongrel inched forward to share the warmth, one of the men shooed it away with a cuss word. Another in the group said with a wheezy cough, "*Kabhi idhar se aati hai...kabhi udhar se aati hai* [Sometimes she comes from here...sometimes from there]."

His interest tickled, Indraneel slowed his pace so he could hear the rest of the sentence: "*Bhosadi ki hawaa* [The **** breeze]!" He was most amused and chuckled at the ease with which people in this part of the country swore. Swearing was woven so smoothly into their day-to-day speech that it ceased to have serious import, almost like punctuation!

Indraneel walked from Triveni Ghaat towards Sai Ghaat. It was just after *purnima* [full moon] and a big fat moon poured its molten silver light lovingly onto the rippling waters of the Ganga. The mist began lifting in the breeze. But for his gnawing hunger, it was a perfect day. He was alone but not lonely. There was not a single tea vendor in sight. He had read somewhere that the body feels colder when one is hungry. How true!

Indraneel had been walking for 25 minutes. The eastern sky was turning a pale pink. He sat down at Janaki Ghaat to meditate. He cursed himself for not having brought his *asana*. Shaman had warned him not to sit on the bare earth. Indraneel muttered to himself as he took off his sweater, shivering in the cold as his warm body was exposed to the chilly air. He placed the sweater on the rough cement slab and sat down. When he ran his fingers through the flowing waters, one step below, he recoiled instinctively. The water was insanely cold.

He began to meditate but his mind refused to become still. The sounds of birds and walkers greeting each other...'*Hari Om* Sharmaji...' came to his ears. He could hear someone taking a dip in the Ganga – someone as crazy as himself, he thought. Having a bath at dawn in this cold was almost suicidal. Though Indraneel bathed in the Ganga every day, it was not something he had got used to.

He hurriedly rose, dusted off his sweater and put it back on. He began to feel better instantly. As he got closer to the dark form in the water, he realised it was a woman. He stopped in his tracks, about to walk away, when he heard his name called between chattering teeth.

Indraneel walked closer and then exclaimed in amazement, "VAZ! What are you doing here?"

She was too cold to reply clearly. Emerging from the water she was about to hug him, but stopped, realising she was dripping wet.

Indraneel asked again, "Vaz! What are you doing here?"

She just pointed at Chandrani Bhawan. "Wait! Lemme change. I'll be down in a minute." She ran up the steps of the *ghaat*, a slim figure in tights and a T-shirt.

Indraneel wondered what Arunodaya's sister, Vasundhara, was doing in Rishikesh, dipping in the icy waters of the Ganga, no less! She had attended the same school as Arunodaya and Indraneel, but was almost 12 years younger. Indraneel remembered her being in nursery when they were in class X. The last he had seen of her, many years ago, was at a cricket match, when she was a scrawny teenager with braces and acne. The woman before him was drop-dead gorgeous, even in the murky light of dawn. Petite, slender and light-eyed, her skin had a translucent quality.

True to her word, Vaz was down in a jiffy, wearing blue jeans and a thick white sweater. Her loose hair hung below her shoulders, the ends still dripping wet. Indraneel was delighted to see her. As she hugged him, he asked if she had gloves. She shook her head. He took her icy hands between his own and rubbed them.

"Vaz, you are crazy!"

"No, not Vaz. I don't like people calling me Vaz. Vasundhara. I've grown up being called by my full name."

"Point noted, Vasundhara ma'am!" Indraneel joked and then asked incredulously, "What are you doing here?"

"I come to Rishikesh whenever I have the time." She had been doing so for seven years.

"Why are you bathing in the freezing water?"

She told him she always bathed in the Ganga for the entire duration of her trip, whatever the season. He was quite shocked. This didn't quite fit in with the image he still had of her.

They were still standing at the *ghaats*. The place was getting busy as the sun rose. Indraneel explained that he was ravenously hungry and could kill for a *paneer paratha* [flat bread with cottage cheese stuffing].

Vasundhara, a twinkle in her eye, said she knew exactly the place. She asked if he had any means of transport? Indraneel replied saying he had his Harley. They took an auto-rickshaw to where he was staying near Ram Jhoola. When he ushered her into his room to pick up his bike keys, she was surprised to find the place crammed with books on spirituality.

Indraneel changed into a leather jacket and handed Vasundhara some leather gloves to wear. They went down again to where the bike was parked. It was a handsome Harley Davidson and she was surprised he had such an expensive bike here.

"I had it transported from Bombay," he sheepishly responded to her unasked question.

She did not comment. It was a beautiful day, filled with golden rays. Strangely, she had no questions for him. Instead, he asked how her jewellery design store was doing and she told him it was doing well. Her partner wanted to open another store in Bandra, but Vasundhara was reluctant. She wanted time for herself. Her current store in Walkeshwar was walking distance from where she lived with her parents, as he knew.

It began to drizzle as they rode along in the chilly wind. The landscape looked freshly laundered. As Indraneel slowed to negotiate a sharp bend, they saw a majestic brown stag with impressive antlers climb up to the road with the possible intention of crossing to the other side. Seeing the bike, it stood transfixed for a few seconds, its body tense, its powerful muscles bunched and poised for flight.

The moment seemed frozen from a postcard. The light rain had stopped and the weak winter sunlight slanted through the trees and dripping branches, right onto the stag, lying glistening on its moist winter coat. Indraneel could see its nose twitching, trying to assess danger. A few drops of water shook it from its reverie and it leapt away with effortless grace into the green thickets from where it had emerged.

It took them a few moments to focus on the road after such an unexpected glimpse of the wild. Indraneel stopped the bike.

"One shouldn't stop in the forest. You can slow down but not stop," Vasundhara advised. But Indraneel did not hear. She moved closer, speaking directly into his ear, explaining that elephants are a huge threat in these parts.

Indraneel nodded and they moved on. He was disturbed by her proximity. He chided himself that she was like a sister... Before they knew it, they had arrived at small, rickety, wayside place called Punj, in Doiwala.

"You want to eat here?" Indraneel asked, surprised.

They could smell fresh dung from the buffalo shed nearby.

"Of course! We'll eat here," Vasundhara affirmed, getting off the bike.

The plastic chairs were broken and had actually been sewn together in places with some sort of sturdy wire. The owner smiled at Vasundhara as she ordered two *paneer parathas* and two *lassis* [beaten yogurt]. As they sat together, waiting for their food, Indraneel aired his concerns about her bathing in the Ganga in the dark. Any scum could come floating onto her.

The piping hot *parathas* arrived, topped with cubes of yellow butter dissolving in golden puddles. They smelt divine. There was no room for conversation as they gingerly tore off steaming hot pieces and put them into their mouths. Indraneel was surprised to see that despite her slight frame, Vasundhara had a hearty appetite.

They ate in silence and almost in unison, signalled for a repeat order. It was tele-synergic and they laughed. Then it was time for *lassi*. It was so thick that they could not avoid making slurping sounds. Indraneel had a *lassi* moustache when he finished. Vasundhara handed him a tissue. He missed a spot, so she wiped it for him. He found the gesture strangely intimate.

Vasundhara insisted on paying. Smiling indulgently, Indraneel let her. Then they headed back. Halfway, in the forest, she asked if she could ride his bike. He was too stunned to respond. It was a beast that weighed nearly 300 kilograms.

"Forget it!" she said instantly, sensing his hesitation.

He asked if she had ever ridden a bike before and she nodded. He corrected himself and asked if she had ridden a big motorcycle? He could hear the smile in her voice when she replied from behind him, "There's always a first time." He adjusted the side mirror so he could see her lovely face.

They had an uneventful ride back to Rishikesh. Indraneel dropped Vasundhara off at Chandrani Bhawan and suggested that if she was free around 5:30 that evening, he could take her to Chilla Road, to try his bike. She happily agreed, peeling off his gloves and handing them back to him. But he asked her to keep them. He could take them from her that evening.

46

Indraneel had been frantically trying to reach Arunodaya for the past 15 minutes. He needed to contact Vasundhara but didn't have her mobile number. He had called Chandrani Bhawan a couple of times but no one answered. It wasn't exactly a date but he had promised to take her to Chilla forest to ride his bike.

A thick soupy mist enveloped the whole of Rishikesh. It was damp and bitterly cold, with the mist billowing off the Ganga. Visibility was practically zero. One couldn't see beyond the tip of one's nose. There was no way he was going to let Vasundhara ride such a powerful bike in such perilous conditions. It was already 5 pm and he had still not been able to contact her.

Indraneel's phone rang. He hoped it was Arunodaya calling back. He had a good mind to call his friend a few choice names. But it was Shaman. He said there was a *katha* [story-telling] session at 6 pm at Ganga Beach Café at Lakshman Jhoola. He was welcome to join in.

Shaman's *katha* sessions were great learning grounds, where people exchanged stories from the *Puranas* and *Upanishads* [ancient Hindu spiritual texts]. One got to hear rare gems, which were then discussed.

"But will anyone come in this fog?" Indraneel asked.

"Whoever can, will. I'll be there," Shaman replied nonchalantly.

"May I bring a lady friend along?" Indraneel asked somewhat hesitantly.

"Of course...bring anyone along...the soul knows no gender. Though the eyes always say the prettier the better..." Shaman laughed at his own joke and hung up.

Indraneel paced the room restlessly. A message alert sounded on his phone. It was from Arunodaya and said: 'Very low battery. Is it something urgent?'

Indraneel began to key in a long message to say he needed Vasundhara's number because he had promised her a ride, but changed his mind and just tapped in: 'Send me Vasundhara's mobile number.'

Arunodaya replied almost immediately with the number and a smiley. Indraneel called Vasundhara. She picked up with a familiar, "Hi!"

Indraneel was surprised."You recognized my voice?"

"No, I have your number saved."

Indraneel told her the bike ride would have to wait because of the heavy fog. However there was a story-telling session with some friends; would she care to join in? If not, they could go to dinner.

"What sort of story-telling?" she asked.

He explained there would be stories from the *Puranas* and *Upanishads*. She immediately said she would love to go. He told her he would pick her up as planned and to dress warmly.

Indraneel was quite surprised she had agreed to go to the *katha* session, but was apprehensive she would be bored. He felt a sense of anticipation about seeing her again and found himself debating between wearing a grey sweater and red scarf or a dark green jacket and a blue scarf. He laid them out on his bed and looked at them. He suddenly realised he was behaving like a teenager going on a first date and quickly donned the grey sweater and red scarf, along with a grey woollen cap. In the mirror he observed his hair had grown back quite quickly. It no longer felt like rough Velcro. He still had no need to comb it, but the characteristic softness of his curls was back.

The sharp cold hit him the moment he stepped out of his room. Despite his thick gloves, the handles of the bike felt as if they were carved from ice. It took him twice as long to get to Chandrani Bhawan. It was like riding blind. Motorists had their headlights on, honking to announce their presence to others on the road. Traffic was minimal.

As he approached Chandrani Bhawan, Vasundhara walked out of the building. She looked like a colourful mummy, her slight frame wrapped in layers of clothing from head to toe. Clad in a deep burgundy sweater, black jeans and a black fleece cap, she had his gloves on as well.

"You look like an Egyptian mummy," he announced laughing, his breath frosty.

"It's the only way I can remain alive in this cold," she said, getting onto the bike.

He turned the bike and they slowly made his way towards Lakshman Jhoola. A bitter wind whipped up the refuse on the streets. Neither attempted to speak. These were treacherous road conditions. Indraneel rode past Ram Jhoola and climbed the sharp incline up to Lakshman Jhoola, using all his concentration and skill. The powerful bike went smoothly.

It got colder and Vasundhara wrapped her arms tightly around Indraneel's waist. He could feel her warmth through the layers of clothing. When they finally crossed Lakshman Jhoola, Gangaji was completely invisible below, hidden behind veils of grey.

They parked the bike and made their way down the steps towards the café, located on the banks. Indraneel held out his hand to help Vasundhara down the steps. Her face was flushed from the cold and her nose red like a child's. He warned her to mind her step as there were often sleeping cows and cow-dung on these steps.

Vasundhara switched on the torch she had brought with her and quickly uttered a warning, "Indraneel, you are just about to place your foot in fresh dung!" She pointed the beam at his feet.

"Oh shit!" he exclaimed.

"Exactly!" Vasundhara laughed.

47

Ganga Beach Café sat directly on the banks of Gangaji, almost on level with the flowing water.

"How beautiful!" Vasundhara exclaimed. "One can hear the Ganga but not see her..."

Shaman was already there, as were Michael and Christina, an American couple, with their two children; and Richard, a Frenchman. When Indraneel and Vasundhara entered, Shaman stood up to greet them

"This is my childhood friend, Vasundhara," Indraneel said.

"Shamantak Srivastava...but please call me Shaman." He folded his hands in a *namaste*. "What a beautiful name! Vasundhara means 'mother earth'. And this is Indraneel, with his new, clean, head-shaven look. He used to sport a stubby pony tail," Shaman said to the group before remarking casually, "It must be awfully cold with no hair."

"You're right," Indraneel agreed, turning to the shake hands with the others.

"Nice to meet you again. It's been a long time since I saw you at Eldorado," Michael said. Indraneel remembered and smiled in greeting.

The small tables had been placed closely so the group could sit together. Each one gave a small introduction. When it was his turn, Indraneel introduced both himself and Vasundhara.

Finally Shaman said, "I am Shaman – bookseller, storyteller and taxpayer." Everyone laughed.

The silence outside imparted a peculiar gravity and resonance to the conversation. Even their laughter was highlighted against the murmuring of the river. It was evident from the way the group interacted that this wasn't their first *katha* session. They spoke of Shaman's earlier sessions: Tales from *Yoga Vashishtha* [classical text on yoga], *24 Gurus of Sri Dattatreya*,

Buddha and the prostitute Amrapali, the eagle and crow conversation in *Ramacharitmanas,* and so on.

"Let's begin with the young people here," said Shaman, turning to the children. "Would you like to tell us a story?"

The youngest, Susan, aged 12, said she would like to tell them about Diwali. She smiled shyly at Shaman. "I read it in a book that mama got from your bookstore. I will tell it in my own words."

Indraneel remembered there was an extensive children's section at Shaman's bookstore.

"What's with Diwali, the Festival of Lights? Why do they light loads of lamps that day? I never got that one, though it looks so nice. But now I know… and here's my story…" Susan took a deep breath. "So look dude, Ram had like a big cool kingdom and people liked him but his step-mom or something was kinda wicked and forced her hubby to send Ram to some jungle. As he was going for 14 years, his wife and bro went along… you know, just to chill…

But dude, the forest was real scary stuff, full of the devil and stuff like that. But this dude killed them with his arrows. But then some bad gangsta jerk – Ravana, kidnapped his wife, Sita. This dude and his bro got cheesed off, so they got an army of monkeys – don't ask how – attacked, and got Sita, and returned home."

Susan paused to take a sip of the mineral water in front of her. "People thought they deserved something. There were no bars or clubs back then. So they lit lamps and that is how it all started..."

Everyone applauded spontaneously for the child.

"It was a wonderful story," Vasundhara told Susan earnestly, though she was amused by the child's choice of words and expressions; she even wondered, 'Is this what it has come to?' but let it go. Times had changed and one had to go with the flow. Besides, it had been a fun narration.

Shaman ordered hot mint tea for everyone. He was going to tell them a story about the importance of *naam*, the Name of God.

"Michael, how long have you been in India?" he asked.

"Three years now," the American answered.

"How many people have you met here, who are known by the names of gods?"

"Ah....let me think....Ganesha, Hariharan, Vedavati, Madhusudan, Swaminathan, Shiva, Radha....well, too many."

"That's the point!" exclaimed Shaman. "This country is full of people with godly names. Here's why..."

"You're gonna tell us a story about that?" Christina asked.

"Yes...from the *Bhagawat Purana* [religious text]. Many, many years ago, there was a Brahmin called Ajamila. He had a great upbringing so he turned out to be virtuous and righteous. He followed the scriptures to a tee. He had terrific control over his senses. But you know, one shouldn't be too sure of one's control, one can lose it anytime. This fellow Ajamila also lost it one day.

He chanced into a forest by mistake and lost his way. He met a prostitute there and became enamoured of her beauty. He forgot all about his upbringing when she said, 'Ajamila! Why do you want to go back home? Stay with me and have fun.' He agreed and stayed on. He had no means to support her and the ten children she bore him. So he took to gambling, highway robbery, stealing and other corrupt ways – things bad people do. In this way he spent his life until he was 88 years old.

Absorbed in his evil ways, Ajamila was completely unaware of the greater forces at work. He did not realise that he had grown old and his lifetime was

WHEN LIFE TURNS TURTLE

ebbing away. His youngest son, Narayana, was just five – a cute kid. Ajamila adored him and was always going…'Baby, baby…my lovely Narayana, my darling Narayana.'

Then ding-dong…death rang his doorbell. Three fellows stood there – the fiercest creatures imaginable – carrying ropes, grinning and beckoning horribly. Appalled and afraid, Ajamila did not recognize them as the attendants of Yama, the Lord of Death." Shaman paused for effect.

The only sound to be heard was the rushing of the Ganga. Then he continued. "Ajamila called out in fear to his child playing outside, 'Narayana! Narayana!' His screams came out with great intensity and passion. It was an all-out kind of cry. As soon as he screamed like that, with all his heart, guess what happened?"

No one answered.

"Narayana appeared. Not his son, the child playing outside the house, but the real Narayana, Lord Vishnu. Actually, he sent his attendants, who confronted Yama's men, asking, 'What are you people doing here?' They retorted angrily, 'His time's up! We've come to pick him up.' Vishnu's men then said, 'Excuse us, but you can't take this man. He called for Lord Vishnu at the moment of death and that frees him.' Yama's men argued, 'No Sir! He dies when it's his time. That is *dharma*.'

That started a heated debate about what constituted *dharma* and *adharma*. Ajamila's bad deeds were recounted. But Vishnu's attendants didn't budge. 'Whosoever utters the Lord's name, even by accident, calls for protection,' they countered. 'As a fire consumes fuel, so the Lord's name, whether chanted with or without faith, destroys unrighteousness. A powerful medicine, even when taken by one who is unaware of its properties, is still effective.'

Finally defeated, the attendants of Yama returned empty-handed. Ajamila attained a place in heaven. Now, for the moral of the story...anyone?"

"Chanting the Lord's name can save a man even from the clutches of death. Whoever utters God's name in his or her last moments is saved. The story of Ajamila gives us tremendous hope," Vasundhara concluded.

"That's very well put, Vasundhara. Let's say cheers to *naam*, the all-powerful Name of God," Shaman finished.

They lifted their glasses and bottles of mineral water in unison saying, 'Cheers to *naam*!' The waiter perhaps mistook their toast as birthday merriment and smiled, asking if they would like to order.

Shaman suggested it would be best to keep it simple. "Let me order some vegetable cheese sandwiches for everyone. Is that okay?" There was general agreement.

The Ajamila story made an impact on Indraneel; he decided that if he ever had children he would give them auspicious names of Gods. That way he would earn merit just by calling them. He smiled at the thought.

Shaman looked around with a twinkle in his eye. "Susan has already told us a story, so who is the youngest left amongst us?"

Everyone answered in union: 'Vasundhara!'

"Vasundhara, you tell us a story now," Shaman proposed, turning to her.

Vasundhara had been making boats out of the paper napkins on the table and was taken aback. She looked at Indraneel in mute appeal, her eyes saying clearly, 'Come on, I can't do this.' But Indraneel just smiled and nodded his head.

Vasundhara had recently visited Rameshwaram. She remembered an interesting story about a place called Agni Teerth, which she recounted to the group now. "As you know, Rameshwaram is a place on the coast of Tamil Nadu, bordering the Bay of Bengal. This holy place has many sacred spots, each bearing its own legends. I am talking about a small place called Agni Teerth. In the *Ramayana*, Sri Ramachandra asked Ma Sita to prove her chastity by entering the fire here. Lakshmanji was in charge of arranging the logs. Ram summoned Agni, the fire god to touch the logs.

"So this happened after the gangster jerk was killed?" asked Susan.

Vasundhara nodded and continued. "Agni arrived riding a ram, seven rays of light emanating from his body in hues of red and orange, and 2000 flickering tongues of flame. He combusted the pre-arranged wood to create an inferno. Then Ma Sita entered the flames. Instantly Agni felt the searing heat of her chastity; it was so powerful and radiant that it burnt even Lord Agni."

There was a collective exclamation from the group.

"Agni, Lord of Fire...was burnt?" asked Richard.

Even the children stopped playing and paid careful attention.

"When Ma Sita stepped away from the fire unharmed, the heavens rained flowers on her. Agni prostrated himself before Lord Ram. Showing him his burns, he asked him to cool his body. Ramji asked

Agni to take a dip in the ocean near Rameshwaram and his body would heal. Thus the sea there is called Agni Teertham."

"Fantastic! Thanks for sharing this one," Shaman said. "Fire purifies gold. But fire itself was purified by Ma Sita. Agni did not burn but was burnt. That's a paradox. You get many such paradoxes in Hinduism."

"You're right," said Michael, who spent much time researching and reading.

Their food arrived and the discussion continued as they ate.

"Imagine Lord Fire, his body burning, seeking refuge in the water," Michael murmured reflectively. Turning towards the waters of Gangaji flowing beside them, he bowed, muttering, "Water...water...."

A feeling of awe spread round the group. Discussion followed about both stories – Ajamila and Agni Teerth. Shaman emphasised that chanting God's name was an easy path.

By the time they finished, it was past 10 pm. The waiter came to tell them sheepishly that they would like to wind up for the night. The group bid each other warm good-nites, telling Vasundhara it had been a pleasure to meet her. Shaman invited her to his bookstore.

"I'm off to Bombay tomorrow, but I'll certainly come the next time I'm here," she promised.

48

Vasundhara felt elated by the session. "Shaman is so knowledgeable," she observed in awe.

"Yeah, he's very good. He is my guide," Indraneel answered. "He seemed impressed with you, too. That Agni Teerth story was awesome."

Vasundhara smiled. The mist had covered everything with gossamer lace. They got back on the bike and started off down the road. It seemed as if they were the only two people alive in the universe, enclosed in a bubble.

As they crossed the circular building of Kriya Yoga Ashram, the mist began to lift. It was so dramatic that for a moment it seemed like a shroud had been snatched away and everything came alive again.

"Have you been on the forest road here?" Vasundhara asked.

"No, I'm not even aware there is such a road..."

"Turn left," she instructed.

Indraneel was rather apprehensive. "Are you sure?"

"Are you scared? If you're nervous, there's no need to go. Otherwise it's a beautiful drive."

Indraneel was affronted by her suggestion that he was scared. "Let's go then!"

They drove along a winding *ghaat* road, through lush dark forest. The deep stillness and quiet was calming. Even the crickets were silent. Suddenly they saw tiny flickering lights. Fireflies! Two, then three...then a whole swarm of them. They looked so pretty...tiny dots of moving fire.

"Could we stop for a moment?" Vasundhara asked.

They watched enraptured as the fireflies wove their way around them, darting here and there. Vasundhara closed her palms over three of them and her hands glowed with light. It was a beautiful sight.

"Look!" she said to Indraneel as she opened a chink between her palms to show him. It looked like she held live fire in her hands.

"Are they hot?" he asked curiously.

"No...it's cold fire..."

He looked at the fireflies buzzing in her hands and then at her happy face in the burnished light.

"I'm so happy we came here. Thank you," she declared as she released the fireflies.

They were confused for a moment and then flew away. Together, Indraneel and Vasundhara watched their fiery path across the dense velvety darkness of the winter night. They alighted near a tree a little distance away. It was full of fireflies and looked like a giant Christmas tree, lit by twinkling fairy lights. They walked closer to get a better look at the sparkling spectacle.

"Wow! I wonder why God put light into these creatures and not into human beings?" Indraneel wondered.

"Fireflies communicate by glowing steadily or flashing. They use it for courtship as well," Vasundhara told him.

Indraneel was struck by her breadth of knowledge. "Is this data from Animal Planet?" he asked jokingly.

Vasundhara smiled. Lost in their own thoughts, they walked back to the bike and rode back in silence.

"Do you want some *masala* milk?" Indraneel asked. "There's a guy who sells it from a pushcart, close to where I stay..."

She nodded, so they stopped beside the roadside vendor. The man was just closing up for the night.

Indraneel asked for two glasses. Vasundhara noticed some lamps stacked in a corner. The man saw her looking at them and said that his niece sold them on the *ghaats,* but due to the cold they had remained unsold that day. Few people wished to venture out in this weather.

When Indraneel pointed out that he was doing good business because of the cold, the shopkeeper grinned and said, yes, it was the grace of God.

As they collected their big steel glasses of hot milk, the vendor told Indraneel, "*Babuji, gilaas kal de dena... ab raat bahut ho gayi hai...main ghar jaa rahaa hoon.* [Sir, return the glasses tomorrow…it is dark now…I'm going home]."

Vasundhara bought two lamps. Indraneel asked if she was going to the *ghaat* now, at this late hour?

"Why not?" she responded casually.

They walked down the steps of the *ghaat,* Vasundhara carefully balancing the lamps in one hand and holding the milk glass in the other. It felt good to sit by flowing Gangaji. Vasundhara peeled off her gloves and curled her fingers round the hot glass for warmth. Taking a sip of the creamy milk, she closed her eyes, savouring the fresh flavour. Within minutes the milk had cooled. They finished and put down the glasses. A dark cloak of serenity enveloped everything. They could hear the river gurgling by, loud and clear.

"I love the sound of Gangaji. I have spent several nights just sitting on the banks, fallen asleep listening to her, and woken to her murmuring by my side. There is something mesmerizing if you just listen with your eyes closed," Vasundhara told Indraneel. "Have you ever listened with your eyes closed?"

Indraneel said he had, but never for long periods of time. "But yes, the sound of Gangaji fills me with a deep sense of peace," he said seriously.

Just then they heard the sound of a flute and the faint sounds of a man's reedy voice singing a *bhajan* [devotional song]...*Sitaram Sitaram*....

"Who are these mad people out on such a cold night?" Indraneel wondered.

"People like us!" Vasundhara replied with a chuckle. "Must be people walking along the road." she said, gesturing to the road above the *ghaats*."

She was right. The sounds of the flute and *bhajan* became clearer and then faded away.

"That man singing God's name in the stillness of night pierces straight through my heart," Vasundhara said softly.

Indraneel was instantly curious but he did not pry. Had she been formally initiated?

"Let's light the lamps." Indraneel was getting restless; it was really late. He looked for a matchbox amongst the flowers. It was not there. He cursed himself for not double-checking.

"No worries," said Vasundhara, taking a lighter from her bag.

Indraneel took it from her. "Do you smoke?"

"Not anymore," she laughed. "But I keep it to light *agarbattis* [incense sticks] when I travel."

Indraneel lit one of the two lamps, impressed by the brand of the lighter – Zippo. Apparently only the best would do for her gods! He handed her a lighted lamp, its flame reflecting as twin images in her eyes.

"Who did you inherit your green eyes from?" Indraneel asked on impulse.

"Surely not from the sea," she chuckled, bending gracefully to set the lamp afloat before adding, "My grandmother! I got my faith in God from her too."

The water gently carried the lamp away. She briskly rubbed her cold and wet fingers against her jeans and then put on her gloves. "Now you light your lamp, make a wish and set it afloat."

Clumsily, Indraneel tried to cup the flame and hold the lamp at the same time.

"Let me light it; you just hold the lamp," Vasundhara suggested.

Finally he set his lighted lamp afloat, gazing at it as it bobbed away.

Vasundhara stood watching him. "When did you cut your hair?" she asked.

"My hair? Actually I shaved it off. When I came here I was coming out of a very intense relationship. It left me broken. Emotionally I was like an empty shell. I heard Shaman say that deep yearnings and subtle impressions exist in the hair; if one cuts it, one feels new. That stuck with me. After a while I shaved my head. I just wanted to make a new beginning. What you see now is my hair growing back." Indraneel took off his woollen cap and ran a hand over his short hair.

Vasundhara smiled at him affectionately. "Both looks suit you."

"I would love a smoke," Indraneel said restlessly. "I'm trying to quit, you know. Sometimes I go for days without any craving and then suddenly it's like an itch I have to scratch. Just when I feel I have got over it, the desperate need makes me feel like a prisoner all over again." His tone was almost confessional. "I haven't spoken about Avani...before..."

"So Avani is her name?" Vasundhara asked, looking at Indraneel knowingly.

But Indraneel continued as if he had not heard. "It's the same with memories of Avani. There are weeks when I don't remember her at all and then all of a sudden I am swamped with thoughts of her. It's so unpredictable. The memories come unannounced, with no apparent connection." He looked pained and confused.

Vasundhara moved closer, saying in a soft, comforting voice, "Don't regret the past. It's over. I once read that Steve Jobs said, in a convocation speech at Stanford I think, 'One's past experiences and events are like dots and we keep joining the dots to make a final picture. So if some dots are absent then the picture that emerges finally is incomplete.' Look at it this way – if it had not been for Avani, you would not have come to Rishikesh."

She had a point. His coming to Rishikesh had proved to be a powerful event in his life.

"And as far as smoking and memories coming again and again are concerned, it will happen...*banat banat ban jaaye*...We have to keep trying; it will get done finally."

Indraneel looked at her with newfound respect. "Now where did you read that Vasundhara, or is it your own *gyan* [knowledge]?"

She shook her head smiling. "They are the words of Lahiri Mahashaya, a great saint from Bengal."

"It's getting really late. Should I drop you?" Indraneel was strangely reluctant to let her go.

"No. I think I would like to spend some more time with Gangaji." Vasundhara seemed to have a plan.

"Mind if I hang around?"

"Of course not..."

It was freezing cold now. Indraneel ran to his room to get a quilt – a king-sized thick fluffy comforter. He handed it to Vasundhara.

"Thank you! That's so thoughtful...but what about you?" she asked, her breath misting in the cold.

"I'm okay."

Vasundhara wrapped herself in the quilt. "I have not done my *naam*...do you mind if I do it now?"

"Please do..." Indraneel responded at once.

"I will do it for 24 minutes," Vasundhara said, setting an alarm on her phone.

"Why 24 minutes?" Indraneel was curious.

"Oh, it's a concept I learnt from astrology," she told him. "*Ghatika* is an ancient Indian unit of time. One *ghatika* equals 24 minutes. A day has 60 *ghatikas*."

"Sure, but why 24 minutes?" Indraneel persisted.

"Well, they say a *lagna* [rising sign in a horoscope] changes every *ghatika* with the movement of the moon. Things take 24 minutes to change or establish. If you do anything for less than 24 minutes, it just doesn't stick; it is not anchored."

"Kind of a threshold for anything to ignite?"

"Yes, a threshold," Vasundhara agreed. She began singing Hare Krishna *naam* in a soft voice:

Hare Krishna Hare Krishna KrishnaKrishna Hare HareHare Ram Hare Ram RamRam Hare Hare...

After a few minutes Indraneel began singing along, barely audibly. Vasundhara sang a line of the *mantra* and gestured for him to repeat it. He did so, hesitantly. Then another line. They fell into a pattern. Before they knew it the 24 minutes were up.

"It's the first time I've enjoyed doing *naam* with another person," Indraneel confessed.

"Initially, I think everyone feels shy, but doing *naam* in a group is also enjoyable."

Indraneel asked what else she did by way of spiritual practice. She told him she did 21 *malas japa*, morning and evening.

"So you missed your evening *japa* today?" he asked, concerned.

"Yes, I did," she said, sounding apologetic.

"Well, why not do it now?" Indraneel suggested.

"I don't have my *mala* with me..."

When Indraneel told her to do her *japa* on her fingers, she looked bewildered. He was glad there was finally something he could tell her that she did not already know.

"Do you have a pen?" he asked.

She nodded. Taking it from her he moved closer, asking her to take off her gloves and switch on the torch. Then he wrote on the digits of her fingers the numbers in the order the *mantra* had to be repeated. He counted and demonstrated, moving his thumb over the digits – clockwise on the right hand, anti-clockwise on the left.

"That makes 108," he explained.

Vasundhara was astonished that one could do *japa* on one's fingers. She ran her thumb over the digits again and again until she got it, then she closed her eyes.

When she opened them again, Indraneel asked, "What time is your flight tomorrow?"

"Today," she corrected, pointing to the eastern sky where a baby pink smudge was spreading.

"Shall I drop you to the airport?" he asked.

"No...I've asked Gagan, the cabbie, to pick me up," Vasundhara replied gently.

49

A few days later, Indraneel and Shaman met for lunch at a small restaurant called Greens, close to the bookstore. Greens served the most delicious Italian food. They ate in silence, enjoying the flavours.

Indraneel suddenly remembered something.

"Shaman, when I went walking near Kartikeya Temple today, I heard the most melodious hymns being sung by a group of women, in a South Indian language. Tamil, I think."

Shaman swallowed the last of his risotto. "Where is this temple? Near Balananda Teertha Ashram?" He wiped his mouth with his napkin.

"Yes, that's it."

"In that case you must have heard the Tiruppavai."

"Shaman, you should have heard them sing... the melody was imbued with the most touching devotion and intense longing. At least that's what I felt when I heard it."

"I first heard them when I was on a trip down south. It is only sung in the month of Dhanur, roughly between 15th December and 13th January. It was composed by the great female saint, Andal. You're right about the longing. It's about a *gopi* and her longing for Krishna. I think it has about 30 verses. In fact, I have the English translation in the store.

"I'd definitely like to buy that," Indraneel said, genuinely interested. "Tell me more."

Shaman drank some water before saying, "Andal was found under a *Tulasi* bush at a Srinivasa temple. The temple priest brought her up as his own child. She grew up helping her father with his duties. She would make the most exquisite garlands for the idol and spent her time singing the praises of the Lord. She also developed an intense desire to marry Lord Srinivasa."

"When I visited the Andal Temple in Srivalliputhur, I saw the huge wooden swing where she would sit making the garlands. One day, her father found a strand of Andal's hair on the garland meant for the Lord. He threw the garland away, rebuking Andal for having worn the garland before it had been offered to the Lord. He then made a fresh one. The garland instantly withered away. He offered another, but it too, withered away. The priest thought the Lord was angry because Andal had given him a used garland."

Indraneel listened intently.

"Later that night, the Lord appeared to the priest in a dream and said he only wanted garlands that had been worn by Andal. The priest realised Andal was no ordinary child. The Lord also said, 'I will marry your daughter on [such a] date.'

The priest faithfully dressed his daughter in bridal finery and took a wedding party to the temple to perform her wedding ceremony. After the basic rituals were done, Andal simply walked into the idol of the Lord and disappeared."

"What a story! I have gooseflesh!" Indraneel lifted his shirtsleeve to show Shaman. "You mean she just walked into a stone idol? I just can't get over it!"

"Yes. We can only imagine the depth of her devotion for her to have attained the Lord in her mortal form."

50

Indraneel found the December cold of Rishikesh merciless, almost demonic in its unrelenting intensity. When he had resolved to do Ganga *snaan* [bath] every day, he hadn't gambled on such life-threatening winter conditions. For the past month he had begun to enjoy singing *naam* and doing long sessions of *japa*. A sense of inner peace was now his constant companion. He loved the early morning darkness and made it a point to get up at 4 am to do his prayers. But the cold was playing havoc with his resolve.

Indraneel went down to the *ghaat*, his teeth chattering. The *naam* he was attempting to sing sounded comical as it came in spurts from between his shivering lips. The normally deserted *ghaat* presented a different picture today. A group of young Caucasian women were sitting on the steps, gently humming Hare Krishna *naam*. Indraneel was surprised. They too, noticed him and joined their palms instantly in a traditional *namaste*. But they didn't stop singing.

Indraneel felt rather embarrassed to bathe in front of this female audience, but then remembered Shaman saying, 'One must be shameless in matters of belief and faith'. He quietly stripped down to his boxers and entered the frigid waters singing *naam*, hoping to stay alive as the water enfolded his body in a bone-crushing grip.

The group of girls were shocked to see someone enter the river so casually on such a freezing morning. 'OMG!' they exclaimed in disbelief. When Indraneel emerged, they were all watching him with awe. One of the girls came over to ask if he was alright.

Indraneel picked up his towel. "I do this every day," he replied, trying hard to keep pride out of his voice.

He went up the steps quickly and back to his room. He had a hot shower, changed into warm clothes, and then returned to the *ghaat* steps. It was still dark. Now he looked more closely at the girls. They were all attractive and appeared to be in their early to mid-twenties. When they saw Indraneel approach, they stopped singing and introduced themselves as

Susan, Lucy, Stephanie, Ruby, Mary, Angelina and Jane.

The last girl said, "I am Maya; that's my Hindu name."

"I'm Indraneel," he responded, and shook hands.

They told him they were all musicians and played various musical instruments. Maya was the vocalist. Indraneel was surprised to hear they had come all the way from Warsaw to attend the Kumbh Mela. They were regulars at the ISKCON temple in Warsaw and sang *naam* there.

"It's time to go to the ISKCON temple at Kailash Gate," Angelina reminded the group.

"This early?" Indraneel asked, surprised.

Ruby answered. "Today is *Vaikuntha Ekadashi*."

Indraneel felt sheepish; he had no idea what she was talking about.

Mary enlightened him. "Today, the doors of *Vaikuntha* [heaven] open. The inner sanctum's northern gate is opened between 4-6 am – *brahma muhurtam* [most auspicious period of 1 hour 36 minutes before sunrise]. This is an auspicious time because God accepts all types of people into *Vaikuntha*, sinner or saint. *Vaikuntha Ekadashi* gives sinners the chance to be cleansed of their sins."

Indraneel was stunned by the girl's perfect pronunciation of the Sanskrit words and the simplicity of her explanation.

"May I come along?" he asked.

The girls were more than willing to have a handsome man accompany them.

Stephanie, who had been quiet thus far, now said, "There is another legend mentioned in the *Padma Purana* [Hindu religious text],' and narrated how *Ekadashi* came to be.

The oldest girl in the group, Susan, turned to Stephanie, trying hard to hide a smile. "Looks like you mugged that up from the temple booklet that was distributed."

Lucy, standing next to Indraneel, interjected, "She's trying to impress Indraneel!" The girls giggled.

But it was a serious moment for Indraneel. He was astounded by the girls' faith in Hinduism. Ruby, the group leader, was the only one who had visited India earlier. She knew her way to the ISKCON temple. The others were just young girls. Where did they get their faith from? What made these young people travel thousands of kilometres to an unknown land?

Indraneel remembered the Canadian he had met on the plane coming to Rishikesh – Madhusudan. He had wept with joy on setting foot on Indian soil. 'We take the spirituality of our homeland for granted,' he thought. It baffled him. Countless foreigners kept visiting this country, famed for its Himalayan wonders, braving inclement weather, spicy food, poor sanitation and unhygienic living conditions. Why?

'Why don't I feel that pull?' Indraneel wondered. 'Do I lack the gravity Shaman spoke of? How do these foreigners believe so plainly, while we who are born here are stricken with doubt and faithlessness?'

When it came to religious faith, believing without questioning was perhaps the way of the West. As for the East, it seemed to him that now, with the modern generation it was just questioning. At one time the questioning must have been in order to believe.

'Well, Rishikesh is belief land,' he told himself.

In the semi-darkness, they made their way to the ISKCON temple. As soon as it came into view, the girls began singing *naam*. Indraneel was amazed at the spontaneity of their singing. He too joined in, surprised to find himself in tears.

They entered through the northern entrance and waited in queue. Indraneel overheard an old man behind him telling his sleepy grandson, "*Aaj Sri Krishna Bhagawan ne Arjun ko Gita ka upadesh kiya* [Today, Lord Krishna gave the *Gita* sermon to Arjuna]…" The child was not interested. "How long do we have to wait?" he asked sleepily.

As the queue inched forward, they finally had *darshan* of Radharani and Krishna, decked in bridal finery, jewels, and pink and white roses. The crush of people didn't bother Indraneel. The girls were oblivious of the crowd, singing in joyful harmony.

When they stepped out, the eastern sky was turning pink. Indraneel asked Ruby, "Shall we all have some tea?"

She looked at the group and they nodded. They walked to Madras Café, which was now open. The girls informed him they were all fasting and would only have liquid. So they ordered tea.

It was embarrassing to ask foreigners about his own land but Indraneel overcame his initial hesitation and asked, "What's the significance of the Kumbh Mela?"

Ruby said they were not too clear about it; they just knew that some of the holy waters of the Ganga turned into nectar at a particular time. Their Guru had said a Kumbh bath was the most important thing a human could undertake. 'Just take a dip and get the hell out of there,' the Guru in Warsaw had added.

"We too, would like to know its significance," Maya added softly.

Indraneel picked up his phone. "If you're free, Shaman, could you join me at Madras Café now? I'm with a group of people you would love to meet."

51

As they waited for Shaman, Indraneel asked the girls how it was that they had taken to *naam*.

"Because of George," answered Ruby.

"George?" Indraneel wondered if there was a guy in their group. Or perhaps their Guru's name was George?

"George Harrison!" Mary exclaimed.

"The Beatle?"

"Yes, the Beatle."

"There's a Beatles Café here," Indraneel told them, promising to take them there. "Tell me how

George got you into *naam*?" Indraneel was intensely curious.

Lucy bit her lip and thought for a second. "Way back, before the dissolution of the Beatles (the most popular music group of all time), George Harrison produced a hit single, *The Hare Krishna Mantra*, performed by him and the devotees of the London Radha-Krishna Temple."

"That must have been four decades ago," Indraneel commented, trying to remember.

"1969," Maya confirmed. "It went to the top of the pops in England. At about the same time, 5000 miles away, several shaven-headed, saffron-robed men and sari-clad women, sang with John Lennon and Yoko Ono as they recorded the hit song, *Give Peace a Chance*."

"We are all great Beatles fans," Ruby said. "We joined a club in Warsaw about four years ago and found many likeminded people there, many of them quite senior. We had discussions, saw inspiring videos, and read a lot."

Indraneel was still curious. "Who initiated George Harrison?"

Mary, Jane and Stephanie answered in unison, "Swami Prabhupada!" They looked at each other and smiled.

"George Harrison was the impetus for the Beatles' spiritual quest of the 60s," Mary added. "And George co-signed the lease for ISKCON's first temple in central London. He did it instinctively."

"What do you mean instinctively?" Indraneel asked, completely confused.

"He just felt he had to do it." A soft voice answered.

Maya, sipping on her tea, commented, "That's the rare voice of Angelina. She hardly speaks, you know. Actually we were at a crossroads...facing isolation and difficulties in our personal and professional lives. We wanted to fill that space. So we thought why not give chanting a chance? We do all kinds of things anyway. So we decided to meet every day at 6 pm at the temple and chant for an hour." Maya rolled her eyes.

"And there was no looking back," Stephanie nodded. "We were happier people. Our circumstances didn't change but our perception of them did."

"And Jane, how did it start for you?" Indraneel enquired.

"In pretty much the same way as the others. I play guitar – George Harrison's favourite musical instrument. I am the lead guitarist of the band I work with. I made a huge effort to go to the temple to be with the girls. I also did yoga."

"It's very good for us," Ruby explained. "We have each other to jam and sing with."

Indraneel was blown away by the girls' faith. The depth of their passion for *naam* enthralled him. He felt at home with their thoughts and feelings.

Looking at her companions for confirmation, Susan said, "Remember the incident discussed at the club... once George was on an airplane in an electric storm. He was on his way from Los Angeles to New York, for the Bangladesh concert. The plane was hit by lightning, thrice, and a Boeing 707 flew over them, missing by inches. As soon as the plane began bouncing around, George started chanting *Hare Krishna, Hare Krishna, Krishna Krishna, Hare Hare, Hare Rama, Hare Rama, Rama Rama, Hare Hare.*

It went on for about two hours, the plane dropping hundreds of feet and bouncing about in the storm. The lights went out and there were unidentified explosions. Everyone was terrified.

George ended up with his feet pressed against the seat in front, gripping his seatbelt. He kept singing

Hare Krishna, Hare Krishna, Krishna Krishna, Hare Hare, as loudly as he could. He knew the difference between making it or not lay in chanting the *mantra* without pause."

"It was direct proof to us that *naam* chanting saved them from an almost impossible situation," Jane concluded.

Maya fidgeted with the ring on her finger for a moment. "There's another thing, we took to chanting to undo the knots in our lives."

"Knots?" Indraneel queried.

"Yes, knots," answered Maya. "Simplistically speaking, life is like a piece of string with a lot of knots in it. The knots are the *karma* you're born with from all your past lives; human life is the challenge of undoing them. That's what chanting and meditation can do. Otherwise you simply add more knots each time you try to undo one. That's how *karma* works. I mean, we're the result of our past actions; in the future we'll be the result of the actions we are performing now. A little understanding of 'as you sow, so shall you reap' is important. Then you can't blame your condition on anyone else. You know that your own actions get you in or out of a mess. Your own actions relieve or bind you."

The group was so caught up in the moment that it took them a minute to notice that Shaman had come. He stood quietly, listening to Maya's words.

"That was beautifully put," he said.

Maya blushed bobbing her head in embarrassment. "The words are not mine but George Harrison's!"

Shaman nodded. "The most spiritually evolved rock star."

Indraneel got a chair for Shaman and introduced him to the group saying, "This is my mentor, Shamantak Srivastava!"

Shaman raised an eyebrow. "That's quite a mouthful...just call me Shaman."

The girls introduced themselves and Shaman nodded to each of them in turn. "Another round of tea...coffee...milk...*lassi*...fresh juice?" he asked. "I'm going to have some fresh orange juice."

"What's *lassi*?" Stephanie asked, intrigued.

"It's beaten sweet yogurt. Try it," Indraneel urged.

"Perhaps I will," Angelina responded.

"We have been honoured with the voice of Angelina twice within the span of an hour. We are all blessed. Cheers!" Maya teased Angelina, lifting her glass of tea.

They all lifted their glasses calling, 'Cheers!' Angelina threw a balled tissue at Maya in mock anger. Indraneel loved the easy warmth and kinship within the group.

"By the way, *lassi* was one of George Harrison's favourite drinks," Shaman informed them all.

This prompted them to order a glass each.

52

For the Polish girls, the Kumbh was a great fair. The thought of seeing bare-bodied Naga hermits; monks performing severe austerities; the silent saints, and over-the-top meditators standing on their heads for hours, was all very exciting. It was such a vast gathering of different sects, saints, *vairagis* [renunciates] and yogis who had renounced the world! They had a preview of it in the documentary, *Short Cut to Nirvana* by Nick Day, which they had seen back in Warsaw.

"Shaman, Ruby and this group of hers, are going to the Kumbh Mela. But they do not know the true significance of the Kumbh. Nor do I! Would you care to throw some light on this for us?" Indraneel asked.

"Yes, please!" Maya pleaded, before asking, "Is he a Guru?"

That put the spotlight on Shaman. Everyone stared at him. There was surely more to the man who knew *lassi* was one of George Harrison's favourite drinks!

"He *is* a Guru...I can feel his aura," Ruby said quietly.

"Oh no! That's just your perception, nothing more. I'm not a Guru but a bookseller. I have no special aura, it's just deodorant." Shaman promptly dismissed his aura and possible elevation with a chuckle.

"Come on, Shaman! Don't be so modest. Tell us about the Kumbh. They're all going there, so it will be helpful to know more," Indraneel urged.

"So you're going to the biggest gathering on earth?" Shaman asked the girls. "Do you know the meaning of *kumbh*?"

"No!" they chorused.

"Well, *kumbh* is a pot, a mud pot."

"Yes, I've seen them sell tea in mud pots," Ruby said.

"Well, that's one kind. This is perhaps more like an urn. Pot or urn, here's the story. Mohini was a divine enchantress; she distributed *amrit* to the gods from a pot. You know *amrit*, right?"

"Divine ambrosia, the nectar of immortality," said Jane.

"That's correct. The Kumbh Mela is named after this pot of *amrit*."

Angelina spoke up. "I believe the gods and demons fought over the pot containing the nectar of immortality."

"Yes, they did. The *kumbh* story appears at the beginning of the creation of the universe. The gods had lost their strength. In order to regain it, they thought of churning the Primordial Ocean for *amrit*, the nectar of immortality. This required them to make a temporary arrangement with their arch enemies, the demons. They agreed to work together, promising to share the nectar equally. So they churned away to glory, gods on one side of the rope and the demons on the other. However, when the *kumbh* containing the *amrit* appeared, a fight ensued."

"Why?"

"The usual thing, much like politicians are wont to do today. The gods did not hold up their end of the bargain and withheld the nectar from the demons. For 12 days and 12 nights, that's equivalent to 12 human years, the gods and the demons fought in the sky for the pot of *amrit*. It is believed that during the battle, Garuda, the vehicle of Vishnu, flew away with the pot of elixir. That was when drops of *amrit* fell at four places on earth – Allahabad, Haridwar, Ujjain and Nashik – the places where the Kumbh Mela is held every 12 years."

"But how can drops of immortality that fell thousands of years ago still be there in the rivers?" Ruby asked sceptically.

"Good question! We're talking of drops of immortality here. How can a potion which overcomes death, die? *Amrit* remains. It can't be lost."

"So why does this a*mrit* come up only once in three years at a specific place?"

"Once in 12 years, the planetary position is exactly what it was at the time of the great churning. It triggers a bubbling of the waters in one of the four spots where the *amrit* fell, creating a high energy point every three years."

"So, there's astronomy to it?" asked Stephanie, surprised.

"Exactly! Scientists know how the moon affects us; they know what happens during eclipses. It's the same principle. A chemical reaction occurs every three years in one of these four rivers."

"What chemical reaction?" asked Jane, somewhat dubiously.

"Cosmic energy starts spurting in the Ganga, Godavari, Kshipra, or whichever river the Kumbh is taking place at."

"But what determines this period?" Ruby wanted to know.

"The *mela* takes place when the planet Jupiter enters Aquarius and the Sun enters Aries."

"So these reactions happen only in the waters of these four holy rivers?" Indraneel asked.

"Yes. Right now, nectar is spurting into the holy waters at Allahabad Kumbh."

"But why water?" Maya probed.

"Because water is the fastest element to be energized. The Cosmic Energy spreads in these holy waters to a radius of 45 kms. When we take a dip in the holy waters, the subtle energy points of the human body absorb it." Shaman sipped his juice.

"Wow! That is a terrific explanation about the Kumbh. But what can a dip do?" Indraneel wondered.

"The dip helps to awaken spiritual energy. The nectar of immortality flows down from the crown *chakra*. Someone with the right receptivity is likely to drink it."

"That's rather unbelievable. If just one dip can bring all this about, what's the point of meditation etc?" Ruby asked, unconvinced.

"Well, it's a tricky business. Let me tell you a story to put it into perspective." Shaman pushed back his chair so he could stretch his legs. "Parvati, Lord Shiva's consort, watched millions gather at the holy Kumbh and grew pensive. She said to Shiva, 'You are compassionate, my Lord, yet to me it seems your compassion has done more harm than good, for only a fool would lead a virtuous life when *moksha* [liberation] can be attained by a mere dip in the holy river on the occasion of Kumbh.'

Hearing her complaint, Shiva suggested they pay a visit to the Kumbh. 'It's true I have offered that boon – that a Kumbh dip will rid one of all sins. But it is not as simple as it seems. Boons are easy to grant, but difficult to earn.' Parvati asked how that was so. 'See for yourself,' replied Lord Shiva, and disguised as a Brahmin and his wife, he lay prone on the ground at Haridwar, where the Kumbh was in progress. Beside him, Parvati sobbed profusely, like a bereaved wife. When pilgrims stopped to enquire, she answered all queries saying, 'Lord Shiva has promised that the touch of a sinless man will bring my husband to life. But if the person is not sinless, he will die instantly.'

On hearing this, everyone recoiled, for none of them truly believed they had been cleansed of their sins after the holy dip. And who'd wish to risk their life? Thus Parvati sat crying until a drunk came staggering along. He readily offered to help. He was certain that the Kumbh dip would purify him. After a quick dip in the river he returned and bent down to touch the dead Brahmin, whereupon Shiva revealed himself saying, 'You have indeed attained *moksha* my son, only you.'

Back in their heavenly abode, Shiva asked Parvati, 'With all my divine compassion I do not seem to have succeeded in making salvation very easy, have I?' That is the reality of the Kumbh Mela and the magical experience of promised salvation for the millions who come for a dip."

"This is a truly profound tale." Indraneel felt touched in a way he could not explain or give a name to.

"Yes, it throws light on the human tendency to want to believe and yet not believe; to trust in divine intercession but check it through personal apprehension; to behold the ultimate reality but never truly believe it is in one's palm." Shaman turned to Ruby. "Tell me, why are *you* going there?"

The question took Ruby by surprise "Frankly, I never thought of immortality or *moksha*. I'm going because my Guru told me it was a good thing to do. I've got an instinct for this, you know. I just think it is positive energy. It *has* to be hugely positive...why else would millions of people go there?"

"True, it has baffled everyone. Mark Twain had a Kumbh bath in 1895, and remarked, 'It is wonderful, the power of a faith like that, that can make multitudes upon multitudes of the old and weak and the young and frail enter without hesitation or complaint upon such incredible journeys and endure the resultant miseries without repining.' He felt it was beyond the imagination of 'cold' whites. I'm not being racist, just paraphrasing Mr Twain."

"He was right. We are the cold whites. India warms our hearts and souls," Jane commented without bitterness.

"Well, I don't believe that," retorted Shaman. "No one is cold and no one is black or white. We're all the same on the common ground of soul reality."

"How true!" Ruby exclaimed, her eyes shining. Shaman's words had reached deep into her heart.

"Coming back to the story about Shiva and Parvati, don't you think it's all a matter of faith?" Indraneel asked.

"If people believe they are cleansed by the dip, they are! If they don't, they are not. Faith has the power to transform. Whether it is the dip which has the power is not the point, it is the belief in that divine power," Shaman pointed out.

"I read something interesting about trust and faith...may I share it?" Indraneel asked.

"Please...I feel guilty about doing all the talking anyway," Shaman laughed.

"A child smiles even when thrown up into the air because it knows it will land in safe hands. That's trust," Indraneel told them, hands clasped between his knees.

"Yes. And if we can take a dip at the Kumbh like the child and the drunkard, we too, can play in the waters of immortality."

Shaman's words ignited in Indraneel a burning desire to go to the Kumbh Mela.

"Where are you all staying?" Shaman asked.

"At Tripathagamini Sadan," Ruby replied.

It was time for them to leave. The girls began walking back to their guest house and Indraneel to his.

Shaman had work at Lakshman Jhoola. He waved farewell saying, "Have a great Kumbh everyone!" Then added, laughing, "And don't be *not* drunk!"

53

Indraneel woke from a deep sleep when he heard the on-flight announcement that they had landed in Varanasi. The temperature outside was only 18° C despite it being almost noon. He was glad for his cableknit sweater and thick jacket. He only had a backpack, and exited the terminal quickly.

Several cabs stood outside. Before he could take another step, a whole bunch of cabbies came rushing up to ask if he wanted to go to the Vishwanath Temple. When he shook his head, they asked if he wanted to go to the University. When Indraneel asked about a trip to Allahabad Kumbh Nagari, most of them backed out. One of them told him, "Sir, you are too late."

"What do you mean too late?" Indraneel asked, all at sea.

"I will take you," one of the remaining cabbies offered.

As Indraneel walked towards the cab indicated, the driver explained, "Sir, tomorrow is the *Shahi Snaan* [Royal Bath]; *Makara Sankranti* [entry of the sun into Capricorn]. It's a very auspicious day, so Kumbh Nagari will be sealed today by 2 pm because they cannot handle more people. We have to hurry."

Indraneel absorbed the information as he got into the Indica. The scenery sped by.

The driver drove with both skill and confidence. "Sir, you have accommodation?" he enquired.

"Swiss Cottage," Indraneel replied.

"You must have booked well in advance then. It's very difficult to get even a single bed now."

Indraneel made a mental note to thank Lily. It must have been a challenge to get a place at such short notice. The first thing he noticed was the movement of people. It seemed like a huge migration of people – travelling in packed tempos, lorries and buses. Some sat on top of buses, others in *jugads* [improvised vehicles]. The traffic moved in only one direction. Cops were everywhere.

The driver cursed the manic traffic as he drove, briefly turning to inform Indraneel, "All these people are going to Allahabad. That's why they are driving so fast."

Vast stretches of the road were covered in mist. The poor visibility reduced their driving speed dramatically.

"How long will it take to reach to Allahabad?" Indraneel asked.

"Sir, I can't say! If we are lucky, we will make it before they close the city," the driver answered, peering through the fog.

After a while the mist cleared and they sped along with the other traffic. Some way ahead, a railway crossing closed in front of them. The driver did his best to get past the closing gate but he was too late.

A guava vendor sitting in the shade of a tree called out to the driver as the car slid to a halt in front of him, "Hey Ram Singh...*itna late jaa rahe ho? Nagari bund h jayegi* [You are going so late...the township will be closed]."

The driver remained unfazed. "If it's in our fate, we will make it."

Indraneel looked at the green guavas with their delicate pink flesh. The vendor immediately said, "Forty rupees per piece, *Saab*."

"Sir, don't eat them. They are unseasonal; not from here. By eating things that don't belong to the natural seasons people fall sick." Ram Singh said, offering free counsel.

Indraneel thought there was a great deal of wisdom in the man's native intelligence. He shook his head at the vendor and let go his desire to eat a guava.

A bus stopped and the passengers stepped out. The guava vendor's entire basket was sold out in minutes. The sharp hooting of the train broke the silence as it rushed by, full to overflowing, with people even hanging from its doors and clinging to the sides. It reminded Indraneel of the grainy black and white pictures of Partition, when trainloads of people had fled to India from Pakistan, and vice versa.

After an hour or so, the kilometre stone read 3 kms to Allahabad. A little ahead, a barricade was in place and the cab stopped at the temporary police station. A cop gestured for them to turn back. Ram Singh got out and spoke to the constable. After five minutes of animated conversation, the barricade was lifted and Ram Singh got back into the car and they passed through.

Indraneel asked Ram Singh why they had been allowed through.

"I bribed them with 100 rupees," Ram Singh stated matter-of-factly.

Once in Allahabad, Ram Singh drove Indraneel towards Kumbh Nagari, which occupied an area of 50 sq. kms., a little larger than the Vatican. Tents dotted the sandy banks of the Ganga as far the eye could see.

Indraneel asked Ram Singh if he could take him back to Varanasi later. But the driver said the city had been locked down and they would only be able to exit once the roads were reopened.

"For now, it's like a jail," he chuckled.

Indraneel took down Ram Singh's number, gave him a missed call so he could save his number, and said he would keep in touch. Then he called the reservation desk that had done his booking and found his Swiss Cottage with ease. It was both luxurious and neat. It had a clean bath with running hot water and a Western style toilet.

It was almost 4 pm and the meagre warmth of the day was quickly dissipating in the evening chill. People, people, people everywhere! A mind-boggling diversity of humanity milled about. All forms of traditional Indian clothing were visible. Indraneel heard many languages and dialects. There were many foreigners as well – Japanese, English, American. He heard accents and languages he couldn't recognise.

Kumbh Nagari was bustling with activity. There were numerous makeshift shops in the narrow lanes between the tents. Temporary bazars had come up behind the *ghaats* and were doing brisk business. There was a roaring trade in *rudraksha,* crystal and black-and-red-thread *malas*, brass and copper *puja* vessels, pictures of gods and goddesses, and *bhajan* CDs, as well as *prasad* packets and eatables of all kinds. Pilgrims thronged the shops to buy memorabilia to commemorate their Kumbh visit.

Indraneel began to feel that the Kumbh Mela was the most photographed event ever. For every little event or place, there was someone taking a photograph. Allahabad wore a festive look. Many of the buildings had been painted and illumined. Faith and joy were tangible in the air. An endless number of people walking towards the *ghaats,* no trace of anxiety on their faces.

Pilgrims poured in – big and small groups, and sometimes hordes that looked like whole villages. All they carried was a bag or two on their heads or shoulders, but they were all imbued with an unshakable faith in the glory of Ganga Ma. Village women came in groups, singing folk songs in praise of Ganga, Kumbh or God. Some played *karataals* or *dhols* as they sang *naam*. They were from Bengal. Indraneel joined them briefly before walking on. He wanted to drink it all in.

A strange energy gripped the whole of Kumbh Nagari. It was a huge affair. There were nearly 60-70 *akhadas* [sects], who had put up camps. In all the *akhadas*, devotees and *bairagi sadhus* [renunciate ascetics], with prominent religious markings on their foreheads, attended to their rituals and singing *bhajans*. There were discourses, *arati* and *prasad* distribution as well as enactments of scenes from the lives of Rama and Krishna.

Some of the camps had huge welcome arches and fancy façades. In one, Indraneel saw an organisation had made the effort to provide free medical care to polio victims. Free surgeries had been done on affected children, who were recouping in a makeshift camp nearby. They also provided artificial limbs. An exhibition about the organisation's activities had been put up.

In another *bairagi akhada*, Indraneel saw people sitting in a circle around a cow-dung-cake-fuelled fire. They were meditating and doing *japa*. The austere silence of the camp amidst the religious cacophony was an inspiring sight.

There were also camps where the Shankaracharyas of Dwaraka and Puri were accommodated. In a relative sense, Mandaleshwar Nagar was rather calm and silent.

As cold night descended, Indraneel noticed that most people had just settled down under roadside trees, having spread sheets to sleep on. They lit the small kerosene stoves they carried, or placed two bricks and lit a fire with wooden chips. Over this they cooked their simple fare of *chapattis* and *dal* [flat bread and lentils], offering it to passers-by as well. The simplicity of their pilgrim faith humbled Indraneel.

As he walked along, he came to the Juna Akhada camp. It consisted of rudimentary tents. A number of *naga sadhus* [unclothed ascetics], occupied them. Besmeared in ash, they sat smoking their *chillums* [clay smoking-pipes]. Indraneel offered his respect to the *naga sadhus*, who in return gave him some ash and touched his head with peacock feathers and strange steel tongs. One offered him a *chillum* as he sat enveloped in clouds of hashish smoke. *"Le lo beta, Bhole ka prasad hai* [Take it son, it is the *prasad* of Lord Shiva]."

"Meherbaani [Thank you]..." Indraneel dutifully took it from the *sadhu*'s hands but didn't smoke it. When the *sadhu* closed his eyes, Indraneel quietly slipped away. He had done all this years ago; he needed no more of this *prasad*.

Signs of modernisation were visible everywhere. Though they wore no clothes, many of the *naga sadhus* were seen talking on mobile phones. Some camps even had TV sets.

There was also a buzz about a rare *sadhu*. His camp was rather isolated but Indraneel went along to catch a glimpse of him. Inside the tent, the bare-bodied *sadhu* sat with his right hand raised – for the last 12 years! He sat in the lotus posture with a stillness that seemed unreal, as if carved from stone.

Indraneel did not go into the logic of such practices, just admiring the *sadhu*'s will power. He remembered Swami Vivekananda's words, that for the sake of a religious purpose, people in India do extraordinary things. 'How true!' he thought, taking pictures.

Kumbh Nagari had a strong, nearly intoxicating, signature odour – a strange amalgamation of cooking fires, incense, and sacred *homas* [fire rituals], mixed with hashish/cannabis and smoke from the campfires people had lit to keep warm.

Food flowed like the mighty Ganga. Everywhere, people were distributing free food – hot *puris* [fried bread], sizzling *jalebis* [Indian sweet], *channa* [chickpeas] in red gravy, plates and plates of *sooji halwa* and round *gulab jamuns* [semolina pudding and milk-solids based sweet] swimming in syrup. Water was being distributed as well. Tea was being served free. Indraneel took some *channa garam* [roasted and beaten chickpeas] and munched as he watched the Ganga. Multitudes of lifetimes were being played out on her banks.

Time moved on, crunching everything in its path. The inconceivably grand scale of the Mela left a deep imprint on Indraneel's mind as he absorbed the carnival atmosphere of Kumbh Nagari. Nowhere was the interplay between the human and divine facets of the Ganga as palpable and magnificent as it was right now, here amidst this immense, peaceful, human congregation.

It was past 1 am when Indraneel walked back towards his cottage. He walked on feeling no fatigue. An inexplicable exhilaration gripped him. Kumbh Nagari throbbed with an electric energy.

Its vibrancy at 1 am could be compared with Vegas at night. Only the texture and source of the energy here was different. There was an immense sense of anticipation and waiting in everyone.

Dawn. *Shaahi Snaan!*

54

Atea-seller sitting on a cycle on the *ghaats* asked Indraneel somewhat hopefully if he wanted some hot tea. Indraneel declined.

The tea-seller muttered to himself, "When tea is being distributed free 24/7, which fool will 'buy' tea?"

Indraneel felt for the vendor's plight. "I will give you 500 rupees if you will take me on your cycle and show me the Nagari," he told the grumpy man.

The tea-seller gazed at him in frustration. "It will take two days!" he said, looking away.

"Let's do it for an hour," Indraneel suggested.

The young man broke into smiles and promptly agreed. *"Sir, mera naam Tinku hai...koi bhi chai nahi khareed rahaa hai aaj* [...my name is Tinku...no one is buying tea today]," he lamented.

They set off on the cycle, the tea paraphernalia tied with rope behind them and adding their own clinking and clanging to the ambient noise.

Tinku showed Indraneel the AC cottages of Hollywood celebrities. "*Iss mein Julia Roberts hai* [Julia Roberts is in this one]!" he announced in a stage whisper. "*Aur woh Titanic ki heroine* [And the heroine from the Titanic]..."

Indraneel just laughed.

They cycled on towards a makeshift stage where the *Ramayana* was being staged. Sita's abduction was being enacted, the audience of men, women and children watching enthralled. Tinku informed Indraneel that the troupe had come from Ayodhya. A child began to cry loudly as Ravana abducted Sita and someone from backstage yelled, "*Bacche ko chup karaao* [Make the baby stop crying]!"

As they cycled on, Tinku said, "Sir, I will take you to the place that sells the best *malai* [skimmed cream] plate..."

"What's *malai* plate?" Indraneel asked.

"I'll take you. You'll see for yourself!" Tinku assured him.

They arrived at a tent located in front of an open area where a mini merry-go-round and a small giant wheel had been set up. A long line of people – *sadhus*, men, women and children – waited patiently for their turn on the rides. The cruel cold seemed to have no effect on the effervescent mood of the crowd. It was an amusing sight to see the *jataadhaaris* [ascetics with dreadlocks], seated on the merry-go-round. The tent itself was full to bursting; *Sheila Ki Jawaani* [a Hindi film song], blasting from a CD player.

Huge, open vats of milk stood at a slow boil, the thick cream being skimmed off and served in plates, generously doused with sugar.

Indraneel hesitated but Tinku urged, "Try it, Sir!"

After a hot mouthful, he realised it was simply delicious. Between him and Tinku, they finished four plates. Indraneel felt replete. But for some *channa*, he hadn't eaten anything since the evening before.

A light rain fell, almost like a spray, making it even colder. A nasty wind had sprung up but the spirits of the people remained jubilant. Hanuman and mace-shaped balloons were being sold. Indraneel took numerous pictures. Tinku told him the queues for the 5 am *snaan* [bathing] started to form by 3 am; he would take him there. Indraneel nodded. He was happy to go with the flow.

By the time they reached the bathing area, the queue was already quite long. After 15 minutes, the barrier was opened and the crowd began walking towards the *sangam* [confluence of the Ganga, Yamuna and mythical Saraswati rivers]. As he walked, Indraneel could see pilgrims bathing –young, old, men, women, *sadhus*. Standing in the frigid water, they made water-offerings to Mother Ganga; others offered lamps and flowers, or milk and honey.

After an hour of walking, Indraneel reached the *sangam*. Dawn was just breaking. He could see the blue waters of the Yamuna mixing with the green waters of the Ganga. Instinctively, he kept repeating the *Mahamantra*. As the sun rose, the entire crowd shouted in unison, '*Surya Bhagawan ki jai* [Hail to the Sun God]!'

Indraneel felt gooseflesh on his arms. In that moment time stood still. He too, raised his hands in salutation. He noticed a number of poles on the bank and hung his backpack on one of them and then walked toward Gangaji. He bent to touch the flowing water with his right hand, seeking silent permission to enter, and then waded in.

Indraneel froze! Though he had been doing *Ganga snaan* regularly, the cold was unbearable. He remembered he had to visualize his sins leaving him but it took supreme control to focus on anything other than the biting cold piercing his body. But once he began, everything else receded. Though he didn't know a soul, he felt a deep sense of belonging. The collective *karma* of the millions present bound him to them. They all had a single motive...a dip in the *sangam*. Literally thousands of people walked shoulder to shoulder with him, but there was no jostling or shoving. It was a peaceful crowd with just one mission...*snaan*!

The Ganga *ghaats* were charged with a strange power. Thousands of people, bound together by an unseen thread, had unleashed a wave of positive energy which was truly exhilarating. Indraneel witnessed a floodtide of faith which spanned the entire Indian sub-continent. Old, young, rich, poor, crippled, handicapped, crawling – they all moved forward, drawn by the same powerful intent.

The sun was up now but Indraneel did not leave the freezing waters. He gazed around him at the spectacular mix of people. A beautiful young woman stood near him, offering water to Lord Surya. The nearly three-carat diamond ring she wore caught and reflected the sun's rays. Nearby, another woman in ragged clothes performed the same action with equal devotion. Indraneel felt deeply moved.

Children frolicked about, some afraid of the ice-cold waters. They pleaded with their elders to spare them the bath. But once in, they forgot their reluctance and splashed around.

When Indraneel finally turned to go back, the scene amazed him. Every inch of the *ghaats* was covered by pilgrims. One could see nothing but people. The air reverberated and echoed with chants of *Har Har Gange*! A million voices were raised in the same prayer. From somewhere there rose a shout of: *Har Har Mahadev*! It spread through the crowd like a wave. The collective consciousness of the crowd was caught in a charged web of faith. Indraneel felt the hair on the back of his neck stand on end. Faith! India! He felt hot tears flow down his cold, wind-kissed cheeks.

His backpack was still hanging on the pole where he had left it. As he changed, he saw some children driving a couple of dogs into the water. Another was pouring water on a calf that was running from the freezing water. Indraneel shooed the kids away, asking why they were torturing the animals.

"They too, need to go to heaven!" a six-year-old replied innocently. Indraneel felt humbled.

He longed for some hot tea or black coffee. But that was too much to long for! He watched a young man carry his ailing and aged mother towards the water. She could barely stand. He saw another man take Ganga water in his cupped palms to pour over someone too infirm to get into the water.

Indraneel heard people saying they should wait at *Shaahi Path*, where the great saints would walk, en route to their dip. He found a tent distributing tea, took a cup, and found a place for himself with a view of *Shaahi Path*. He sat down behind the barricade. A group of young girls were handing out pamphlets and serving hot coffee in small mud pots. As they came closer, one of them exclaimed loudly, "That's Indraneel Barua!" All the girls stopped what they were doing and stared at him. After some hesitation, they approached. Despite the fact that she could see he was already drinking tea, the tallest girl in the group held out a pot saying, "Care for some coffee?"

Their nonchalant sophistication, urban upbringing and convent educated English seemed at odds with the setting. Indraneel accepted the coffee with a smile and tossed aside the nearly empty plastic glass of tea. One of the girls, wearing disposable gloves, immediately picked it up and put it into the large waste disposal bag she was carrying.

The girls said they were from Bangalore and had come to spread the message of the green initiative by their Guru Sri Sriji. They told Indraneel they were big fans of his movies and asked for a picture. When he agreed, they happily took a group selfie with him in their midst.

Before they could indulge in any further chatter, the police shooed away everyone who was standing. The girls walked on with much waving. Police sniffer dogs came to check *Shaahi Path*.

"It's called *Shaahi* because all the *akhadas* go in a royal procession to bathe in the *sangam*," the elderly man sitting next to Indraneel explained. "The time and order of the *Shaahi Snaan* is predetermined. When the *akhadas* take their holy dip, the public is not allowed there." He introduced himself saying he was a Hindi Professor from Gorakhpur College.

"So you are a film-maker? *Lukkhey* was your film?" he asked.

Indraneel nodded but suggested quietly, "Let's not talk about that now." Instead, he asked what was going to happen.

The Professor was ready to educate him. "*Akhada* processions are called *peshwai* in Hindi, meaning 'presentation'. It is a great public attraction during the Kumbh. Monks from different *akhadas* are given time slots for the *Shaahi Snaan*. Accordingly, they gather in their camps. They have already set out."

Indraneel found the man very interesting. "Some of these saints, the absolute recluses, emerge from their remote places of meditation only during the Kumbh Mela. They go nowhere else, but they surely come for a dip at Kumbh. One glance from them and you are cleansed."

Indraneel felt lucky to have found a spot in the front row. They waited for the saints to appear while the police moved the crowds behind the barricades. Camera crews from news channels around the world sat on their wooden perches and waited with the same anticipation as the devotees.

Lo and behold, the saints appeared! An awed hush fell on the millions gathered. Everyone stopped what they were doing and gazed at the procession. First the Naga Babas of Juna Akhada appeared, not a stitch of clothing on their ash-smeared bodies. They strode along *Shaahi Path* like kings, chanting *Har Har Mahadev*! There were hundreds of them, carrying tridents. They had blackcat commando protection but walked looking straight ahead, exuding the raw power of their deep austerity. They all had long, matted hair. Some sat on horses...others beat drums. Some threw flowers and *gulaal* [colour].

Some *gulaal* fell on Indraneel as he reached forward to pick up a flower.

"That is a rare blessing!" the Professor commented, palms joined together.

Indraneel felt tears fill his eyes. It was mesmerizing. All the Naga Babas had their hands raised in blessing. What assurance! Indraneel knew he would carry this moment, in all its vividness, with him to his dying day.

The mounted police got off their horses to do *pranaam* to the Naga Babas. A helicopter flew low over the procession, scattering rose petals on the naked *sadhus*; the delicate pink petals sticking to their ash-smeared bodies briefly.

Thousands of other *sadhus* set out in decorated 'chariots', with the head of the camp, the *Mahamandaleshwarji*, sitting on a throne-like seat, wearing a garland. He had a *chattri* [ceremonial umbrella] held over him. Some were attended by disciples waiving hand fans. Other *sadhus* came riding horses and camels. With every decorated vehicle walked followers and devotees bearing yellow or orange flags, or insignia. They chanted *bhajans* [devotional songs] and *stotras* [hymns], and shouted *Jai*! every now and then. Several bands walked along, playing popular *bhajans*. One *Mandaleshwar* came riding an elephant with an elaborately decorated *howdah* [seat], flying a red satin flag. He stood on the elephant on one leg, his hand upraised in blessing.

The various processions represented the different *akhadas*. At the head of each *akhada* was a *dharma dhvaja* – the flag of their sect. Then came the chariot carrying the metal image of their deity or Adi-Guru, with two Naga Sadhus on horses, playing drums. This was followed by the decorated chariots of the various sects and sub-sects of the *ashrams* and *mathas* [monasteries] affiliated to the *akhadas*.

Many *sadhus* carried staffs tied with ochre cloth, others had tridents. Some *Mahamandaleshwars* were quite young. Women *Mahamandaleshwars* could also be seen and there was one group of Westerners, with a foreign *Mahamandaleshwar*.

'That is surely the most Indian a foreigner can get,' thought Indraneel in amused admiration.

The procession finally ended. As he prepared to leave, Indraneel saw some women devotees quietly slipping through the barricades to collect sand from the road on which the *sadhus* had walked. Holy dust. For Indraneel it seemed to sum up the spirit of the Kumbh – the deep sense of devotion and its sanctity. It had been truly humbling to experience the religious fervour and solemnity that pervaded the place. The Kumbh was effectively the spiritual and cultural integration of India. The gaudy and garish blended seamlessly with the pristine and sublime. It was an unforgettable experience.

A lady was heard telling a group of women, "I asked every member of my family to come, but no, they refused. It seems our sins cling to us so strongly that they play a key role in preventing us from going to a Kumbh *snaan*."

As Indraneel walked away from Kumbh Nagari, he heard someone else say, "It's not just sins, it's their *sanchit karma* [performed *karma*]."

Indraneel's mobile rang. It was Ram Singh. "Sir, they will be opening the exits now. Come to Prayag Hotel. I will be parked there. We can leave for the airport from there."

Indraneel thanked Ram Singh. He had forgotten he had a flight to catch back to Delhi and then to Dehradun. He had stumbled upon an infinity of faith. It was going to be hard to stumble back into a life of limitations.

55

The cold velvety darkness coiled itself firmly around Rishikesh. It was past 11 pm. Indraneel sat gazing at Gangaji. Where had the time gone, he wondered? In fact, he could hear Gangaji more clearly than see her at this point.

The phone in his pocket vibrated again. He thought of ignoring it but it occurred to him that it could his mother. Before he could take the phone from his pocket, the caller hung up. It was Shaman. A text arrived within a minute: 'Alive or dead? Or lost in *mela*, Hindi film style?"

Indraneel smiled and called back. Shaman picked up immediately.

"Where have you been holed up for the last 15 days? Or should I ask with whom have you been holed up?" Shaman cackled. "Indraneelbhai, you've been incognito!"

The *bhai* felt warm and affectionate. Shaman's concern was evident. Indraneel apologised for not staying in touch. He told Shaman he had been so overwhelmed by the Kumbh experience; that it had taken days just to process it all. He knew Shaman understood completely.

"Can I come and see you now if you're free," Indraneel asked, knowing Shaman had *japa* targets to meet; he didn't want to impose.

"I'm at the shop," Shaman responded.

Indraneel laughed. "So who are you holed up with this late?"

"I had an inventory of old books to cross-verify and put away – a consignment from Delhi. Come to the store."

Indraneel went back to his room to put on a warm jacket and then sped on his bike across Ram Jhoola to Shaman's shop. He thought once again that the closest one came to an absolute feeling of freedom was on a fast bike. He arrived at Shaman's shop within minutes though those minutes were enough to freeze him to the bone. His teeth chattered.

Bells jingled as Shaman opened the door. The rich aroma of freshly made coffee welcomed Indraneel.

"I figured you would need to thaw before you could talk," Shaman commented, holding out a steaming cup.

Indraneel took a sip and closed his eyes in bliss though his tongue felt scalded. Shaman was busy putting away the books after keying the titles into his computer.

Indraneel described the Kumbh Mela experience enthusiastically but concluded with the question which had been niggling at him. "Shaman, as I was leaving the Mela, I overheard a conversation which refuses to leave my mind."

Shaman poured himself some coffee. "What was it about?"

"There was a woman who said, *karma* prevents people from going to have a dip at the Kumbh Mela. What is *karma* and why should it stop people from taking a dip? I didn't get that...I thought I'd ask you. If someone wants to go to the Kumbh Mela, he can go. Isn't that how it is? It may seem a clichéd question, but I'm still confused about the concept of destiny and free will. Are we free at all? Where does everything come from? Is there someone sitting up there calling the shots? Why does some shit hit us that we can't figure out?"

"First of all, there's no one up there calling the shots," Shaman said, taking a sip of his coffee. "The one calling the shots is in here, inside you and me. *We* are calling the shots."

"Sure." Indraneel made as if to fire a gun. "Yes, we're calling the shots," he laughed.

Shaman gave him an amused look. "And it's not a clichéd question. It's a very important one. Free will and things being predestined is actually a matter of *karma*. If you understand the concept of *karma*, more than half the puzzles of human life are immediately sorted."

"It's *that* important?" Indraneel raised his brows.

"Yes, *karma* is the acme of wisdom in Hinduism. It's the greatest *gyan*. You can make no sense of anything without the *karma* theory."

"Yeah, everyone talks of *karma*. But I have to ask you Shaman, what's *karma*? I mean we all know what goes around comes around. But how does it really work?" Indraneel glanced at the titles of the books lying on the table.

"Listen Indraneel, I want all your attention. Try to understand this like you would a principle of science or engineering." Shaman stopped doing the inventory and turned.

"I'm all ears..."

"Most Masters agree that we can control most of our lives," Shaman began, sounding like a Master himself.

"What can we control in our lives?" asked Indraneel sceptically.

"I'm coming to that. *Karma* is of three kinds – *accumulated karma*, *fructifying karma* and *current karma*. *Accumulated karma* is quite simply everything you have already done thus far."

"Done things! That's a good term."

Shaman stopped and listened to the sound of footsteps and a stick on the main road. Who could be out this late, he wondered.

"How old are you, Indraneel?" he asked.

"Thirty-nine."

"What you are, as of this moment, does it contain what you've been over 39 years?"

"In a way, yes."

"Not in a way," Shaman corrected. "That's *exactly* how it is! We are full of our past. We may not know it, but all our past is sitting in us."

"But I thought things passed." Indraneel observed, not too happy with the thought of a past which never went away.

"No, they don't. They change, they transform, but they don't pass."

"And where is my past or *accumulated karma*, Shaman? Where are the done things of all these years? Where are they sitting? I can't see them."

Shaman chuckled. "They are stored as *vasanas* or impressions. You see, events happen and then they are gone, but they leave memories and impressions in their trail – that's the storage format. The past is stored as impressions. What happened to your feelings of yesterday?"

"Well, they are gone," Indraneel was prompt to respond.

"You are mistaken. They are stored. Everything is stored. Like on a hard drive; tonnes and tonnes of data. Don't think that because you're 39 years old, the hard disc is full. You could be carrying 3900 years."

"3900 years...what the hell?"

"Actually, hell may be a pertinent word here. The fact is this isn't your first life. You have lived many times. This particular incarnation of yours is 39 years long so far. Add all the years of your yester lives and you will know what you're about."

"Am I a prehistoric creature then?" Indraneel asked, appalled.

"Yes, you are. It's just that life is renewed. The body changes. The *yoni* [form] is altered. Life remains the same," Shaman said as if repeating a nursery rhyme.

"That means humongous *karma* is attached to every one of us," Indraneel murmured. "What a thought!"

"Yes, *accumulated karma* is humongous. It's a huge bag."

"Does it have a say now or in the future?"

"It's an action-reaction thing. What's done must have a payback. If a simple hangover shows, past lives must show too. Life's greater than four pegs of Scotch, right?"

"Any sober man would agree... so that's how you mean destiny is self-made?" Indraneel observed.

"Bingo!"

Shaman picked up Stephen Knapp's book, *Reincarnation and Karma* from the pile he was classifying. Indraneel had noticed the title too. What a coincidence! Both men smiled in silent acknowledgement.

Indraneel finally broke the silence. "Okay, I get *accumulated karma*. It's a storage thing. A hard drive. Done deeds. The hangover of many lives."

Shaman nodded in affirmation. "Right! Let's move to the second one – *current karma* – that which is in action now. *Current karma* is what you're doing presently...talking about *karma* theory in a bookshop called Eldorado. If *accumulated karma* is the past, *current karma* is the present." Shaman put one book in front of another to indicate the order.

"Good. We're moving from the past to the present, from done deeds to doing deeds," Indraneel commented, trying to keep pace with Shaman's narration.

"Yes. We're always doing that anyway, moving from past to present..." Shaman cleared his throat. "The done thing is gone, but this, the *current*, what we're doing right now, is totally in our control. We're doing it now."

"Understood. Which is the third – *future karma*?"

"Not future...*fructifying karma*," Shaman corrected. "There are certain givens in this life. You were born to certain parents, have a certain body, etc. That is *fructifying karma.*"

"You mean it is something that has surfaced from the bag of *accumulated karma*?" Indraneel asked.

"Yes, but only a part. Call it a present instalment from *accumulated karma*, which has begun to bear fruit. It cannot be avoided or changed, only exhausted by being experienced. So, at every moment, we have some part that's determined and some part that's free."

"Let me get the math right." Indraneel picked up a paper and wrote out in large letters:

Future = Destiny coming from *Accumulated* (Determined) + *Current* (Free) *Karmas*.

"So it's destiny plus free will?"

"That's right," confirmed Shaman. He had nearly reached the end of his new books inventory.

"I had no idea life had such mathematical continuity. And all of it bound by a seamless principle!" Indraneel felt rather bemused.

"That's the law of *karma*." Shaman was happy Indraneel had asked about this following his experiences at the Kumbh Mela. He was glad to share what he knew.

It was past midnight. Shaman had finished sorting his books. Indraneel could see he was tired. But Shaman merely laughed, saying the night was young.

"There are a few other, finer points about *karma* theory..."

"I'd love to hear them, but let's save them for another time. Let me digest what you've said today." Indraneel rose to leave.

"Fine, some other time," Shaman murmured, rubbing his eyes. He shut down the computer.

56

The doorbell rang at its usual volume but to Indraneel, doing *japa*, it sounded very loud, shattering the silence of the night. He sighed, rose from his *asana* and opened the door. Vasundhara stood there smiling. His heart did a strange little flip-flop as she hugged him spontaneously.

"So Indraneel, aren't you going to invite me in?" She grinned seeing him frozen in surprise.

Indraneel composed himself and held open the door, shutting it again quickly against the blast of the chill air. He noted Vasundhara was casually dressed in blue jeans and a thick baby-pink sweater, nevertheless she exuded an air of stylish chic. Feeling somewhat bemused by her sudden presence in his room, he didn't hear most of what she was saying, catching only the words, Kumbh Mela...she wanted to know about his trip.

Vasundhara gazed at the series of pictures he had taken in Allahabad, which now formed his screen saver. "How exquisite!" she exclaimed, rubbing her cold hands together. "So grand, magnificent, intriguing!" The images dissolved seamlessly one into the next.

She pushed back her hair, gently picked up the laptop and came to sit beside Indraneel on the bed. "I know they say a picture is worth a thousand words but this time pictures alone won't do. Tell me the story behind each one," she demanded with childlike enthusiasm.

Indraneel felt rather unnerved by her proximity but gathering his thoughts, he spoke about his trip. The passion with which he described the Kumbh Mela enraptured Vasundhara. She was no longer looking at the laptop screen. Indraneel drew her attention to a picture of a *mahant* entering the Ganga, seated on his elephant; he zoomed in for greater detail.

Vasundhara looked at Indraneel's hand on the mouse and said abruptly, "I have always thought you had beautiful fingers. Long and well formed, almost delicate like an artist's." She paused, wondering about the appropriateness of her confession, before explaining, "You know, I used to watch you doing ordinary things like stirring sugar in your black coffee, lighting a cigarette..."

There was a moment of awkward silence. Indraneel's gaze fell to his own fingers. Suddenly, his phone rang. It was Shaman.

"Yes, I'm ready," he said and hung up. "That was Shaman. I need to take your leave now, Vasundhara. I've got to go."

"Where are you going in the middle of the night? I didn't think there was any night life in Rishikesh!"

"No, nothing of that sort. There is a task to be accomplished. We're going to distribute blankets to the homeless."

"Now?"

"Yes. That's the plan."

"Terrific! Would you mind if I joined you?" she asked as eagerly as if it was a trip to the mall.

"I don't think it's a good idea for you to come. It's late and it will be very cold. We'll be in an auto-rickshaw."

"No, no...I would love to come. I must! Are you afraid of me?" Vasundhara asked laughing.

Indraneel gave up. "Fine. If you're okay with the cold. Just give me a minute." He quickly put on his Mountain Hardwear Chillwave jacket and shoes and turned back to Vasundhara.

"Let's go," she said, pulling on her own cap.

Indraneel locked the door. "I had no idea you were so keen on the homeless. I'm glad you're coming."

"I'm glad too," she said happily.

"You will be useful, I must confess. We need more hands to carry the blankets."

Vasundhara looked straight into Indraneel's eyes. "I must confess the opportunity to spend some time with you is my chief motivation."

He laughed boyishly, enjoying her attention.

"I leave tomorrow," she added.

This additional piece of information suddenly felt important to Indraneel. Just then they heard Shaman hooting his car horn.

57

"What a lovely surprise! It's good to see you!" Shaman exclaimed when he saw Vasundhara with Indraneel.

"Hi!" Vasundhara greeted him, her palms joined in a *namaste*.

"Indraneel, did you manufacture her from thin air?" Shaman asked, laughing.

"I'm in Rishikesh for just a couple of days," Vasundhara explained.

Indraneel opened the car door for her and then got in beside Shaman in the front.

"Shaman, I hope you don't mind me piling on...I just thought it would be a good experience for me," Vasundhara said from the back seat.

"Not at all. You're welcome."

"I'm really excited. This is a novel thing for me. Whose idea was it?"

As Shaman drove towards the *ashram*, Indraneel replied, "I don't know how the idea originated. Not distributing blankets, but the manner in which they should be distributed. Perhaps it came as a flash of genius into Shaman's head."

Shaman turned to look at him. "Indeed!"

"You know it was your inspiration," Indraneel insisted. "As soon as the idea was mooted, friends from Chennai, Mumbai and Hyderabad contributed money for 100 blankets. Thick blankets were bought, but not the double-sized ones, because they are unwieldy and most of the homeless we choose for distribution are wandering fakirs, minstrels, dervishes and beggars, who carry the blankets around with them. They had to be easy to carry."

"Good thinking," Vasundhara approved.

"The new age heads of charities and NGOs are from IITs and IIMs," Shaman told her, parking the car at the *ashram* gate. "And, of course, we also have this gentleman from MIT, to help distribute blankets on the streets of Rishikesh," he added, pointing to Indraneel.

It was Indraneel's turn to say, "Indeed!"

They transferred 30 blankets and a torch from Shaman's car into an auto-rickshaw, driven by Bhuwan, who had agreed to go on this expedition at 10 pm. It was a bitterly cold night. Rishikesh is a small town and most people retire by 9 pm. By 10 pm the streets are deserted and the silence almost uncanny. Some *yaatris* [pilgrims] were returning to their guest houses; eatery owners were bringing down the shutters; here and there street urchins warmed themselves at small fires. Occasionally one could see someone by the roadside, huddled in a blanket or sheet.

The lane behind the ISKCON temple was their first port of call. The *ghaat* there, constructed during the previous Haridwar Kumbh, was where Shaman thought they would find worthy recipients.

After nearly two hours of distributing blankets, they sat down at a small tea shop and waited for the hot brew to be served. *Tip tip barsaa paani,* from the soundtrack of the film *Mohra*, played softly in the background.

"I have always loved the rain but I can't imagine enjoying getting wet in this insane cold," Indraneel remarked as he zipped up his jacket all the way to his throat.

"Now that depends entirely on who you are with!" Shaman laughed.

Vasundhara smiled at Shaman's words but Indraneel just shook his head, saying firmly, "No way!"

The steaming tea arrived. The three of them drank in silence, curling their frozen fingers around the glasses.

"Thanks for letting me join you tonight," Vasundhara said, her words heartfelt.

"The fact that you came seems to have been a satisfying experience for our friend here," Shaman chuckled, taking another sip of his tea.

"Yeah, I'm happy to be on this mission," said Indraneel, skirting Shaman's comment.

But Vasundhara would not let it go. "Indraneel, Shaman is not saying you're happy to be on this mission, he is saying it was a satisfying experience for you because I was with you."

Indraneel said nothing. He paid for the tea and they stepped out of the tea stall. Shaman grinned.

Vasundhara caught up with Indraneel's quick strides. "Is it true? Is my company satisfying to you?"

Indraneel felt embarrassed. He said nothing, just shrugged his shoulders.

Shaman, right behind them, commented gleefully, "I guess the lady deserves an answer, my friend."

"I'm happy to be with both of you," Indraneel answered evasively, refusing to be drawn in.

Shaman laughed loudly. He was enjoying this cat and mouse game with his friend.

Vasundhara threw Indraneel a teasing look. "I don't know about you, but it was a very satisfying experience for me to be with *you*."

"That's honesty. I love it!" Shaman was emphatic.

Indraneel was happy about Vasundhara's presence. They made good team mates, according to Shaman. They slowly made their way back to the car, the icy wind in their faces hampering their progress.

Vasundhara asked contemplatively, "Shaman, sometimes I wonder...is it not enough to serve people? Isn't service to humanity the same as service to God? I mean, acts like giving away blankets or food... isn't that service to God?"

Shaman listened to her question while pulling at a piece of paper that had got stuck to his shoe. "Yes, service to humanity is enough as long as we recognize human beings as God. If you do not understand this principle in its entirety, then it is ego operating in your charity and service. If you are sitting on a higher pedestal and throwing alms to a beggar, where is God in that? There is nothing divine there. On the other hand, if you envision God in every being, your heart automatically fills with the desire to serve. You don't need lofty ideals of philanthropy. Service happens because God is in those you serve. This was achieved by Swami Vivekananda. He coined a beautiful term: *daridra Narayana seva*, service unto the poor and lowly. That's humanity and God rolled into one."

Vasundhara nodded, happy with the answer. Indraneel, who had been listening intently as well, felt enlightened.

A howling, bone-chilling wind was blowing at Ram Jhoola; it made conversation impossible. The bridge swayed slightly. The lights on the hills looked exotic in the darkness. They crossed the bridge and a little ahead, on the *ghaat* opposite Gita Bhawan, Indraneel found a young *sadhu*, sitting on the steps.

"*Hari Aum* Babaji," Indraneel greeted him.

"*Hari Aum*," was the response.

"Would you like a blanket?"

"No! Cold is good!"

The *sadhu*'s eyes were powerful and penetrating. While everyone around was asleep, this young hermit was busy reading the *Kena Upanishad* [a Vedic text]. There were other books in his bag as well as a notebook in which he had been taking notes. He was from Orissa and spoke perfect English.

"A future head of an Order," Shaman whispered. "Such souls become Shankaracharyas one day."

They had learnt much from their night mission and drove around for another hour to see if they had missed anyone. But they did not find anyone else in need of a blanket. At several places they found people sleeping under the blankets they had just received.

"Hopefully, there's no one in Rishikesh sleeping without a blanket tonight," remarked Indraneel.

"That is a comforting thought," Vasundhara said seriously. She was to leave for Mumbai the following day, taking the 12.30 flight from Jolly Grant Airport, Dehradun.

"I would have dropped you to the airport but I have to meet Nitya Shanti Maharaj at 11.30," Shaman told her.

"No problem. I'll drop you," Indraneel offered.

Shaman hid a smile. "Great! I was hoping you would."

"I wish I could have stayed another day to meet this *mahatma*," Vasundhara sighed.

"You don't have to stay back just to see him," Indraneel told her. "You can always meet him the next time you come. You must get home to Bombay."

"Oh, so I belong to Bombay? What about you, Indraneel Barua, Bollywood film-maker? Don't you belong to Bombay too?"

"I don't know...I don't know..." Indraneel murmured. "I don't know if I ever want to step out of Rishikesh again."

"You'd better, Indraneel!" she warned. "Another day won't kill me. I want to stay back because life is short."

Indraneel nodded. "Yes, life is short. I agree with you on that."

58

Indraneel prepared to kick-start his bike; he was to drop Vasundhara at the airport and he was running late. The phone in his pocket rang. He muttered to himself as he reached for it. It was Vasundhara. Sure that she was annoyed at his lateness, he quickly silenced the phone and rode off quickly towards Chandrani Guest House to pick her up.

The powerful Harley Davidson quickly ate up the short distance. The sleepy man at Reception informed him that Vasundharaji was in room 102. Indraneel swiftly ran up the stairs and pressed the bell.

Vasundhara opened the door, asking without preamble, "Why didn't you pick up my call?"

"I was riding the bike," Indraneel answered. He added sheepishly, "Actually, since I was late, I thought you would be annoyed..."

Vasundhara bit back a smile.

Indraneel looked around. "Are you packed?"

"I have one backpack, but that's not the point. My flight to Bombay has been cancelled," Vasundhara said with resignation. "The fog in Delhi has played havoc with the flight schedule and 45 flights have been delayed or cancelled. That's why I called, to tell you not to come."

"The fog can be really bad in Delhi this time of year." Indraneel made himself comfortable on one of the two chairs in the room. "So now what? You wanted to see the *mahatma*? Shall we go?"

Vasundhara occupied the other chair. "I've already called Shaman but he said Swamiji is not feeling well." Her face suddenly brightened. "Indraneel, remember you promised to let me ride your bike on Chilla Forest Road? Can we go today?" She paused and added hesitantly, "That's if you are free."

Indraneel thought for a moment; he had nothing planned. "Did I say I would take you to Chilla or that I would let you ride the bike?"

Vasundhara's green eyes twinkled mischievously, suddenly reminding Indraneel of the little girl he had known. "You said I could ride your bike. In fact, you promised."

He looked at her grey jeans and thin black sweater. "You need to wear something warmer. Muffler, cap, jacket, gloves...it will be cold on the bike. Plus the forest is always colder."

"Okay, gimme a minute." Vasundhara quickly rummaged through her backpack and fished out her cap and gloves.

Relaxed, Indraneel watched. There was something fascinating about women getting dressed, he thought.

Vasundhara pulled on a heavy beige jacket and then turned and looked at him. "Happy now?" she asked, pulling the zip up to her throat.

Indraneel nodded. Vasundhara locked the room and they went down together. It was a bright, crystal clear day, but intensely cold. The sun did not warm, it merely illuminated.

Indraneel looked at his bike. "Vaz...I mean Vasundhara, are you sure you want to ride the bike?" Vasundhara looked fragile next to the big, mean machine.

But she merely took the keys from his hand, got on, and started the bike with consummate ease. Astride the roaring bike she yelled, "Hop on!"

Indraneel got on behind her and the bike glided off smoothly. He was astonished at the ease with which she handled the big beast.

"Tell me the way to Chilla," Vasundhara addressed him in the mirror.

"Take the first left," Indraneel directed, adding, "You drive well. In fact, really well. Where did you learn?"

"Just enjoy the ride for now," Vasundhara laughed.

They were soon on the empty stretch past the barrage, along the Ganga canal. The wind tore into them even though they were not travelling at high speed.

Vasundhara's hair blew into Indraneel's face. Noticing it, she slowed the bike to a halt and tucked her hair into her jacket. "Better?" she asked.

"I didn't say anything," Indraneel remarked.

She smiled. "I could see my hair blowing all over the place. I should have worn a helmet."

After 20 minutes Vasundhara stopped the bike on a grassy knoll and handed the keys to Indraneel.

"Thank you so much. It felt like flying, or the closest thing to riding the wind." She closed her eyes in pleasure. Her cheeks were pink from the cold and she looked happy.

Indraneel realized there was a lot more grit and strength in her than was evident on the surface.

"Where did you learn to ride a big bike like this?" he asked again.

"Arunodaya's bike," Vasundhara replied matter-of-factly. "Shall we go for a walk?" she asked, pointing towards the trees.

Indraneel hesitated. "We could encounter some wildlife."

"Isn't that the whole point of coming to Chilla?"

Indraneel pushed the bike behind a tree and they set out, walking in a companionable web of soft silence. The deeper they walked into the forest, the darker it got. Though it was only mid-day, the dense canopy of trees didn't allow sunlight to filter in. There was an unusual silence in the jungle. They spotted many peacocks. As they walked further in, they saw herds of deer. Vasundhara was fascinated. She stood absolutely still, watching the grazing deer a few feet away. The lush and thick undergrowth barely made a sound as they walked.

Suddenly, she felt strong fingers clamp over her mouth. She was steered into the hollow of a gigantic tree. Instinctively, she began to struggle.

Indraneel whispered, "Shhhhh..." into her ear. With his free hand he pointed at something.

His warm breath on her ear caused shivers to run down her body but she instantly relaxed against him, following his pointing finger. A magnificent leopard was slowly striding through the dry riverbed, just a few feet from them. Her fur glistened in the afternoon sunshine. Three cubs, the size of medium-sized domestic cats, followed her.

Indraneel was acutely aware of Vasundhara's proximity. He could feel her soft mouth against his fingers and quietly removed his hand. He could feel the softness of her body pressed against him within the cramped space afforded by the hollow of the tree. The subtle fragrance of her perfume enveloped him. He felt a sharp pang of awareness and wanted to get out. But it was impossible; he had to wait for the leopard to pass.

To Indraneel the leopard seemed to be walking in slow motion, stopping once in a while to play with her frolicking cubs. Vasundhara too, was aware of the tension in Indraneel and turned to look at him. He was watching her, not the leopard.

A little later, Indraneel gestured they could step out. They emerged from the hollow but now there was an awkwardness between them, an odd tension that had replaced the earlier sense of easy comfort. They walked back in strained silence, discussing neither the leopard nor their attraction to each other.

Indraneel dropped Vasundhara at Chandrani Guest House and went back to his own room.

59

The days rolled into weeks and the weeks into months. Winter withdrew reluctantly. Then the last buds of spring gave way to harsh summer. Looking out one day, Indraneel found a dark, overcast sky. He picked up his umbrella, realizing for the first time that over the last two months he had lost cognizance of the weather. It was early morning and he wanted to walk to clear his head before returning to his room.

Indraneel's entire stay in Rishikesh now had a surreal quality, due to the sheer quantum of change it had wrought in him. He wanted to somehow put it all down on paper. He was brimming with experiences to which he wanted to give expression, capturing them forever. The urge to write was all consuming; it was as if he was being commanded to write by a force within.

He began to write, initially putting down his thoughts on paper, with an autobiographical slant. The writing became a spontaneous overflow that demanded expression. He wrote for long hours every day, sitting at his laptop, keying in. Being a film-maker, his writing had the inherent potential of a script. Once he realised this, he began working on it with the intention of making it into a film.

He constantly referred to the numerous photographs he had taken, right from his first day in Rishikesh. They transported him to particular moments and evoked emotions connected to them. He was astonished by the number of pictures he had taken of the Ganga in all weather conditions, in early dawn, mist-clad or sparkling in bright sunshine, to the low exposure pictures at midnight. He strove to find words to capture his silent communion with the Ganga.

The images from the Kumbh Mela made his heart ache with joy. The incandescent impressions of faith and collective *karma* were branded forever on his mind, heart and soul.

His mind was constantly occupied with the script. He mentally searched for a title, but nothing seemed to encapsulate the narrative. He decided on a working title: *Incandescence*.

The hot dry summer went on but Indraneel was unaware of it; the drive to write remained paramount. Before he knew it, he was sitting at a tea stall in Lakshman Jhoola watching the rain come down in torrents.

60

When Indraneel first saw the grainy images of the houses crumbling away like toy structures, he was struck not by the violence of the river but by how unreal it looked on TV. In fact, he wondered for a second if he himself could have shot it better. Then it hit him that this was a national disaster. He was sipping tea at a wayside *dhaba* [eatery] in Lakshman Jhoola, watching the footage on the small TV set. The heavy rain pummelled the tin roof of the *dhaba* with relentless ferocity. It was so loud that Indraneel looked out to see if it was hail. No, it was rain. He could barely hear what the news anchor was saying; it was frustrating. He struggled to read the scrolling in Hindi but it moved too fast. The TV sat perched high up near the ceiling. There were many people gazing up at it, watching in mute horror.

Indraneel finished his tea, picked up his umbrella and walked out with the intention of buying a newspaper. Everything was shut. He returned to his room, hoping the Internet would work. By some miracle it did. He quickly browsed the *Times of India* and *HT* sites and was horrified by what he read. How could this have happened? He looked out of the window. The rain fell with unabated vigour. The dark, low hanging clouds spewed raindrops like bullets.

Indraneel felt a deep sense of anger at himself. Here he had been smoking a cigarette in a warm room when half the population of Uttarakhand was being simply washed away! He had to help. He had to do something. He didn't know what or how but he had to get into action. It was as if the coiled energy within him was spinning faster and faster in ever-widening circles, urging him to do something.

Indraneel called Shaman...he didn't pick up. He lit another cigarette as he stared out of the window. He saw a whole grove of trees washed away like toothpicks in the turbulent waters of the Ganga. When he put the cigarette to his lips again, it was just a burnt out stub. He went closer for a better look and froze with horror when he saw a bus and several cars carried away like toys in the swirling waters. The river looked bloodied with red mud. His mind refused to register the scope of what he was seeing. They were just images. Little did he know that they would remain etched in his mind till his last breath.

He called Shaman again...he did not pick up. Bloody stoic! Indraneel called him a few more unkind names. The sound of the rain was driving him crazy. He felt so restless that he could not bear to sit down. The hammering of the relentless rain was finally broken by the shrill ringing of his cell phone. Asheem, a photographer friend, was calling from Bombay.

He said a friend of his, Cathy, was part of the CNN crew who were driving up from Delhi to cover the floods. He wanted Indraneel to help them out. Cathy was heading the crew; she was from London. Asheem had already told her that Indraneel was a film-maker, now in Rishikesh. Indraneel immediately agreed.

The crew had left Delhi late the previous night, when the story broke. There was no saying when they would get to Rishikesh. Indraneel told Asheem to give Cathy his number.

As he hung up, there was a call from Shaman. Indraneel told him urgently that all of Uttarakhand was under the threat of flood; that thousands had died. Shaman was nonplussed and said it was the will of God. Indraneel urged him to look out of the window...at Gangaji.

"I am on Ganga *ghaat*, dear boy!" the stoic announced.

"In this rain?" Indraneel was astonished.

"One's prayers must go on. Even if she is furious on a given day, she does not cease to be the Mother..."

Indraneel was not in the mood for prayer or philosophy. They seemed worthless on such occasions.

"I feel impotent at not being able to do anything." He almost yelled into the phone in order to be heard.

"Don't think too much about wanting to help, *bhai*. You can pretend to help, and full marks to you for that, but the main thing is to feel impotent. It's a great feeling! It means you *are* impotent. God will do everything, not you," Shaman laughed.

Indraneel was angered by Shaman's jeering laughter. Just then he received a call from Cathy. She wanted to buy dry biscuits, bottled water, medicines, bug spray, and a solar lamp if possible.

"We could meet at Madras Café and then pick up the supplies," Indraneel suggested, and gave her directions. "Is there room for one more in your truck? Could I come along?" he asked on impulse.

She considered a moment and then said quickly, "Yes, yes, you can come."

Cathy was a small, wiry girl, barely five feet tall, with a mop of blond curls tied into a ponytail. She wore sturdy hiking boots. She was an avid mountain climber and talked incessantly. Full of energy and verve, she loved going to new places and worked long hours. 'The kind of character we see in movies,' Indraneel thought. 'Only I too, appear to be in this particular horror movie!'

61

They bought supplies and headed towards Kedarnath, the epicentre of the tragedy that was being called the 'Himalayan tsunami'. There was slush everywhere. An unbelievable volume of rain fell as they slowly made their way up the hills towards Dev Prayag. The roads had turned into torrents as rainwater rushed down them.

"Smoke?" Cathy's voice broke into Indraneel's reverie.

He automatically reached for the offered cigarette, taking a deep drag while continuing to stare out unseeingly.

Suddenly the truck stopped. There was a huge landslide ahead. The driver said they would not be able to drive any further, so they got out. In 14 hours they had barely covered 100 kms and now seemed to be stranded in the middle of nowhere. It was 2 am. There was no rain thankfully!

Indraneel's body felt cramped but he had managed to sleep on the truck despite the bumpy ride. In the light of the truck's headlights they could see and hear the angry roar of the Ganga below. Indraneel sat down on what looked like a rock only to leap up with a yell. It was the bloated, half-submerged corpse of a cow.

Cathy came running, as did the truck driver. They surveyed their surroundings more closely. The carcasses of cattle were strewn here and there. As they went further up, they saw human bodies as well. Nothing had prepared them for the horror. Indraneel retched helplessly by the side of the road.

As they walked on through knee-deep slush, they saw scores of bodies, smothered in the mud, life snuffed out. Indraneel was beyond shock. 'They are dead and I am alive,' he muttered, shivering in the cold. Cathy poured him a cup of tea from the thermos she was carrying. He took a sip but his stomach revolted. He ran into the bushes, nearly slipping in the mud, and vomited again. Cathy waited patiently behind him and handed him a cup of water. Indraneel rinsed his mouth. Feeling exhausted, he sat down, making sure it was a rock this time. Suddenly it began to pour down again. Cathy had on her jacket but Indraneel just sat in the rain, getting soaked to the skin, waiting for day to break.

As the darkness gave way to the dull grey light of dawn, Indraneel found himself wishing the dark cloak of night would continue to hide the wretchedness around them. But as it got brighter, the stark reality of death and destruction everywhere became overpowering. There were bloated bodies all around – women, children, men, dogs, cattle, mules. The squelchy mud made movement almost impossible. One had to first pull one's leg out of knee-high sludge before stepping forward again into the gum-like mud.

Cathy and Indraneel decided to try and extract the bodies from the mud and place them on the rocky overhang ahead. But it was easier said than done. The truck driver refused to touch the bodies, so it was just Cathy and Indraneel, with the cameraman filming them avidly.

The body closest to them was that of a middle-aged man. Cathy held the legs and Indraneel the torso, and they heaved with all their might. Nothing. The body was so bloated and heavy that they could not move it at all. Cathy asked Harpreet, their cameraman, to stow away his camera in the truck and lend them a hand. He was a well-built Sardarji. The rippling muscles on his forearms became evident when he rolled up the sleeves of his soggy shirt. Together, they heaved the body out of the slush. By the time they made it to the rocky overhang, it was nearly an hour later. They were physically and mentally exhausted.

Cathy was emotionally the toughest of them. "Don't look at the faces," she commanded like an army officer. "Just focus on the job. Don't think."

She was right. Looking at the faces was terrifying. One inevitably wondered about those last frightful moments before death finally crushed them. Some of the eyes were still open, filled with grey mud. Cathy closed them, making the sign of the cross over each one. In the face of tragedy all faiths merged into one.

The rain kept pounding down. The grey mist became more and more dense. They had been working continuously for six hours but had managed to move only 14 bodies. They felt mentally numb though their limbs ached from the back-breaking work.

"Guys, take a break!" Cathy called at noon, wiping the face of her waterproof watch.

Indraneel tried his phone but the battery was dead. They walked to the truck, which was relatively dry, and sat in silence. Cathy offered biscuits and Indraneel took three. He was ravenously hungry, but as he bit into one, it turned to mud in his mouth. He chewed on it deliberately, forcing it down with a few sips of water. Harpreet refused. He sat with his eyes closed and hands clasped between his knees

Cathy consumed a whole packet of glucose biscuits, slowly chewing her way through them. She shook her hair out to dry, saying, "Guys, I know it's difficult but we have to eat to keep up our strength."

The enormity of the human tragedy had hit each of them. Cathy told them of her experiences doing relief work during hurricane Sandy. But Indraneel and Harpreet had never been involved in disaster relief and they didn't know what to do. It was a job for trained professionals like Cathy, or the Army.

By the time they had moved all the bodies from the mud – a total of 29 – they felt ready to be buried themselves. Tired, hungry and soaked to the skin, even their ability to think seemed to have become frozen. The rain was relentless, never letting up in intensity or intent. As they hauled the last of the bodies, daylight faded rapidly. Now only the bloated carcasses of cattle remained.

From their anklets and remnants of their tie-and-dye clothing, they assumed the people who had died were not locals but a group from Rajasthan. The *tulasi malas* around their necks said they had come to meet God, not death.

Cathy, Indraneel, Harpreet, and Pradeep – the driver who had sat watching them all day – spent the night in the truck, sheltering as best they could from the rain. At 3 am, Indraneel turned over, trying to ease his aching body. He saw a movement but could not make out what it was. He leaned across the sleeping driver and turned on the truck lights. A panther! It was dragging the body of a child into the thickets. Human... corpse... prey! Indraneel leapt from the truck, yelling like a mad man.

The others awoke abruptly. Harpreet grabbed a crowbar from the toolbox and came running. But the panther had vanished. They decided to keep watch over the bodies; they were not safe from wild animals. Rajaji National Park was no longer a place of amusement. Cathy and the men sat beside the bodies in the steady rain, the Ganga roaring below them. How quickly they had become used to the sight of the dead.

"The dehumanisation process is very rapid," Cathy said to them, thinking back to her own first encounters with those who had managed to survive inhuman conditions.

Indraneel craved a cigarette but it was next to impossible in the driving rain. Cathy and Harpreet sat exchanging stories about their growing years – his in Ludhiana, and her's in London. Indraneel felt strangely disconnected from everything. He even stopped trying to wipe the water from his eyes. It was easier to keep them closed. After an hour they put their heads on their knees and napped.

It was a little past 4 am when they awoke to the sound of vehicles moving towards them. It was a convoy from the NGO, Banyan Tree. They had four trucks equipped with medicines, water, tents etc. They also had a medical team of one doctor and two nurses. But the tragedy was that there was no one left to help here, only dead bodies that needed the dignity of last rites.

The Banyan Tree team leader came forward. "I'm Avinash Dutt," he said, holding out his hand to Cathy.

He walked over to where the bodies lay and examined them, making clicking sounds with his tongue and shaking his head. Then he called another unit and gave them their exact location, telling them that 29 bodies needed to be cleared.

Turning to Cathy he asked, "Can you wait until they come to pick up the bodies?" He was in a hurry to move on to where there were still people to be helped. "I'll find an alternate route; we'll have to backtrack about 60 kms. We need to get to those who need medical help."

Cathy nodded silently. They watched in stoic silence as the medical team left, leaving them to their death-watch.

They waited till 11 am for the other team to arrive. The putrid stench of rapidly decomposing flesh became overpowering as the day progressed. The wind had picked up, tugging at the remaining clothing on the bodies. Bent against the cold wind, Indraneel went forward slowly and tucked the clothes around the stiff bodies, trying to give them some dignity in death. Rigour mortis had set in.

Indraneel's legs and body ached, his head throbbed. He was aware of every bone in his body. A filmmaker's work was often hard but nothing compared to these grotesque circumstances. Perhaps only filmmakers and actors could put up with this sleepless trial, he thought morosely.

They heard a truck groaning its way up the mountain. *Banyan Tree* was neatly etched on its side. There were four trained men in the truck, with two stretchers. They quickly tied scarves across their faces before beginning the task of loading the bodies onto the stretchers. They worked efficiently but it still took them three hours because of the knee-deep slush and driving rain.

Cathy and Indraneel tried to arrange the bodies as neatly as they could but in the end they had to be stacked in the truck like inanimate objects. There was simply not enough room to lay them out individually. Indraneel felt deeply saddened, aged and weary. For some strange reason he remembered Marquez's *Love in the Time of Cholera*.

At last the ghastly task was done. The truck reversed with great difficulty in the small space and poor visibility. There was next to no road left, just the Ganga raging on one side and a quagmire of mud on the other. They all helped the vehicle to turn around. As it finally moved off around the bend, Indraneel saw the plastic sheet they had used to cover the bodies blow away in the tearing wind, revealing the macabre arrangement of stiff limbs. He closed his eyes; he could no longer feel anything.

Cathy gestured for everyone to climb into their own truck. It was easier for them to turn as the vehicle was much smaller. They drove in grim silence. Cathy opened her iPad and began keying in her notes. Indraneel peered at the screen, wondering what she could possibly find to say. She gave him a quick smile and turned the screen for him to read. Indraneel felt emotion return to his tired mind. He remembered how she had toiled for all those countless hours in the rain and mud. This woman was truly heroic, he thought.

Her note read: *I have said this many times before; nothing replaces time. The greatest effort one can put forth in my line of work is good old fashioned hours. It is very simple – if you fully commit yourself and do the hard time, everything you need, will come as a result. We did a lot of things to provide relief to some of the hardest hit areas during Sandy, but the most valuable thing we did was simply to be there. It's been the same everywhere I've worked in the world – all the greatest developments through our relief efforts came organically, showing up day by day while we worked...*

Indraneel looked out of the window. He realised the rain was finally easing off. After another 15 kms and it had stopped completely. They passed a small cascading waterfall and Indraneel asked Pradeep to stop. They took turns to wash the caked mud from their bodies; it seemed to have clogged every pore.

Indraneel felt like a new person after he had washed and changed his clothes, as did the others. He wanted to chant *naam* but, overwhelmed by his recent experiences, he couldn't bring himself to do so. They drove on. After 60 kms there was another small road leading to Kedarnath, but their truck was too big to pass. Cathy and Harpreet decided to go on with another team, some of whom Cathy already knew. She told Pradeep to take the truck back to Delhi, after dropping Indraneel off at Rishikesh.

Indraneel hugged Cathy and shook hands with Harpreet. It was impossible to name the bond that had formed between them. He climbed in beside

Pradeep. As the truck rumbled off, he began to ponder. He was surprised to find a multi-point charger in the truck and quickly plugged in his dead Blackberry. As it revived, a flood of emails and messages beeped in.

Sitting at an awkward angle because the charger cord was so short, he wrote to Arunodaya: *The simple fact is that it doesn't matter where disaster hits — the need is always the same. We are ALL human and need the same basic things to survive. Mother Nature doesn't discriminate; humans do!*

62

Indraneel was bone-weary when he finally got back to Rishikesh. The rain fell in a steady downpour, everything shrouded in an opaque, watery curtain. Indraneel dragged himself up to his room, surprised to see everything untouched. Somehow, he had expected the destruction to have struck here too.

He longed for a hot shower but there was no power. He made do with cold water, soaping and shampooing himself vigorously, as though to wash away the pain in his soul. Finally he rubbed himself dry till his skin burned. He never wanted to be in the rain ever again!

Indraneel fell into bed, giving in to the fatigue of his sore body. But his brain refused to sleep – a collage of horrifying images kept gnawing at his mind. Finally, in the early hours of the morning, he dozed off, dead to the world.

The sound of his daily alarm woke Indraneel. He had intended to switch it off but had forgotten to do so in his weariness. Still feeling fatigued and deeply sad, he got up, used the rest room and then looked out of the window. He peered intently, not believing his eyes! The beautiful, two-storey high Shiva idol on Paramarth *ghaat* was no longer there. The cynosure of all eyes at the daily *arati*, the object of so much devotion, had simply disappeared! He quickly took his binoculars from his bag and focused carefully, his heart pounding. No Shiva!

Indraneel ran down to Reception and asked the boy there, "*Woh Shivaji ki murti kahaan gayi* [Where has the idol of Lord Shiva gone]?"

"*Shivji beh gaye... Gangaji unako le gayi* [Shivaji has been washed away...the Ganga has taken him]," the boy answered philosophically.

Indraneel was shocked! He ran down to the *ghaat*. The Ganga raged like an ocean. Huge waves rose and fell. The roar of her turbulent waters was deafening. She was a terrifying sight!

Indraneel fell to his knees in supplication, beseeching Gangaji to return to her benevolent form.

63

A s Indraneel sat praying to Mother Ganga, his phone rang. He pulled it from his pocket. It was his mother. His heart heavy, he took a few moments to gather himself before pressing the green button on his handset.

Revati was extremely concerned about her son. "I didn't even know you were going to the disaster zone," she said. "It was only when Ahalya called to say you were safe that I knew you had gone."

For a moment Indraneel was confused but then recollected the mail he had sent Arunodaya. Ahalya Aunty was Arunodaya's mother and their parents often played bridge together. Indraneel assured his mother he was safe. The normally calm Revati was still very worried; she had seen the horrific images on TV.

"Please tell Dad too, that I'm fine," Indraneel added, thinking about his emotionally reserved father.

"Your father has gone to Berlin on work, but I will tell him," his mother said.

Indraneel hung up after once again assuring her he was safe and promising not to go anywhere dangerous without informing her.

64

Indraneel couldn't believe the huge idol of Shivji had simply been washed away. That empty spot on the *ghaats* was a continual and chilling reminder of the uncontained fury of the Ganga. He felt the burden of human loss at the core of his being; the scale of destruction burned a hole in his heart.

After his trip to the disaster zone, a great transformation came over Indraneel. He felt sad at a primordial level. Deep, existential questions plagued him. His eyes gazed vacantly. Silent and morose, he had nothing to say anymore. He moved like a sluggish automaton. He had the burnt-out look of someone who had just emerged from a protracted illness...

Indraneel dragged himself to see Shaman. His steps felt heavy and it took him twice as long as it normally did to get to the shop. A light drizzle fell and there was dampness everywhere. He carried his umbrella like it weighed a ton.

As Indraneel approached the shop, Shaman spotted him. Happy at first, Shaman became concerned as Indraneel drew closer.

"What's with you, Indraneel? You look run down. Are you unwell? Fever?" Shaman touched his friend's forehead.

"I'm alright." Indraneel brushed away Shaman's hand. He put his umbrella in the basket by the door and then turned and walked to a seat by the window. After gazing out in silence for a while, he finally whispered in the voice of the tortured, "Shaman, I feel wounded by what happened."

"I can see that," Shaman responded seriously.

"Even the bright day fails to soothe my bruised soul. The brutal images of the dead constantly gnaw at the edges of my consciousness."

"You must put it behind you," Shaman said firmly.

"I want to....I want to...but I'm assailed by those haunting images. I wish I could delete them from my memory." Indraneel's voice throbbed with desperation.

A middle-aged man wearing steel rimmed glasses walked into the shop. "I want some stories about survival...a book that recounts the psychology of survivors," he said.

Shaman pointed to the corner where the book could be found and turned back to Indraneel. The gentleman soon returned with a book, but seeing Shaman engaged in intense conversation, he stopped and listened.

"It was a great tragedy and people still haven't got over the damage."

"But what a mix of courage, strife and hopelessness was out there! Nothing like this has ever been witnessed in this region," Indraneel added.

The gentleman finally spoke up. "Your friend here seems to have just returned from the tragedy," he said to Shaman. "You're right, something extraordinary happened. I personally witnessed it. I am Ashutosh Sinha, Deputy Inspector General of Garhwal Range. I have been supervising the rescue and relief operations in Gauri Kunda and Kedarnath."

"From all accounts I must say your people have done a great job," Shaman complimented the official.

"We do our duty," Ashutosh answered quietly.

"Do you think relief will reach all areas soon?" Indraneel enquired.

"It isn't easy. The roads are all gone. It will take time, I won't lie. But there's hope. There is always hope in God's kingdom. I have witnessed one of the greatest miracles in the face of adversity," Ashutosh told them.

Shaman dragged over a chair and offered it to his visitor. "We're all ears. Please tell us about it."

Ashutosh sat down heavily. "I have read in many books over the years that surrender is an act of courage and strength. That surrender is not passivity but calm acceptance. A surrendered soul remains calm in the midst of the storm. Till now it was just something the books said. But during this tragedy, I witnessed it personally. Many people were drowned or washed away, with no means of escape. But when the violent, deathly wave of water was seen approaching, hundreds of devotees took off their footwear as a mark of respect and surrendered themselves to the flood, folding their hands in prayer, in the hope of attaining *moksha* [liberation]."

Shaman and Indraneel were astonished by the account.

"That is humbling." Shaman's voice held none of its usual assertiveness.

"Blue-blooded pilgrims! They had come to meet God. By their calm gesture, they perhaps gained Shiva," Indraneel observed.

"The gigantic, sweeping waves of the Ganga seemed to them a call from God. They surrendered silently, prayerfully," Ashutosh narrated. "Just think about it: a pigmy-sized human standing before a gigantic water divinity, with hands folded, saying, 'O death, take me! I smile as you carry me in your lap to a safe place.' The very next moment he is carried away. Whatever it is, it needs strength!"

"This is true courage, true faith, true surrender!" Shaman said quietly.

Over the next hour, Ashutosh Sinha discussed various events from the tragedy. Indraneel shared his experiences. Shaman heard them both with great attention.

"There's a possibility these people will attain *bhakta veer svarga* [heaven of the courageous believer], as against *veer svarga* [heaven of the courageous]. It cannot be ruled out," he commented reflectively.

Indraneel stood up to go. "Shaman, there's no guarantee to human life...I want to give myself wholeheartedly to *naam* and *japa*."

65

It was hard to recognize Indraneel in his present *avatar*. A full beard covered his handsome face and a thick curly mane touched his shoulders. Almost two months had passed since the Kedarnath tragedy. Indraneel had engaged in deep austerities, almost as if he was trying to burn away his mortal body through the heat of his penance. He found meaning and peace in doing *japa* and singing *naam*. Everything else seemed shallow, trivial and fleeting.

Indraneel ate just once a day – some fruit. But he drank copious amounts of Ganga water. *Japa* consumed him for most of the day and he sang *naam* for another three hours. He also did *japa* standing waist-deep in the Ganga at night, or sitting beside a blazing fire in the heat of the day. He yearned only to look inwards and concentrated all his energy in repeating the Name and listening to its repetition.

He had lost weight. Always lean and athletic, Indraneel now looked emaciated and bony. Strangely enough, his face had a radiant lustre, and he was happy. His sunken eyes burned with a strange intensity. He barely spoke to anyone, practising *mauna vrath*, the vow of silence, at least thrice a week. He was aware that of the sense organs, the tongue is the most difficult to control, with its dual function.

The horrific images of the flood began to slowly recede from Indraneel's mind. He found inner peace as he did more and more *japa*. It gave him tranquillity but he felt he couldn't tap into the deeper recesses of his self. He longed to close his eyes and push past the darkness.

'Am I afraid? What does this darkness mean?' he wondered.

Concentration on breath followed as he focused on inhaling and exhaling; it provided him with a rhythm in the silence of solitude.

Indraneel gave up wearing footwear. The initial blisters burst painfully, leaving hardened calluses. He thought of the great sages who had gone on long *padayatras* – the Shankara, Mahatma Gandhi, Swami Vivekananda... He slept on the floor using a thin sheet, trying to eliminate body consciousness. He rose at 3 am every day so he could begin his meditation at *brahma muhurta* [the moment of Brahma], and bathed in the Ganga thrice a day. Indraneel began to practise closing his eyes and ears and listening to the sound of the natural fire in his body.

Shaman worried about his friend's health. But Indraneel hardly came to see him, immersed in solitude. He loved the silence of being alone. He walked deep into the Chilla forest and did *japa* there. He even gave up his favourite activity – reading, and switched off his cell phone. He wrote one postcard a week to his mother, with just one sentence – that he was fine and she was not to worry.

Indraneel's mind grew free of clutter, fear and longing. He lost track of the days and the date. They no longer mattered to him. He lived only in the all-powerful Now.

66

Shaman had left several messages with Madhusudan, Vedavati and Nagaraj, but none of them could tell him much about Indraneel. He had been spotted occasionally, wandering along the banks of the Ganga. One of Vedavati's German friends had seen Indraneel at 2 am, sitting on the *ghaat* with a little mud lamp lit next to him. That seemed bizarre. The *ashram* people reported that he had come in one day and performed an elaborate worship of the cow.

Shaman decided to take things into his own hands and went to Indraneel's room to check on him. He found the place locked. A tea vendor nearby told Shaman that it was impossible to predict Indraneel's behaviour these days.

"There must be some place he goes to every day?" Shaman asked.

"Ganga *ghaat*...look for him there. He goes to Gangaji daily," the tea boy replied, nodding his head vigorously.

Shaman walked along the *ghaats*. Behind Dayananda Ashram he found Indraneel, sitting like a statue, in deep meditation. Shaman was shocked to see the change in him – the weight loss, the beard, the wavy locks, the glow on his face – it was all beyond his comprehension.

"Indraneel Maharaj! I'm glad I found you before you left for the Himalayan points of no return."

"Shaman! Why would I go anywhere?" Indraneel greeted his mentor, coming out of his meditation.

"One never knows! The way you've been behaving recently, I wouldn't be surprised if you disappeared among the Nagas, or buried yourself in a cave in Badrinath."

Indraneel smiled briefly. There was too much on his mind. Shaman's words no longer seemed humourous to him. They sat on the steps beside the flowing waters and talked. Shaman cursed him for not being in touch and probed till Indraneel confided the details of his austere life.

"I am really happy with what I'm doing. I don't want to do anything but spiritual practice for the rest of my life," Indraneel said finally.

"That is a good state, but I hope you're not rushing into it prematurely," Shaman cautioned.

"No, no...I'm fine. But I have so many questions. For instance, whenever I close my eyes to meditate, I feel extremely uncomfortable. I am afraid. Bizarre images of death appear – other people's deaths, my death, random things...but so real! Can I meditate with my eyes open? I feel afraid of the dark. What should I do?"

"How do you hope to progress if you refuse to go deeper within?" Shaman asked in a matter-of-fact way. "When you close your eyes to meditate, you are going within yourself. There's darkness at the door, but once you get in, there is only light. Just like when you enter a dark room, you feel blinded, but only for a minute. If you stay, you begin to see."

"True. I have experienced it often," Indraneel agreed.

"It's the same with inner darkness. You may have to strain a bit but as long as there's even a wee bit of light, you can see. It's only in absolute darkness that you cannot see anything."

"It's never absolute darkness," Indraneel remarked.

"That's right, engineer *babu*! Darkness and death are just doors. Beyond them, there's light," Shaman declared emphatically.

"I heard someone talking about *Mahanishaa* [the Great Night] at Devi Puja at Ananda Ashram. Is that linked to this?" Indraneel asked contemplatively.

"Yes. It's another name for *Diwali* [festival of lights]. *Mahanishaa* is the great night of Kaali. She is said to have appeared on this night, along with 64,000 *yoginis*. Think of the word *Kaali* – *Kaal* is Time, *Kaal* is also darkness. If it was negative in its connotations, why would we have a goddess called Kaali? *Diwali* is a night, as is *Mahashivaratri*. But they are dark doors to eternal light."

Shaman's phone beeped. He quickly looked at the message and then continued. "The dark is beautiful. If ghosts dwell in darkness, why do people make love in the dark? Darkness is one of the most misunderstood things in this world. When you close your eyes to meditate and plunge within, it feels dark. But it's not really darkness. There are streaks of indigo, orange and deep blue. Relax the tension in your eyelids. Become still. The darkness of colours that floats before you will become steady. Enlightened ones reach the light within. Do you know the sign of a true *jnani*, man of wisdom?"

Mutely, Indraneel shook his head.

"When we close our eyes we see darkness; when the *jnani* closes his eyes, he sees light. That's an arrived soul!"

"Is there anyone really like that?"

"There's my Guru, Naam Yajnananda Maharaj, at Ananda Ashram. He sees light all the time."

"And you? You've seen it too, haven't you, Shaman? You seem to know this so well," Indraneel stared into Shaman's eyes with unnerving intensity.

"Well...yes, but I haven't been able to go the whole way," Shaman admitted. "The well within is deep, but there's no safer place. We cannot afford to remain on the brink; we must take the plunge."

"So true, Shaman! We get so accustomed to the external world that we are afraid to go within. But I *want* to go all the way." Indraneel's voice shook with earnestness.

"You can't get there on your own, my friend. You need a Guru," Shaman warned.

"I am already practising and finding it; I don't need a Guru," Indraneel declared.

"Mister Buddha, don't get over-confident. There was a guy like you in the US – Swaminathan – a married man. He'd sit and meditate far into the night, in a ramrod posture, in the puja room. His family could never tell when he would finish. One day, I got a call from his wife at 5 am. Apparently, Swaminathan had been meditating late into the night. When she rose to go to the loo, she found him in the same position. Worried, she called out and shook him, but there was no response. Frozen from rigor mortis, he was carried in an ambulance to the hospital, still in the lotus posture. You see, these things happen when you have no Guru energy protecting you. You have already gone far beyond the limits of safety; it's time you met your Guru and took proper initiation," Shaman insisted.

"But I'm not ready," Indraneel protested.

"What do you mean not ready? I'm not asking you to get married."

"But Shaman..."

"No but. Tomorrow is auspicious – *Guru Poornima*. You will be initiated tomorrow. Get up at 4 am, have a Ganga bath, put on a cotton *dhoti* [traditional Indian lower body garment for men], and don't eat anything until your initiation happens. I'll pick you up."

Indraneel ceased to protest. It felt right.

67

Indraneel rose at 3.30 am, eagerly anticipating the new dawn. It was a significant day in his life, more important than the premieres of his movies. He walked down to the Ganga and bathed, then meditated for an hour, trying to go beyond the darkness Shaman had spoken of. Perhaps a gentle nudge from his Guru would get him over the threshold.

When Shaman came, they went to the *ashram*. On one side of the *ashram* gate, they saw a carpet of Parijata flowers, strewn abundantly beneath a tree.

WHEN LIFE TURNS TURTLE

An old woman was picking up each fragile white blossom with its orange stalk, chanting the *Hare Krishna mantra*. As they walked in, they could hear the chanting of Sanskrit *mantras* by a group of young voices; they were from the Sanskrit school in the *ashram*. A festive air of harmony, peace, calm and prayer pervaded the place.

"Tell me about *diksha* [initiation]," Indraneel asked Shaman.

"*Diksha* is one of the *mahasamskaras* [great ceremonies] of life. The naming ceremony, the thread ceremony, marriage, last rites...these are other prominent Hindu *samskaras*. But *diksha* is superior to all these."

"So what does this *samskara* achieve?"

"It touches you with divinity. We call ourselves human but there is much in us that is animal-like. *Diksha* helps us to rise above the animal to the human, and then to divine levels. In the olden days, *diksha* was mandatory for all students who went to a *gurukul*. Today, one rarely meets a real Guru, so few can say they are really educated."

"One does meet Gurus at school and college," Indraneel remarked.

"There are two things: *shiksha* [disciple] and *diksha* [initiation]. *Shiksha* is about formal education in school, college etc., and *diksha* is about education regarding the Self. One can indeed go through life without *shiksha*, but travelling through life without *diksha* is a dark tragedy." Shaman emphasised his words with an upraised forefinger.

"What did you mean by *diksha* making us divine? Aren't we divine already?" Indraneel tried to understand the implications of Shaman's words.

"Life is cast in *maya*, Indraneel, continuously perpetuating desires. The cycle of birth and death, a boring thing, never really ends until one *wants* to put an end to it and be free. *Diksha* is the first step towards such freedom. *Diksha* is the ignition of the soul – dynamite for worldly dross. It makes a disciple more pure, more enlightened, more successful. *Diksha* means 'initiation'. It is the subtle transfer of the Guru's divine energy into the heart, soul and body of a disciple."

Shaman seated himself on a wooden bench under a tree and motioned to Indraneel to sit too. Under the same tree, a group of women sat talking as they briskly wove *malas* from bright red hibiscus and orange marigold flowers, alternating them with thick bunches of green Tulasi leaves.

"I assume all this happens eventually. So the ritual today will do all of this? Is it elaborate?" Indraneel asked.

"*Diksha* is a simple affair and may not impress you. Just 15 minutes, nothing romantic. You may even feel nothing has happened. But it has... inside, where you cannot see. As the years pass, the awareness about the role of *diksha* in your life will keep revealing itself."

Shaman picked up a flower one of the ladies had dropped and handed it back to her with a smile. Indraneel was amused by Shaman's awareness of the world around him.

"Thank you for today, Shaman."

"Don't thank me; thank the Guru and his grace. You are fortunate that the events of your life have ignited interest in the ultimate reality and the science of spirituality. *Diksha* is not a thing you can have because you want it; it's a gift bestowed upon the rare few who are ready. God chooses who is ready, creating conditions to lead them to a Siddha Guru. The rest follows. It is only to those who have performed good deeds (*punya*) over many lives that a Satguru's grace comes and *diksha* is obtained. For most, it simply does not happen despite their best efforts. How many people do you know who have received *diksha*?"

"Not one!"

Shaman nodded. "That's the point. It's a rare thing."

"What will the Guru do? What's the initiation protocol?" Indraneel continued to shoot questions.

"You will be taught a simple ritual on how to do *japa*; be given a *mantra* in your ear, and an *asana* for meditation. That's all. But it's a serious moment. You will return carrying a great deal in your soul. Just practicing what you have been told at your *diksha* will see you through everything in life."

"Are there strict rules to follow after *diksha*?" Indraneel was somewhat apprehensive of what might be required.

"Don't worry about rules and regulations. Be at ease. Our Gurudeva never commands anyone to give up things; he suggests and urges us to do it at our own pace, one step at a time. Of course, there are some do's and dont's, but they can be implemented over time according to one's own will and effort. There is no compulsion. If we were perfect we wouldn't need *diksha*. It's because we are weak that we take *diksha*, so that its power can move us from darkness to light, from weakness to strength."

"That makes sense. So Guru is going to give me a *mantra* in my ear? Is that standard?"

"When the Guru gives *diksha*, a flow of energy takes place from him to the disciple. It can be in any form – spoken words as a *mantra*, subtle radiation emitted from the eyes, or gentle warmth from a touch on the forehead with the thumb, or by touching the Guru's *padukas*. But the Satguru is not limited to these; he can transfer his energy across continents and give *diksha* through the medium of a photograph or book as well."

Indraneel and Shaman chatted on, waiting for Naam Yajnananda Maharaj to call them to the hall where *darshan* and *diksha* were to be given. Maharaj was in the hall, finishing his morning prayers, the door closed.

68

As soon as Indraneel entered the hall where *diksha* was to take place, the electricity went off and sudden darkness enveloped the room. The day outside was grey, with dark rolling clouds pregnant with rain; ominous thunder clashed periodically. A clear voice chanted the *Hare Krishna Mahamantra*, which the gathering repeated.

From the chorus of voices, Indraneel realized there were many people in the hall, even though he could not see them clearly. He remembered Shaman's description of darkness and smiled. They made their way towards the erect figure who sat facing the crowd.

Indraneel negotiated his way between those already seated, clutching his *dhoti*. The garment felt unfamiliar and he was concerned it would come undone.

Shaman prostrated himself before the Master, remaining so for a minute before rising. The chanting continued. Shaman urged Indraneel to seek the Guru's blessing. Indraneel too, prostrated himself. As he rose, he looked into the Guru's face.

Light from the *ghee* lamps illuminating the large picture of the butter-eating Sri Krishna, beautifully decorated with *Tulasi malas* [garlands of Holy Basil], fell on the Guru's face as well. Indraneel noted the long ash-grey *jatas* [dreadlocks], piled on his head like a crown. A wispy white beard covered the lower half of his gaunt face. A vibrant *vaishnava tilak* adorned his wide, wrinkled forehead. Below the overgrown moustache, the lips were barely visible as they moved in the *Mahamantra*. The Guru's voice was not loud but it had a clear, bell-like quality. His eyes were the most dramatic feature of his face – though sunken into folds of wrinkled skin, they shone like polished ebony in the lamp light, emanating a kindness and grace difficult to describe. Indraneel could not tear his gaze away from those eyes. He remained frozen on his knees, palms folded.

The Guru's frame appeared emaciated, even in the weak light of the *diyas*. Translucent skin barely covered the sharply protruding bones. His upper body was bare. Only a *janevu* [sacred thread] crossed his bony rib-cage. He wore a simple white *dhoti*. His fingers were bare of rings. No watch graced his wrist. The Guru was the picture of austerity; divine energy radiated from him.

Indraneel felt Shaman tap him on the shoulder. He looked back to see his friend indicating that he should move as there were others waiting for the Guru's blessings. It was *Guru Poornima* and there were about 1000 people waiting to see the holy man, among them, heads of *ashrams*.

Once everyone had offered their *pranaams*, the *diksha* ceremony commenced. Indraneel was pleasantly surprised to see Shaman reappear, clad in a *dhoti*, to give a prefatory address on the importance of the *diksha* ritual. He was apparently an official assistant to the Guru. He asked the aspirants to face east and then handed each a woollen prayer mat. Then he explained the ritual.

Guru Maharaj smiled at everyone. "Happy birthday to all of you! You are reborn today!" Everyone smiled. Guruji then went from person to person, speaking a *mantra* into the ear, requesting them to do *japa* with the *mantra*.

Indraneel received the Krishna *mantra*. His mind flew back to when he had met Anasuya Ma. She had unerringly predicted that his Guru would give him the Krishna *mantra*. Tears filled his eyes as the Guru placed his hand on his head. He closed his eyes and did *japa* with the given *mantra*. A sense of fulfilment flooded his soul.

After the *diksha*, everyone chatted for a while and then went to the dining hall for lunch. Indraneel did not speak. He picked up his mat and went to the Guru Mandir and sat there with eyes closed, repeating the *mantra*. The image of Gurudeva flashed in his mind, bringing peace and light.

At 2 pm, Shaman came to forcibly take him to lunch. "Are you happy?" he asked gently.

Indraneel reached out to hold Shaman's hands warmly between his own, and nodded silently. He could not utter a word.

69

It was close to noon on a hot day. The sun had climbed right overhead. It had been nearly two months since Indraneel's initiation. Though not a stranger to the practice of *naam* and *japa*, his experience of both practices changed radically post his initiation. He felt an internal explosion of awareness and bliss. The mortal plane of his existence was now suffused with inner radiance.

Indraneel sat, lost in the sweet octaves of the *naam* singer at the Guru Mandir. Entering the heart of the *naamic* sound transported him to a faraway place. He felt a sensation of indescribable coolness, as if he were sitting under a gurgling cascade of sparkling water. The chill water fell on his head and slid down his neck, leaving a trail of gooseflesh. His limbs were soaked. He longed for the icy water to soak him through.

Indraneel felt that the drops of water were the syllables of *naam* permeating his being. It felt familiar, a place he had bathed several times in the past. As the water sluiced over him, it patterned a deep path of *naam* over his physical body. He felt the 16 words of the *Hare Krishna mantra* slide over him. His scalp was chilled. His eyes closed, Indraneel trembled from the sensation of nearly being frozen in the Himalayan brook.

Indraneel had never imagined he would ever experience such a surreal connection between the physical and the sublime. It was like the physical presence of *naam*, a bodily experience so calming that when he came out of it, he felt he had been asleep for hours and woken rejuvenated, in another realm.

He told Shaman about this experience.

His friend looked at Indraneel with affectionate admiration. "That is beautiful. It is the experience of ecstasy that poets try to explain. It is the consciousness throbbing with the divinity within. I have not heard a more eloquent description of the Real; surreal though it may seem to others!"

Indraneel was deeply moved.

70

It was just before dawn. A dark inkiness still spread its mantle over the heavens. Indraneel made his way towards the Ganga more by instinct than by actual sight. There were no firm definitions, just dark shapes. As he approached the *ghaats*, chinks appeared in the dark skies. A slow grey began squeezing out of apertures, turning the heavens a dull mauve. From the quality of light it was difficult to know whether it was dawn or dusk approaching. Transience was the only real thing.

Indraneel went down the *ghaat* steps slowly, gingerly finding his foothold in the half dawn. He knew from long familiarity with the place that the platform leading to the Ganga had a fine layer of sand, brought down by the river. The clean wet sand seemed to have been uniformly spread with the precision of a surgeon. For a moment Indraneel marvelled at nature's handiwork.

He discarded his clothes but hesitated before putting his foot on the virgin sand. It seemed almost blasphemous to sully something so pure and untouched. His feet formed perfect impressions as he moved forward. As he walked to the very edge of the water, he saw two perfectly made infant footprints. He was intrigued. A baby here at this hour? Where were the footprints of the accompanying adult? Indraneel looked around but found none. How could the child have come alone, negotiating the steps in the treacherous semi-light? There were no answers.

Indraneel bathed in the cold waters of the Ganga and then returned to the platform, dripping. He gazed once again at the tiny footprints imbedded in the wet sand. Instinctively, he bowed and touched his head to the imprints, tears in his eyes.

'It's not often that we meet Little Strangers,' he thought.

71

The days that followed Indraneel's *diksha* flowed with a smooth, joyous energy. He rose as usual at 3 am to catch the pre-dawn, and the rest of the day just whizzed by. It was as if he was riding an energy wave of *naam* and *japa*. He had found Life. He wondered where he had been all these years.

He loved the *Ishta Mantra* [*mantra* of a personal deity], that Naam Yajnananda Maharaj had bestowed on him; its utterance brought him a deep sense of peace. Alone though he was, he felt filled to the brim. His world comprised of the syllables of the *mantra*.

Though he had felt great peace and calm from the austerities he had practiced before his *diksha*, post-*diksha* he felt filled with a luminous joy. Initiation was real, he told himself. Indraneel was filled with a secret happiness. It was like he had found the key to unlock the chamber of treasures in his soul. He experienced a strong sense of completion.

Indraneel's past life as a famous film-maker in Mumbai, now seemed like a fake bubble. He couldn't imagine how he had lived for 39 years. The past seemed to have been an animal existence. He loved his life and he awoke each day with a sense of joyous anticipation. He now understood that each day was a gift. Each day brought him closer to his Maker.

One day he saw a man making an idol of Ma Durga on Ganga *ghaat*. Indraneel calculated that it must be Durga Puja time again. A whole year had passed since he came to Rishikesh, and almost two months since his initiation. He had lost track of time. He recalled that Naam Yajnananda Maharaj had mentioned he would be in Rishikesh again for Durga Puja. Indraneel remembered the Master's ebony eyes, filled with love and compassion.

He asked the idol-maker, "When is *Dussera* [Indian festival marking the victory of Lord Rama over Ravana]?"

The artisan replied without glancing up from his work, "I'm late. This idol will only be installed on the fifth day. *Navaratri* starts today."

Indraneel ran up the steps of the ghat towards his room. He quickly changed into a *dhoti* and began walking towards Ananda Ashram. He had decided in a flash that he never wished to return to Bombay and his old life. All he wanted was to be here in Rishikesh, by himself. All his worldly possessions and connections meant nothing now; he was happy to let them go. The very thought of renunciation filled him with tranquillity.

Indraneel decided to ask Naam Yajnananda Maharaj to initiate him into *sannyasa*. He had an overwhelming, soul-wrenching desire to start life afresh without the encumbrances of his dreary past; to be free. With this resolve, Indraneel almost ran to Ananda Ashram. As he entered, he knew his Guru was there. He felt a palpable energy in the air. Some of those present turned their heads, wondering who the handsome, lean man in a demented hurry was.

Indraneel did not know where to find the Guru. He hurried in, searching blindly. The Guru was in the cowshed, petting a new-born calf. He knelt on the ground, drawing three fingers over the creature's small forehead, as if he was drawing an invisible *vaishnava tilak*. The moon-white calf edged closer to the frail Guru, seeking comfort. The mother cow stood by, proudly showing off her calf to the saint. As Indraneel came closer, hesitant about intruding on the beautiful moment, the cow sensed his presence and mooed loudly.

Naam Yajnananda Maharaj saw him and beckoned him closer. "She is Gauri," he said, pointing to the wobbly calf. "She was born today at 4 am, on the first day of *navaratri*."

Indraneel prostrated himself at the Guru's feet, on the mud floor of the cowshed.

The Guru blessed him with *"Jai Guru...Jai Ma,"* and then walked towards a bench outside, beside a row of *Tulasi* plants. Their heady fragrance was intoxicating. He sat down and gestured for Indraneel to sit as well.

Indraneel lowered himself to the ground, at the Guru's feet. Shaman had once told him that all the four *Vedas* reside in the feet of the Guru. For the first time in months Indraneel wished he had his camera with him. He would have loved to have taken a picture of his Guru's feet.

"What is it, *beta*?" the saint asked. "Do you have a question? Do you want anything?"

"Actually, I don't know how to put it..." Indraneel's tongue stumbled over the words.

The Guru smiled. "When one's mind is made up, words humbly serve that intent. But when the soul's call has not come from within in a simple and straightforward way, we find it difficult to articulate things."

"Gurudeva, I wish to take *sannyasa*. I want to be a *sannyasi*," Indraneel blurted out.

Naam Yajnananda Maharaj gazed for a long moment into Indraneel's intense eyes.

Indraneel had come with a specific purpose. He was afraid of any contrary possibility. He wanted to be a *sannyasi*, to never go back to the life he had once lived.

"So you don't wish to return to the life you had?" asked the Guru, verbalising Indraneel's thoughts accurately.

Indraneel was taken aback. "No, I cannot return to that life," he stated emphatically.

"My child, seeking freedom and seeking to be liberated from bondage are two different things. Just because one wishes to be freed from bondage does not mean one wishes for freedom. It just means one wishes the bondage to cease." The Guru's words were compassionate.

"But when bondage goes, doesn't freedom follow?" Indraneel asked.

"No. Only bondage goes. Freedom is something else."

Indraneel thought this sounded paradoxical. Removal of bondage and gaining freedom – he couldn't quite see how they were two different things, even though he realised there *was* a difference.

"We are not to give up anything. We are only to get closer to ourselves, our true selves," the saint said, closing his eyes meditatively. In a few moments he opened them again. "If you had *sannyasa* in you, I would have said, 'Come, I'll give you the ochre robe', but it's not in you, my son! You are an artist and must go back to being one." The Guru paused and then asked, "What were you doing before you came here?"

"I made films," Indraneel replied, feeling stripped of all hope by the Guru's surmise.

"Then go back and make films. Don't live on the periphery of life. Settle down. Get married and lead the life of a householder, performing your own *karma*."

"But Maharaj...I don't see myself getting married." Indraneel started to say something more but stopped.

"*Bete*...tell me...don't hesitate."

433

"Baba, I have been married and divorced. Then I wanted to marry again...but that too, ended on a bitter note. I feel scarred. I don't think marriage is for me."

The Guru looked at Indraneel, then closed his eyes for a few seconds before saying, "You *will* marry. You *will* find a girl who will be a partner in your life. She will have similar inclinations in the pursuit of spirituality. Things will happen, just follow the path...that's your only duty. There's nothing to be gained by throwing away one's *swadharma* [one's duty]. Making films is your *swadharma*. Follow it. Your *dharma* may seem boring, monotonous, difficult or unromantic, but it will liberate you."

Indraneel's reservations dropped away. He felt free to speak his heart. "But Gurudeva, I seem to have drifted far from film-making and worldly life. To go back to it now will be very difficult."

"Yes, it will, my son. But you're living a dream, Indraneel. You've drifted far from those things in this dream. In reality, you have merely taken a break. You stand exactly where you were, just more enlightened. And that's enough. Really enough."

"Gurudeva, life drags me down. I want to renounce it," Indraneel pleaded.

"How can life drag anyone down, Indraneel? What *is* there except life? Isn't the idea of renunciation also life? Don't *sannyasis* have a life? How can you be so foolish? Don't you realise that it is only life that can transcend life? That we make our freedom from the same stuff from which we make our bondage? Trust life, Indraneel! Your salvation lies in your life, not in your mind."

"I have begun to enjoy my life here in Rishikesh. Isn't that life too?" Indraneel persisted, unwilling to believe the way forward lay in the way back.

"Of course, it is. But it is someone else's life, not yours. God gives each one their own life. Whatever that is, it's invaluable. However mundane that life may be, the only way is to embrace it as the way to eternity."

"But my life is worldly," Indraneel agonised.

"The world is worldly; it can't be anything else. But *we* need not be worldly, need we? Bring God into your life and your life will cease to be worldly. And you can do this anywhere in the world. Yes?"

"Yes, Gurudeva. What you say is true. It's just that I wasn't prepared to hear the truth," Indraneel confessed sadly.

"What you are to do has already been spun by the Almighty. Just go with the flow." Naam Yajnananda Maharaj placed his hand on Indraneel's head.

"When do you wish me to go back to Mumbai?" Indraneel asked, half afraid of the answer.

"Stay till *Vijaya Dashami* and leave on *Ekadashi*."

"As you wish, Guruji. Please give me your blessing."

There were tears in Indraneel's eyes. He was going to miss Gurudeva...miss Rishikesh, the Ganga, the Himalayas... But his heart was now freed of doubt. He would return to being a film-maker. He didn't know how and with whom he would settle down; it seemed beyond the bounds of possibility at the moment. But he took solace from his Guru's words: *What you are to do has already been spun by the Almighty.*

72

Indraneel's mind churned with possibilities after speaking to his Guru. He felt an urgent need to talk to Shaman. He was apprehensive and troubled by his Guru's advice to marry and turn into a householder. His previous relationships had been acrimonious and bitter. So who was this person the Guru had mentioned, the one who would be his partner and share his circumstances? Who had such spiritual inclinations, he wondered? The only name that came to mind was Vasundhara. Indraneel sighed. Arunodaya's sister was like his sister. Besides, she was so much younger than he. His mind continued to go round in circles.

Indraneel walked to Shaman's shop, hoping to find him there. He had stopped using a mobile phone but he now wished he had one to locate Shaman. Payal was behind the counter and said Shaman was at his afternoon prayers.

Indraneel waited outside the shop, on the steps leading to Ganga, gazing at the majestic Himalayas towering over the town. He felt a deep sense of despair. How could he leave all this and return to the concrete cage of Bombay? Once again he told himself his role was to fulfil the advice of his Guru.

As he sat staring at the flowing waters, Payal came out to tell him Shaman had finished. Indraneel immediately rose and went into the shop.

Shaman was happy to see him. "*Hari Aum*...some black coffee?" he offered.

"No thanks," Indraneel declined abruptly, before adding, "I stopped drinking coffee a while ago. Shaman, I have something important to ask you. I went to see Maharaj this morning."

"I too, went for *darshan*, but I didn't see you," remarked Shaman casually.

"That's not important," Indraneel replied impatiently. "Gurudeva advised me to return to Bombay. He said something about *swadharma*..." Indraneel sounded agitated as he paced the floor of the bookstore.

"Calm down. What exactly did Gurudeva say?"

Indraneel thought for a moment. "Shaman, it was something about *swadharma*. In fact, everything he said sort of hinged on *swadharma*. I need to know exactly what he meant. I know vaguely that *swadharma* is one's own thing, but what is the real meaning? What did Gurudeva mean by asking me to follow my *swadharma*? And what was the thing about each person's own life being the only way to eternity? Is there no flexibility in life? How does one know what one's life is, one's lot?"

"That's a barrage of questions, my friend. Let me address them one by one. Why don't you sit down?" Shaman gestured to a chair. Indraneel sighed and sat down.

"*Swadharma* is the property of one's self. *Swa* means 'own'. *Dharma* means 'way'. So *Swadharma* can roughly be described as 'one's own way'. It's a scientific thing."

"How is it scientific?" Indraneel interjected.

Shaman was quick to answer. "The way of water is to flow, that's the water's *dharma*. The way of fire is to burn, that is its *dharma*. The *dharma* of gold, silver, platinum etc. is not to react, to remain unaffected. In the periodic table these may be noble metals, in humans you could term them royalty. Everything in this world has an inherent characteristic, its *dharma*." Shaman stopped to gauge Indraneel's reaction.

"But I thought *dharma* was about truth and non-violence and things like charity, forgiveness etc."

"Sure. That's *dharma* too. When one sticks to something, holds onto it, when it becomes a characteristic, then it becomes *dharma*."

"But what about what is inherent, what one is born with? One can acquire any quality by practice, can't one? Then how can we say this or that is a person's *dharma*? Take my case. I did not begin as a film-maker; I studied engineering. But I took to film-making. So how is it that engineering is not my *swadharma*?" Indraneel really wanted to understand the conundrum.

Shaman took off his glasses and rubbed a thumb and forefinger over the lens. "You're right," he said. "Over many lifetimes, we change our *dharma*. We like to do something and become good at it. That becomes our *dharma*. Then our desires take us in another direction and we chuck the thing we were good at and try the new thing. The whole process begins again."

"But what's wrong with that? Isn't life all about experimentation?"

"There's nothing wrong with that, Indraneel. Stupid perhaps to throw something hard won away, but not wrong. I take up a job and leave it after a while. Then I take on an entirely different job, and so on. What's wrong with that? Nothing. I live in one place and then leave it. I build a house all over again in another place. What's wrong with that? You know the answer, don't you?"

"Yeah! Basically, it's like trying to do too many things in a limited span of time. Maybe something like a Jack of all trades and master of none?"

"In a way that's what it is. But more importantly, it's like building multiple identities for oneself."

"I'm sorry but what's wrong with that?"

"You just keep asking what's wrong with it. That's what the world has come to. Nobody asks

WHEN LIFE TURNS TURTLE

what is right with it." Shaman sounded irritable. He closed his eyes and felt calm return.

"Anyway, life is already complex. We are identified by what we do – water with wetting and flowing, fire by burning. And that's the problem with creating new *dharmas*. Each *dharma* is an identity. We become confused and lost; we don't know who we are, because life after life we keep changing ourselves, chasing new desires, building new identities."

"So are you saying one should restrict oneself to a single identity?"

"Yes. An Arjuna should stick to warfare and not confuse himself by trying to be a Brahmin *pundit*. He is good the way he is! That's what Krishna tells him. You see, with one identity one can go deeper. It's not restriction, it's definition."

"Not restriction but definition," Indraneel repeated, memorising it.

"A man who lives all over the world belongs nowhere. But a man with a fixed abode, travels all over the world as a global citizen. Committing to something, one thing, helps to define yourself. Then you can expand that identity."

"And is this definition of *swadharma* and what comes with it, is it what Gurudeva called 'one's own life'?" Indraneel bent forward in his chair, hands clasped between his knees.

"Yes. The location of *swadharma* is in your own life. *Swadharma* is not something one goes hunting for and finds. It's the most obvious, fundamental thing; perhaps not the most desirable or most romantic."

"Could you explain that, Shaman? I'm not quite on board with this." Indraneel was finding this bit of wisdom difficult to come to terms with.

"It's natural for a round ball to roll. No effort is needed. Just a gentle push and the ball rolls. That is the way it is with *swadharma*. Whatever is natural to us we do effortlessly because that's our *dharma*. And because we do it effortlessly we have no ego about it. An unnatural thing requires great effort, and that brings in ego. So you see, *swadharma* eases the ego and our identity gets unselfish. A natural writer has no ego about writing because it just comes to him. Gurudeva told you to continue film-making. You're already successful. You know it. It comes to you naturally. So, with a little bit of God in your life, you can easily duck the monster called Ego. Think about it Indraneel, do you think *sannyasa* is a natural thing for you?"

"No...not really," Indraneel confessed, though it pained him to admit it.

"So it's settled," Shaman said. "Adios on *Ekadashi*! Go, get your life...and your eternity."

73

As the flight approached Santa Cruz airport in Bombay, it flew low over the Arabian Sea. The setting sun turned the water into a dazzling expanse of molten gold. Its vastness was overwhelming. Indraneel joined his hands and bowed to Varuna, Lord of the Waters. He now had a palpably sharp awareness of God, and remembered Him often through the day. He took nothing for granted.

Disembarking, Indraneel headed for the slowly circling conveyer belt. He collected his luggage and walked out of the terminal. He was surprised to see his parents outside, anxiously scanning the arriving passengers. They looked suddenly older and more frail. He felt a pang at not having been to see them for over a year. Weaving his way through the departing masses, he finally stood before them. It was a wordless moment of poignant joy. Indraneel bent low and touched their feet.

"Welcome home, son! Welcome home!" his father said in a gruff voice full of emotion.

Her eyes full of tears, his mother kissed him on the forehead and gently patted his cheeks in the age-old gesture of maternal love. She didn't say a word. Indraneel put an arm around her shoulders and pulled along his suitcase with the other hand.

The moment he spotted them, Govind driver came running to take the suitcase from his hand, his face wreathed in smiles. "Good evening sir," he said happily.

It was only after they were well on their way that Revati finally collected herself and said softly, "So happy to see you, Indoo."

"Me too, Mum." Tears choked Indraneel.

The drive back to Cuffe Parade was in frenzied traffic. The evening rush hour was in full flow. How could he have forgotten the pace and density of Bombay? His parents were silent but he could see them glance at him, unable to believe he was finally with them again. They listened to whatever he had to say but didn't pry. He loved them all the more for their restraint.

Bombay was like a seasoned courtesan, trying to lure an old patron back with breathless charm and seductive overtures. There was an undeniable beauty about her. As they drove over the Sea Link, lights twinkled as far as the eye could see, and rose in towers, piercing the dark sky. Despite himself, the familiar energy and verve of the city struck a chord in Indraneel. The traffic eased somewhat as they approached Cuffe Parade and home.

When they rang the bell of their penthouse apartment on the 27th floor, Big Gomati opened the door.

"Look who's come home!" Revati said, giving a small whoop of undignified joy.

"*Chote saab*!" Big Gomati exclaimed.

An air of happiness filled the house.

"Now close your eyes," instructed Balarama Barua. "We have a small surprise for you."

Indraneel instantly felt he was eight years old again. He obediently closed his eyes.

"Indraneel, no cheating now," his father cautioned as he led his son forward, a hand on his shoulder. "Now open your eyes."

"Wait...wait...Indoo..." his mother called in excitement. "Let me open the door..." Indraneel heard a door open. "Now you can open your eyes."

Opening his eyes Indraneel was amazed to find that his parents had converted his father's study into a *puja* room for him. They had restored his grandmother's silver *mandir* and installed her beautiful marble Radha and Krishna. Brass lamps hung from the ceiling, gently illuminating the *mandir*. The aroma of incense and fresh flowers filled the air. The whole effect was beautiful.

"This is exclusively for you, Indoo. No one will disturb you here," Revati said, watching her son's face anxiously to see if he liked their surprise.

Indraneel hugged both his parents, holding them in a warm embrace. He felt overwhelmed, amazed by his parents' thoughtfulness, touched by their unconditional love and willingness to do anything to make their child happy, even if the child was 39 years old. He could not find the words to express his emotions. Nevertheless they understood.

Later that night, after a grand dinner supervised by his mother, Indraneel opened his laptop and looked at the familiar script he had been working on. Mentally seeking the blessings of his Guru, he began keying in. The words flowed easily and smoothly as he found his groove. Before he knew it, four hours had passed.

Indraneel went into his newly created *puja* room and bowing, placed there the picture of Naam Yajna Maharaj that he had brought with him from Rishikesh. It fit right in.

The tired but happy film-maker walked up to his room, fell onto his bed and dropped off to sleep, a peaceful smile on his lips.

74

It was three months since Indraneel had returned to Bombay. The time had just flown. He had established a routine of getting up at 4 am to do his *japa* and three hours of *naam*. His *puja* room was a source of joy for him. No matter how late he returned, he would shower and do his late night *sandhya*. Prayers, thrice a day, helped him stay centered.

Indraneel made it a point to breakfast with his parents every day, and then left for office by 9 am. He worked diligently on his script and came home for lunch, to spend an hour with his parents. They were overjoyed to have his company. He told them about Rishikesh. They were avidly interested in all that he had experienced. Revati ensured vegetarian food on the table, with no onions and garlic, since he was now an initiate. There was always plenty of fruit.

Lily, Indraneel's efficient assistant, was delighted to have him back. She had seen him through his worst drinking binges and was relieved to see her old boss return. But she soon realised Indraneel had changed in a fundamental way which she could not quite put into words. A deep spirituality was now reflected in his eyes.

When Lily's mother took ill, she went to Indraneel and said, "Boss, will you please pray for my mom?"

Indraneel was surprised at the request but replied seriously, "I will pray to my Guru."

He wound up in office by 5 pm and then went home to shower and perform evening *sandhya* before going out to catch up with Arunodaya, Prabhu Da, and others from the film fraternity. Everyone was happy to see him. Everyone commented on the strange peace he now exuded. A few asked what he had been doing in the past year but most did not. In Bombay, the city of transactions, few really wanted to delve deep into the private lives of others.

Arunodaya was delighted to have him back. He immediately saw the change in Indraneel but didn't ask any questions.

When Prabhu Da saw him, he shouted with unaffected joy, "Hey Indraneel! Thank God you're not in saffron! I thought I would find you holding a big trident like a *tantric*!" Indraneel laughed at the image.

The script was shaping well and was now in the final stages. Even his harshest critic, Arunodaya, liked it. He said it left him contemplative.

On an impulse, Indraneel sent it to Shaman, who commented on it in just two lines: 'Art draws from life. It is *rasa*...brilliant!'

Prabhu Da felt that to do justice to the narrative, it had to be mounted on a large canvas. "I'm telling you with all my experience, that this film should reach international audiences," he advised. "See Indraneel, international audiences love Indian mysticism. They are in love with the magic called India. Take advantage of it. Your script is solid. Talk to some international production houses. Besides, there is an elephant in the script. That makes huge sense to the *phirangs*," he laughed.

Indraneel took his mentor's advice seriously and connected with 20th Century Fox Pictures. The script of *Incandescence,* was semi-autobiographical and deeply personal – about a successful fashion photographer, his subsequent disillusionment, and how he finds himself in Rishikesh.

Much to his own surprise, Indraneel heard from Fox within the month. They felt the material had promise and asked him to fly to LA to lock both the contract and the final script. Indraneel sat for a long time gazing at the email, feeling strangely free.

The next day, Lily booked him on a flight to LA.

75

Immersed in last minute changes to the script, Indraneel finally looked up to find there had been eleven missed calls from Arunodaya. Expecting his buddy to spew forth like a volcano for not having answered so many of his calls, Indraneel gingerly tapped in the number.

But Arunodaya was uncharacteristically subdued. "Indraneel, Vasundhara is in hospital, in a critical condition. She has dengue," he said. "Her platelet count and BP have fallen dangerously low and she is slipping in and out of consciousness."

Indraneel was shocked. "Why didn't you tell me earlier?" he asked. "We meet every day."

"She had fever but we didn't know it was dengue. Or that it would be this serious. She was admitted this morning," Arunodaya explained quickly.

"Which hospital? I'm on my way," Indraneel said even as he picked up his car keys and walked out of the office.

Arunodaya told him it was Breach Candy, room 303. Indraneel asked if he should inform his own parents, who would certainly want to know. But Arunodaya said they were already at the hospital.

"So I'm the last to know..." Indraneel muttered to himself.

"Indraneel, one other thing," Arunodaya spoke hesitantly. "Vasundhara has been asking for you continuously. The doctors feel you should see her."

"I'm on my way," Indraneel assured him again.

The traffic was light and Indraneel reached the hospital in record time. Knowing that hospital lifts take forever, he ran up the stairs, taking them two at a time. When Indraneel knocked on the door of room 303, Arunodaya opened it, his eyes red, as if he had been crying. Indraneel walked in. Vasundhara lay on the bed, a nurse seated next to her. On a sofa against the wall sat Vasundhara's mother, crying softly. Sitting next to her was his own mother, holding her friend's hand, her eyes wet with tears. Vasundhara's father and Balarama Barua sat in stoic silence beside them.

Above the beeping of the machines, Indraneel heard a soft voice rambling in delirium. "Indraneel...has Indraneel come? Where is he...?"

Vasundhara, her eyes closed, looked like a small child in the big hospital bed. Arunodaya tapped her hand gently. "Vasu...open your eyes... Indraneel has come."

The nurse looked up at Indraneel and said in a typical Malyalee accent, "Patient is critical. Only five minutes."

At the mention of Indraneel's name, Vasundhara opened her light green eyes. A spark lit in them when she saw him. "You came!" she murmured, smiling through cracked lips.

Indraneel was shocked to see how the illness had ravaged her. Her naturally fair complexion looked blanched and bleached of all colour, save for the dangerous flush of high fever. He immediately took her hand in his and sat on the stool vacated by the nurse.

"Did...you...become...a *sannyasi*?" Vasundhara's words were barely audible.

"No, no...I did not," he replied, surprised at the question.

"What a waste! I thought you would." Her fingers fluttered in his warm clasp.

"Let's talk about it later. You need to get well first," Indraneel said, trying to mask his deep concern.

"I'll be fine... or maybe I will die... But I must talk to you. Why not *sannyas*?" she persisted.

"I wanted to, but Gurudeva told me to return here." Indraneel breathed a sigh.

"I guess he knows better. In any case, I wanted to tell you that I love you very very much. In fact, I have loved you for as long I can remember." Vasundhara spoke in a rushed whisper, as though she just had to get the words out before it was too late. Everything else in the world could wait.

She closed her eyes, exhausted. Indraneel wanted to stop her but did not know how.

"If you had become a *sannyasi* I would never have told you. I was very angry with Revati Aunty when she got you married to Chitra. I have wanted to marry you all my life!" Vasundhara declared as vehemently as she could, her green eyes sparkling with fever.

"You were just a child then," Indraneel reminded her.

"I was 22. People have kids at that age. I spoke to Shaman...told him I loved you. He said I should tell you. But I was shy Indraneel, I wanted to but I didn't know how. To you I was always Arunodaya's little sister to you...a pest...not someone to love..."

"The patient is getting agitated. Please let her rest now," the nurse said.

"Remember the night we spent on the *ghaats*?" Vasundhara words were barely audible but Indraneel heard her mother whisper in disbelief, "They spent a night together!"

She was obviously eavesdropping. Arunodaya quickly shushed his mother, asking her to be quiet. Indraneel now realised the whole family was paying close attention to what was being said.

Vasundhara sighed. "It was the happiest day of my life."

She paused, gathering her strength, then she said so softly that only Indraneel heard, "When we saw that leopard with the cubs in the forest, I thought for a moment we had something special, but maybe I imagined it."

Indraneel bent down to hear. She was almost inaudible.

His mother exclaimed quite loudly, "She went to his room at night!"

Vasundhara was oblivious to all this

"Indraneel I know I'm very sick, that I may not make it. I didn't want to die without telling you. Will you marry me? I will pray with you, sing *naam* with you..."

Indraneel was so touched by her unconditional love that tears came to his eyes.

"Vasundhara, I don't know where I'm headed. I may take some drastic decisions. I don't know if I'll ever live up to the expectations of a householder."

"What drastic decisions? Giving up films? Relocating to another country?"

"I don't know…"

"As long as you know you are following your Guru's advice, I don't think there can be anything drastic." She moved in the bed trying to ease her aching body.

"I cannot deviate from his advice; he gave me new life." Indraneel spoke with utter conviction..

"Will you marry me if I survive? Will you?"

"You will survive."

"I didn't ask if I'd survive. Will you marry me?"

"I will." Indraneel's decision was as sudden as it was final.

Vasundhara's face broke into a smile. She closed her eyes but didn't let go of Indraneel's hand. Slowly, he extracted his fingers from her frail grip and stood up.

The doctor on duty came in. Asking them to wait outside, he completed his examination and then emerged to say they would be doing a plasma transfusion, which they hoped would improve Vasundhara's condition.

They sat on the plastic chairs in the waiting room to continue their vigil.

Revati Barua asked her son, "You love her?"

"This is neither the time nor the place for such a discussion," Indraneel said and walked a little away from the group.

Sitting down, he began to do *japa* and was soon lost in it.

***

Hours later, Arunodaya tapped Indraneel on the shoulder. He opened his eyes and noticed it was dark outside.

"Though she is still very sick, she has turned a corner," Arunodaya told him, his voice breaking with relief. "You have been praying for nearly six hours without moving an inch." There was awe and wonderment in his voice.

"Can I see her?" Indraneel asked.

"She is sleeping, but yes, you can see her."

Indraneel walked into the room. The dangerous flush on Vasundhara's face had disappeared and she looked like she was sleeping peacefully. Revati and Vasundhara's mother were both dozing on the sofa.

"Now it's a matter of time, rest and good food. She will recover. She is young," the nurse said, as if youth was the solution to all ailments.

Indraneel felt greatly relieved. "Arunodaya, I have a plane to catch in a few hours," he told his friend.

Arunodaya hugged him. "Thanks for coming." He added with solemn sincerity, "You saved her life!"

"Message me as soon as she wakes up. I will call and speak to her," Indraneel said as the elevator doors closed.

76

After checking in for his flight and clearing immigration and security, Indraneel sat down in the waiting area and looked at his watch. It was almost 4 am. He decided to call Shaman, knowing that he would certainly be up.

Shaman picked up on the second ring and Indraneel briefed him about Vasundhara.

"Indraneel, I have been interacting with her regularly. I believe she is the right person for you," Shaman responded without hesitation. "She has a deep, unshakable faith in the Almighty, perhaps more so than you. Vasundhara has a great subterranean depth of devotion; she is a pure girl and that's a rarity in today's world. And another thing, she will provide you with centering, gravity and levity."

Indraneel was happy to hear this from Shaman but felt hesitant nevertheless. "Shaman...I hope I'm not making a mistake by marrying again."

"Just go with the flow, Indraneel. Wait for things to unfold. For now, go to LA and concentrate on the film. Our Guru will take care of every need. And yes, Vasundhara is right for you," he reiterated.

Indraneel could hear his flight being called. He thanked Shaman and hung up.

77

Indraneel returned from LA three months later. He was happy to be back. It had been exhausting.

The team at Fox had worked minutely on the script. Though frustrating at times, and comical at others, when they did not understand the local nuances, he greatly admired their professionalism and zeal for perfection. Finally the script was locked.

Indraneel missed his *puja* room. He missed the serene peace of the altar. Only he knew how difficult it had been to do his three *sandhya puja*s.

Initially, during his stay in LA, he had tried to get in touch with Vasundhara, but her mobile remained switched off. However, Arunodaya kept him posted. She was discharged from hospital after a month, still painfully weak. One good thing to happen due to Vasundhara's illness was that Arunodaya moved back home in order to spend more time with his sister. The crisis brought the family together. Arunodaya and his father ironed out their differences. Though they would never agree on many things, they were finally able to let them pass.

After long thought, Indraneel decided to wait to speak to Vasundhara till he returned to India. Throughout his hectic schedule she remained in his thoughts. He wondered again and again whether she had really meant all that she had said, or even if she remembered any of it? After all, she had been delirious at the time.

78

Indraneel arrived at the old bungalow on Walakeshwar as the afternoon sun was glinting off the waters of the sweeping bay beside Marine Drive. He gazed at the wonderful view for a quiet moment before turning to ring the bell.

The old family staffer, Ramu Kaka, opened the door. He looked exactly the way he had for the last 30 years. Ramu Kaka never seemed to age, nor could Indraneel remember him ever looking young.

"Indoo Baba...*namaste*!" he said affectionately.

Indraneel smiled warmly. "Vasundhara *hai*?" he enquired.

"Vasu baby is in her room upstairs," the old man informed him.

'Vasu baby!' Indraneel chuckled to himself. Well, if he could be Indoo Baba at 39, she could certainly be Vasu baby.

Indraneel felt a sudden urge to see her. He walked up the marbled stairs on silent feet. Vasundhara was on the balcony overlooking the sea. She sat on an antique wooden swing, making the most beautiful garlands he had ever seen. Dressed in a canary yellow sundress with a halter neck, her hair was tied in a French braid. Her face was devoid of make-up, her creamy complexion flawless. She looked young and lovely.

Bent over the garland she was making, Vasundhara reminded Indraneel of Andal, the lady saint of south India, who would adorn her Lord with the floral offerings she made. Tying a final knot, Vasundhara put down the garland and picked up the notebook and pencil which lay beside her and began sketching a design.

Indraneel walked quietly down the verandah. "Vasundhara," he said softly.

Intent on her drawing, she was startled to hear his voice and jumped up, the sketchbook and pencil falling to the ground unheeded.

"Indraneel! When did you come?" she breathed, hand on heart, as if to stop its sudden pounding. She looked healthy and beautiful, her cheeks full of colour, her eyes twinkling.

"I've just arrived," replied Indraneel, sitting down on the low chair next to the swing.

Vasundhara poured him a glass of buttermilk from the pitcher near her and handed it to him. Then she picked up the *mala* and went on with threading the flowers.

Indraneel picked up the fallen notebook and flipped over the pages. "These are beautiful designs," he commented, trying to break the awkward silence.

"I get inspired...perhaps 'inspired' is too lofty a word... I get ideas for my jewellery design from these garlands and flowers. I try out different colour combinations and motifs based on them."

"That's beautiful and unique!" He paused for a moment and then said quietly, looking up at her on the swing, "Could you stop for a few moments, Vasundhara? I need to talk to you."

She continued with her task, saying nothing. Indraneel could see she was nervous. He rose and gently took the *mala* from her fingers, putting it into the basket of flowers on the floor. She didn't resist.

Holding her face between his palms Indraneel asked, "Do you still want to marry me?"

Vasundhara's eyes remained downcast, rooted to the floor.

Indraneel lifted her chin so he could look into her eyes and asked her gently again, "Do you want to marry me, Vasundhara?"

After a heart-stopping moment, she nodded, looking up at him, her eyes swimming in tears. Indraneel smiled and bent down to kiss her. Sunshine flooded his heart.

Ramu Kaka's voice interrupted the special moment. "Vasu baby, mummy-daddy have come with Baruaji. They are calling you both down.

Indraneel and Vasundhara smiled at each other in sudden amusement. Some things never changed!

As they walked down the stairs together, both sets of parents watched them expectantly, almost afraid to breathe.

79

Two years had gone by so quickly. Walking along the ghats of Gangaji in Rishikesh, Indraneel reflected on how the wheel of his life had turned inexorably. The cool breeze on his face felt wonderful.

Following his divorce from Chitra, Indraneel and Vasundhara had been married in her family home, in a simple and intimate, no-fuss ceremony, attended only by their families. Chitra too, had wished to remarry and move on. It had been long enough for both of them. They parted without acrimony or regret, Indraneel signing the generous terms without hesitation.

The shooting of Indraneel's film *Incandescence* had been completed and was now slated for worldwide release. The media was already full of it and a positive pre-release buzz surrounded the movie.

The sun was beginning to set.

As he walked on, Indraneel saw Vasundhara in the distance, sitting on the *ghat*, silhouetted in the dusky twilight. She had two large baskets of lamps with her. As he got closer, he saw at least sixteen lamps floating downstream, one after the other, like the bogies of a train at night.

Vasundhara was his wife – the mother of his identical, three-month old twin daughters! In her blue jeans and white shirt, she looked like a young girl and not at all like a nursing mother. She had regained her pre-pregnancy slenderness almost immediately.

There was sudden clap of thunder. Vasundhara turned towards the double baby stroller parked under a tree, to see if the babies had woken up. She noticed Indraneel walking towards them and smiled.

"Are they awake?" she asked.

Indraneel bent to look into the strollers and told her they were just waking. Dakshayani had an orange thread tied to her right leg. Katyayani was the one with no thread. The babies were splitting images of Vasundhara, with her green eyes. They had also inherited dimples from their maternal grandfather, Kapil Garg. They both wore soft cotton white and peach sleeveless smocked frocks, similar in design. On their wrists were adjustable gold baby bangles.

Refreshed by their nap, the babies gurgled at their father, wanting to be picked up. As Vasundhara watched, busy with her task of lighting the lamps, Indraneel lifted the babies expertly and came to sit on the *ghat* steps beside her. The babies sat of his lap, happily exploring their fingers and making slurping sounds.

Indraneel could now see more than 40 lamps in the water. "Those are little prayers," he told his daughters. They stared back at him with unblinking eyes, waving their hands aimlessly.

A family of peacocks was making its careful way towards the water when suddenly they began to dance, just a few feet from where they were sitting. Indraneel wished he had carried his camera.

Vasundhara stopped lighting the lamps to watch. The iridescent feathers glittered in jewel bright tones as they moved in quivering motion.

Indraneel felt gratitude flood his heart. He bowed his head, silently thanking God and his Guru for blessing him with so much – his beautiful babies and a life companion who walked the same spiritual path as he.

It was all His grace.

80

It had stopped raining. The sultry summer day was transformed as the earth cooled. Indraneel lifted his face heavenwards breathing in the divine fragrance of the wet earth.

The Ganga had found an abode in his heart. He remembered Shaman telling him how Bhagiratha had brought Gangaji down from heaven to earth... And here she still was, never stopping for a moment. High and low, everyone bathed equally in her waters – the Canadian Madhusudan, the German Viktoria, Michael from America – she embraced them all without argument.

'What is the gospel of the Ganga?' wondered Indraneel for perhaps the hundredth time. The answer eluded him, yet again.

A Sarus Crane flew over the river into the distance. Indraneel's gaze followed the smooth flight of the bird and then dropped to the river below. As he sat in the gloaming beside the swirling waters, the answer came to Indraneel with utter clarity.

Equality! That was the Ganga's *dharma*. Travelling the breadth of this vast land, like a singing mendicant, she brought oneness and universal brotherhood. No arguments, no cults, no duality. All distinctions and disputes were simply washed away in her waters. Everyone was equal in her presence. She flowed in the same way she had done for thousands of years, eradicating differences among people, giving life.

The river of eternal grace...

A passing *sannyasi* called, *Hari Aum* and Indraneel responded to the greeting in similar fashion.

'A *sannyasi*...' he thought. 'A great soul who has renounced everything. The ochre of his cloth is the same hue as the yellow leaves of the Himalayan birch that are carried on the river. Sometimes Man finds it in his heart to give, but Mother Nature does

WHEN LIFE TURNS TURTLE

it all the time! True *sannyas* is in the act of continued giving.'

Indraneel felt humbled. The Ganga didn't argue; why should he? What was there to debate about when everything was God? This was his life, his *sannyas*, his *dharma*. Suddenly Indraneel recalled his Guru's words: *Living is Giving*.

'Nothing in the world is impossible,' he thought, closing his eyes. He too, would live like the Ganga – a simple life of soulful giving; a life without argument.

"*Sharanaagatoham*…' he intoned, 'I surrender to the Almighty." Peace embraced him.

The Ganga flowed on...

Have you also learned that secret from the river;
that there is no such thing as time?
that the river is everywhere at the same time,
at the source and at the mouth,
at the waterfall,
at the ferry,
at the current,
in the ocean and in the mountains,
everywhere and that the present only exists for it,
not the shadow of the past
nor the shadow of the future.

~ HERMANN HESSE, *Siddhartha*

To Ramya, Swarup, Chandralekha, Abhilasha,
Vickie, Vikas,
Shubhadip, Muneesh,
Benjamin and Ruskin,
I give due and grateful credit.
Their contribution to this novel has been invaluable.
~ AUTHOR